Kenneth Lo is the foremost expert on Chinese cuisine writing and broadcasting in English. Born in Foochow, China, in 1913, he studied physics at Peking University and then English Literature at Cambridge and London. He has pursued a variety of careers during his time in Britain: as a diplomat, a fine-art publisher, an industrial relations and welfare officer for Chinese seamen, a journalist, a lecturer, and as a professional tennis player. He is best known, however, for his many authoritative books on Chinese cooking and eating. He has contributed articles and columns to innumerable journals and magazines, and has appeared many times on television. The Mayflower edition of his *Cooking the Chinese Way* has been successfully in print for twenty-five years. Now in his sixties, Kenneth Lo is still extremely active and productive, and this he attributes to the fact that he follows his own advice – about cooking and eating the Chinese way.

D0626453

Kenneth Lo

Cooking and Eating the Chinese Way

MAYFLOWER
GRANADA PUBLISHING
London Toronto Sydney New York

Published by Granada Publishing Limited
in Mayflower Books 1980

ISBN 0 583 13136 0

A Mayflower Original
Copyright © Kenneth Lo 1980

Granada Publishing Limited
Frogmore, St Albans, Herts AL2 2NF
and
3 Upper James Street, London W1R 4BP
866 United Nations Plaza, New York, NY 10017, USA
117 York Street, Sydney, NSW 2000, Australia
100 Skyway Avenue, Rexdale, Ontario, M9W 3A6, Canada
PO Box 84165, Greenside, 2034 Johannesburg, South Africa
CML Centre, Queen & Wyndham, Auckland 1, New Zealand

Set, printed and bound in Great Britain by
Cox & Wyman Ltd, Reading
Set in Monotype Times

Granada ®
Granada Publishing ®

Contents

Eating Chinese

Introduction

The number of people who eat Chinese food these days runs into millions, and a good proportion of these do so with regularity. It is not at all unlikely that within the next few decades Chinese food may become accepted as a part and parcel of the routine western diet. Yet up to now westerners who know exactly what to do when confronted with a Chinese menu of over one hundred dishes, or even two to three hundred dishes (which is not uncommon), are very few and far between. The purpose of the first part of this book is to give some practical guidance in ordering Chinese foods, or composing a Chinese meal, and to provide westerners with some general acquaintance with Chinese dishes.

The Chinese meal is essentially a buffet – a hot sit-down buffet – where the keynote is balance and variety. Where a greater number of people are sitting at a table and dining together (up to ten or twelve), a greater number of dishes can be served. Hence, with numbers, there can be a great variety of foods provided and better balance achieved. A Chinese dinner is essentially a communal occasion. A full-scale meal with eight to a dozen dishes could not be served to one person sitting down to his meal – unless he were the Emperor, and even he would look pretty small and ridiculous, surrounded by mountains of food and dishes (the last Emperor of China, Pu Yih, thought so too in retrospect when, after Liberation, he became a gardener in the Peking Botanical Gardens!).

Balance

Balance is achieved at a Chinese meal by varying the food material and the character of the dishes served. When there are rich meat dishes there must be plain cereal foods; when there are crisp dry dishes there must be saucier dishes; where there is poultry there must be fish; when there is a meaty, meat-broth soup, there is usually a vegetable soup. In this way, not only is variety achieved, but also, it seems, nutrition. The majority of the health-experts in the world today seem to agree that what the human body requires to be healthy is not a lot of nutritious food (which can often be supplied and consumed in excess) but a wide variety of foods, supplied and consumed in comparatively small quantities.

Variety

Variety in Chinese food is also achieved by selecting dishes which are cooked in a number of different ways, instead of limiting oneself to just one method of cooking (say, roasting). When you have a roast dish you should also have a steamed dish, a quick-stir-fried dish, a long-simmered dish, a boiled or poached dish, an 'assembled' dish, a deep-fried or dry-fried dish, a braised dish, or a smoked dish. Thus when you have foods cooked and prepared in different ways, you are likely to get also variety of colour, shape, size, and flavour. Talking about shapes and sizes, most food materials can usually be cooked whole (e.g. poultry or a large piece of meat or a whole fish) or they can be shredded, julienned, diced into cubes, or cut into thin slices. When these different methods of presentation are 'married' into mixed dishes, where several food materials and ingredients are mixed and cooked together, the number of the dishes proliferate. Some people have said that the number of dishes in Chinese cuisine runs into tens of thousands. We certainly have no shortage of variety!

'Red-Cooked' and 'White-Cooked' Dishes and The Chinese Home-Cooked Meal

In China, for over two and a half thousand years, we have been using soya sauce in our food preparation and cooking. Since soya sauce is dark brown and slightly reddish in colour, all food cooked or stewed in soya sauce is called 'Red-Cooked'. And those in which no soya sauce is used are called 'White-Cooked'. These stewed and long-cooked dishes (often steamed for a lengthy period of time in a closed receptacle) form the backbone of Chinese domestic cooking. Since these dishes are often prepared in quantity, or are just as good or even better when re-heated (and we have no inhibition about re-heating, which we *know* is quite wholesome) Chinese housewives are hardly ever found to be climbing up the walls just because a few extra relatives or friends arrive unannounced for dinner. All she has to do is to re-heat these long-cooked dishes, and prepare two or three quick-fried dishes (none of which requires more than five or six minutes to prepare *and* cook), and put out three or four extra bowls of rice (which is always available anyway in the Chinese kitchen) and everyone will be satisfied. If she has pots of 'jellied meats' in reserve in the pantry, or pieces of Chinese 'salami sausages' hanging from the shelves, she will cut these into slices (in the case of the 'sausages' the pieces can be inserted into the hot rice to cook for a few minutes) and serve them as 'extras'. Most of these cold or hot 'extras' and the re-heated 'stews' are universally appreciated by all irrespective of social class or wealth. If anyone drops in for dinner unannounced, these are what they will get, and enjoy. One of the freshly-cooked quick-stir-fried dishes is likely to be a vegetable dish: it is likely to be glistening green and succulent – whether it consists of spinach, spring cabbage, or french beans – or ivory in colour and crunchy, like well-sprouted bean-sprouts or celery, and this vegetable dish is also an integral part of the domestic meal, which makes it so appealing. For here the richness of the stews is balanced with the freshness of the vegetables. The whole meal is enlivened with a few well-chosen quick-cooked fish dishes, which may consist of quick-fried seafood or perhaps a freshly quick-steamed piece of fish or a quick-fried meat dish. At times when no fresh fish is available, salt-fish, which, like the 'salami sausage', is always hanging in the pantry, can be brought out and a few small pieces are sliced off and given a few minutes of slow-frying. The result is a cheesey substance which, when consumed with plain boiled rice, gives the same satisfaction as a good cheese when eaten with hot crisp-crusty bread!

Eating in Restaurants

In a restaurant the choice is of course much wider. Your choice requires your acquaintance with a much greater range of dishes, and is partly dependent upon your knowledge of the quality of the particular restaurant and its specialities. There is no point in ordering foods which are not in the restaurant's normal run of dishes, as they have to be prepared in a very short time without much time to think and deliberate. To ask for special dishes to be cooked just for you, or some items culled out of the corner of the menu which you had spotted but which are not normally on tap – because you have done some eating in the East in your time – is tantamount to asking for a tailor-made shirt in a shop at sale time when they normally sell only different coloured tee-shirts!

My own somewhat unusually wide experience in eating and ordering in Chinese restaurants is derived partly from the time when I was for over half a decade a restaurant inspector, or consultant to different famous Food Guides, such as the Egon Ronay Guide, or the Good Food Guide, and consultant/advisor, or promoter-of-products, to such establishments such as the M. & S. Sharwood (R.H.M.

Foods Ltd.), Coral Leisure Group, Mars Ltd., and Bird's Eye, and these latter days to an electric-wok manufacturer. These experiences have given me the opportunity to eat more widely in Chinese restaurants than anybody in his right mind would care to do. In more recent times, as founder and chairman of the *Chinese Gourmet Club*, I have had to organize and eat at 400 Chinese banquets in five years, in the course of which I have taken some 15,000 people to eat in scores of London restaurants and have paid over £75,000 in restaurant bills! Although this overwhelming experience of eating has probably left bean-sprouts sprouting out of my ears I cannot say that I know Chinese restaurants and their menus as well as the back of my hand (of which I know very little!) – for the experience seems to have shown that the more one knows, the more fascinated and humble one feels. (Drink deep, or taste not the Pierian spring!) I can therefore say with honesty that I am very pleased to have the opportunity of putting my 'little experience' of eating in Chinese restaurants to the help of the reader in ordering from Chinese menus and sorting out some of the intricacies, which may seem puzzling because of the range, or because of one's lack of knowledge of what the items or dishes really are, or how they should be arranged and grouped together.

When confronted with a Chinese menu, one must bear in mind the principles of ordering Chinese food. These principles are that one must have:

Variety and balance: 'white-cooked' and 'red-cooked' dishes, crispy dishes, saucy dishes, 'soupy' dishes, spicy dishes, aromatic dishes, and fine-cut 'cold spread', items for nibbles, as well as 'big dishes' consisting of large chunks of meat or whole poultry (roasted or long-cooked) or large whole fish, to be dismembered and shared on the table. One must not just be confined to the small- or medium-sized quick-stir-fried dishes, which the restaurants are too inclined to serve because of the speed and ease of production.

Of course one does not need to order all of these things,

but one must have the possibility of variety, range, and the need for balance in mind.

It should be remembered that 'variety' means not just variety in food materials (meat, fish, poultry, vegetables, etc.) but also in the cooking methods employed in preparing them (i.e. when one has a quick-fried dish, one should also have a long-cooked simmered dish etc.). 'Variety' also means variety in texture, colour, size and shape. After a number of small dishes to start with (in China even at top-grade banquets the starting dishes are always small – seldom more than 15–20cm (6–8in) in diameter even for a table for ten people: one is meant to nibble rather than wolf!) one should come to a large dish or dishes to satisfy the greedy. Here in the West one should arrive at the 'large dish' fairly early in the proceedings, because in the West the 'natives' who are afficionados of Chinese food are very inclined to wolf, especially after the initial parade of small dishes, which seem to remind them of the belief which has never been properly laid or exorcized that 'You can eat your fill of Chinese food, but you'll be hungry again in an hour!' (I have known eaters who, after a full-scale Chinese meal, didn't feel hungry for three days!)

Balance in a Chinese meal really means bringing variety in food into a sharper contrast: when you have had a rich meat dish you will need to contrast it with a large green vegetable dish (the richness should be contrasted with the freshness of the vegetable); when you have had a soft tender dish (of say, *Soft Oil-Poached Sliced Fish in Wine Sauce*) you will need to contrast it with a crisp dish (say, *Crispy Prawn Balls Covered with Croutons*); a roast dish will need to be contrasted with *Steamed fish*; when you have an extra spicy dish (say, *Diced Pork Cubes in 'Red Oil' Sauce*, or *Szechuan Hot Dry-Fried Shredded Beef*) you will need to eat it with plain boiled rice, or wash it down with a copious amount of soup or wine. The balance in the meal is built up through the juxtapositions and continual contrasts in a whole series of dishes. Indeed, the wholesomeness of the domestic Chinese meal is built on the basis that savoury foods with their matchless gravies are consumed with quantities of plain bland bulk foods, be the latter boiled rice, steamed buns, or noodles. When you have balance and contrast, in material, colour, texture, shape, form and size, the quality and character of each dish becomes more pronounced thus making them more easily enjoyed and appreciated.

Soups

Since we do not always drink tea or wine at a Chinese meal the soup, and 'soupy' dishes have a somewhat different function in a Chinese meal compared to a western meal. In a western meal the soup is a 'starter', which is sometimes made and served thick to provide added bulk to the meal. Chinese soup is seldom thick; it is usually a consommé with different items lightly cooked in it served throughout the meal (placed at the centre of the table for the individual diners to help themselves from), taken in occasional mouthfuls to help to wash down the mouthfuls of savoury and bulk food consumed. In this era when wine has become *de rigueur* for every respectable western meal, the drinking of clear soup impregnated with a variety of flavours to wash down bulk and savoury foods in the mouth is a fresh and enjoyable sensation which is worth while trying.

Because of this added function and enjoyment of soups, there is an extra range of dishes in Chinese cooking which can only be called 'semi-soup' dishes. These often consist of duck or chicken long-simmered in a copious amount of soup, with vegetables added (to add freshness) towards the last stage of cooking (and if the principal material is fish, the latter is often added into a meat or chicken broth to simmer for only 15 minutes before the vegetables are added). The result is a 'semi-soup', 'white-cooked' dish, which is enjoyed for both its matchless consommé and for the extraordinarily tender meat (or fish), which acts as an important contrast to the richer stews, as well as to the quick-fried, or deep-fried drier dishes – thus providing a further element of 'balance' in the meal as a whole. This is an aspect of the cuisine of Shanghai and Lower Yangtze, an area where vegetables, poultry, fish, and water abound, but this cuisine has not as yet caught on in the West, where in several of its centres the palate has been carried away in recent years by hotter and spicier Szechuan food – a type of cuisine which is more easily noticed and appreciated. In recent decades during which the geography of China has noticeably contracted due to unification and improvement in communication, a good Chinese meal usually consists of menus which are drawn and constructed from dishes orig-inating in different regions. In this context I submit that the lighter Lower Yangtze dishes should be used as a contrast to the spicier western Szechuan dishes, in order to strike the ideal balance.

Pattern or Grouping of Dishes in a Chinese Meal

When confronted with a sizeable Chinese menu, apart from constantly reminding yourself of the need for *variety* and *balance*, which cannot be over-emphasized, you should also bear in mind the normal tradition or style of serving Chinese food and dishes, both at home, or when dining out, or at dinner parties or banquets.

Dining at Home

When eating or serving food at home, where one eats reasonably well, there may be one or two soups: a meaty soup (or 'semi-soup' dish) to go with the vegetable dishes, and a vegetable soup to go with the meatier dishes. There should be at least one big meat dish (usually a pork dish), a fish dish, a dish of mixed ingredients, a tou-fu or bean-curd dish, and a pure vegetable dish. To supplement these, there may be a beef, mutton, lamb, or seafood dish, or anything which might be in season or has just come on to the market. These supplementary dishes are called up, or thrown in, especially when there are extra mouths to feed, due to guests dropping in unexpectedly or unannounced. When there are no special foods or ingredients available in the kitchen or pantry very often this supplementary dish may consist of no more than two or three lightly stir-fried eggs, a large pinch of freshly-chopped chives or chopped spring onions thrown over them, sprinkled with a spoonful of 'yellow wine' (or dry sherry). The aromatic effect of the chives and wine is often quite capable of lifting this very ordinary and mundane dish to the level of haute cuisine. At a family meal all these dishes are served at the same time on the table, around which some five, six or even a dozen persons might sit and gather, each with a bowl of rice (which can be replenished). They would consume the hot savoury dishes on the table as in the West you would eat a buffet. However, there is a difference which is that the Chinese would not gather all the foods they required from the 'communal dishes' all at once at the beginning of the meal, and place them on their own rice-bowl or side-dish, but they would do so slowly and gradually as the meal progresses, drinking mouthfuls of soup as they proceed, taking only bite-size pieces of food one at a time. The last morsels of food on the communal plate, bowl, or dishes, are meant to be eaten only when the meal has come to the very end. It would be considered the height of bad manners, or even abnormal, to gather the best morsels of foods from the communal dishes, all at once, and start stuffing yourself. The Chinese dinner is not only a communal meal in practice, it is also communal in spirit. Each person should be concerned that his or her neighbours, and all the persons around him, have had a good share of all the best bits of foods which are on the communal dishes. If some dishes are situated too far away on the table they should be passed on to them; or individual choice bits of foods may even be picked up with the chopsticks and placed on their rice-bowl or side-plates. In polite or well-brought up families, and especially at parties, this communal spirit and expression of mutual concern should be all-pervading. In the end the host or hostess, after having given all their attention to their honoured guests and the elders, may end up with having eaten next to nothing after a dinner of more than a dozen courses. However, at home this seldom happens. But out of respect for the older people, the choicer bits are always offered to them before they are offered to juniors. In the present day world of 'smash and grab' perhaps it would not be amiss to re-emphasize this old fashioned spirit of orderliness, mutual concern within the community and self-denial.

Party Dinners and Dining Out

The pattern of eating when dining out or at a party or banquet is somewhat different. Whilst at home, as already mentioned, all the dishes are served more or less at once – although some quick-fried or quick-steamed dishes may be brought out later in the course of the meal as these have to be served immediately they leave the stove. However, when eating out or at a party dinner the dishes are served in courses, one after another. Or some other dishes, such as cold hors-d'oeuvres, are served in groups.

At a full-scale party dinner, the cold hors-d'oeuvres – if they are served at all, since dinners do not necessarily have to commence with hors-d'oeuvres (which usually consist of four to six dishes of 'cold cut' foods, often very finely cut, frequently in artistic patterns) – are placed on the table before the diners sit down around it. In recent times these hors-d'oeuvres items are often arranged and served together on one large impressive dish. The diners will commence by picking small morsels of these items, and nibbling them. The host or hostess, whilst urging the assembled people to commence with these 'starter' dishes, would also pass the wine around. The wine usually consumed at a party dinner is the 'yellow wine' which is a rice-wine, similar in flavour to a dry sherry. The 'yellow wine' is usually served warm in a pewter pot, which is encased in a jacket of hot water in a china pot. At more formal or polite dinners the host or hostess would go around the table to drink the health of the individuals, especially that of the 'guest of honour', and all the 'honoured guests'.

The dishes which follow the hors-d'oeuvres are called the 'wine-drinking' dishes. There may be three or four or more of these, and they are brought out at intervals of five to ten minutes. Every time they are brought out fresh and sizzling from the kitchen, the host or hostess will once more urge the guests to drink their wine and attack the dishes. These 'wine-drinking' dishes are seldom large (usually served in dishes of not more than 20cm (8in) in diameter), but they should be all quite different in flavour, texture and colour, crispness or tenderness – being dishes of different food materials, which have been quick-stir-fried or deep-fried. These dishes are eaten in somewhat larger quantities than the hors-d'oeuvres, but still the diners should not exactly stuff themselves.

At this point of the proceedings quite often a soup will appear and this will act as a 'punctuation mark' between the two groups of dishes. The group of dishes which will now follow is usually known as the 'big dishes'. They will consist of the roasts, the casseroles and stews, served in large deep bowls rather than dishes, and a whole fish which may be over 45cm (18 in) in length. These are the impressive dishes, and the food from them is attacked, divided, and eaten in larger quantities than that from the previous group of 'wine drinking' dishes. They give the diners for the first time the chance to stuff and gorge themselves if need be. By this time, when a fair quantity of foods have been eaten and wine consumed, the proceedings will have become less formal, and the host and hostess could afford to be less insistent in urging the guests to eat and drink, and the 'eating party' will have achieved a momentum of its own to carry on its own impetus. The foods in the 'big dishes' are usually served whole (poultry in whole birds, meats in large chunks, or in piles of large slices) to emphasize their character, which is that they are rich, big and succulent.

If a second soup is to be served this is the time to do it. This soup is very likely to be a 'sweet soup' – often an 'orange' or 'tangerine soup' with miniature dumplings floating in it. This 'sweet soup' is not exactly a dessert as we have not yet come to the end of the meal. It acts more like a 'second punctuation mark' to indicate the end of the three or four 'big dishes', and the beginning of the 'rice-eating' dishes.

The 'rice-eating' dishes are meant to help to settle the stomach. After a long series of mostly very rich and savoury dishes especially when eaten on their own (without bulk food) the stomach is bound to become somewhat uneasy, due to over stimulation. The consumption of something as bland as rice – especially soft rice – is calculated to dilute the contents of the stomach and make it feel easier and more comfortable, which it does. The rice when served is supported by a small selection of very plain and simple dishes, mostly consisting of vegetables, pickles, tou-fu (bean-curd) or eggs. These will only be nibbled at by the diners, and washed down with a few mouthfuls of rice or soft rice. This 'tucking down' is like the comforting sensation of being tucked at night into a well-made bed. If there is a soup this is likely to be a largely vegetable soup, or if *Peking Duck* has been one of the courses, the remainder of the duck or the duck carcass will have been boiled with a good amount of Chinese cabbage into the conventional, if not institutional *Duck Carcass Soup*. So the Chinese dinner would start slowly although stimulatingly, but end in a low key like a lamb. It is only in its middle reach that it rises to its phoenix; tigers and dragons.

When eating Chinese in the West one could hardly follow this pattern, even when dining out. First of all one hasn't the time (such a full-scale meal may take three hours or more to consume), secondly, the expense could be prohibitive, thirdly, what westerners truly appreciate in Chinese food is its delicious savoury spiciness, and the sumptuousness of its range and variety. These, together with the exploitation of textual contrasts, the refinement of bringing out the freshness and true flavours of food by the studied application of heat, the aesthetic blending of different foods and ingredients and the cutting of them into different shapes, sizes and forms, are indeed some of the more characteristic qualities of Chinese cuisine. The problem of appreciating and eating Chinese food today in the West or elsewhere is how to bring out these qualities in a more manageable form without adhering to all the traditional forms and formalities of bygone China. This I feel can be done simply by contracting the menu somewhat and moving to the heart of the matter more rapidly by dispensing with the frills.

First of all we can dispense with the whole concluding section of 'rice-eating' and stomach-settling dishes, which in themselves may number half a dozen. We can dispense with these because few westerners are likely to appreciate plain bland dishes with watery rice. Secondly, we can compound the hors-d'oeuvres with the 'wine-drinking' dishes, by serving the former as one large dish or just serve the latter dishes without the hors-d'oeuvres. If hors-d'oeuvres are served, the 'wine-drinking' dishes could be reduced to just two or three, and made into somewhat larger dishes (25cm (10 in) double-portion dishes).

The soup can naturally be reduced to one, and since Chinese restaurants (certainly in China) regard sweets and desserts as belonging to the sphere of confectioners, which has little to do with them, they can best be replaced by well-chilled fresh fruit salads with one or two items of Chinese fruit thrown in, such as lichee, lungaan, and chow-chow (crystallized ginger). After a long series of savoury dishes when the mouth tends to become very dry, a dish at this concluding point which is long, cool, and fresh can be very refreshing. If one wishes to be elaborate nothing could be more impressive and attractive than having the fresh fruit salad placed inside a large artistically-carved and excavated melon, which has itself been well-chilled, and served steaming in a mist of frost. When such a dish, which has the 'ice mountain' effect, is served to conclude a Chinese meal, it provides that unexpected icy 'twist in the tail' which is how all good stories should end. So a Chinese meal need not end 'like a lamb' but in icy splendour!

Bearing in mind the principles of ordering Chinese food, and using the patterns of conventional Chinese meals as a constant reference, how does one go about ordering a meal in a Chinese restaurant which has a reasonably large menu?

EATING CANTONESE

What to Order in a Cantonese Restaurant

Cantonese restaurants are the ones which are situated in or around chinatowns. Nowadays a few have spread into the suburbs. They are usually hung with roast ducks in the window, and inside there is normally at least a sprinkling of Chinese customers, if they are not thronging with them. These restaurants generally have a reliable minimal standard, as otherwise the Chinese customers would disappear in a day. Being mostly in the catering trade themselves they all know where the good foods are to be found, and where one gets the best value for money. The restaurateurs would hardly try to pull wool over the eyes of fellow 'card-carrying' members of their own trade. For authentic, reasonably-priced Chinese (Cantonese) food, these are probably the best places for appreciative westerners to go to. They have something of the atmosphere of bourgeois French restaurants, where families often dine together in groups, and the children are not only tolerated but welcomed. If one likes that kind of atmosphere of 'eating for eating's sake' in a bustling world the best time to go to them is on a Sunday.

Cantonese cuisine is strong on seafoods, steamed fish

dishes; roast-duck; *Cha Shao Quick-Roast Fillet of Pork* and
Crispy-Skin Pork (best eaten with boiled rice with a dab of
soya sauce) or if you wished to be classy, *Crispy Suckling
Pig*; meats and chicken in *Black Bean Sauce*; beef and
vegetables in *oyster sauce*; small casseroles of long-cooked
meat (mostly beef) sometimes flavoured with wind-dried
foods and sometimes containing a mixture of eel and roast
pork; *Sea-Salt Baked Chicken*; the varieties of *Congees*
(self-contained bowls of 'soft rice' with varieties of flavours),
and finally, *Dim Sums* (varieties of 'Tea House Snacks'),
which are consumed in the afternoon accompanied by tea or
wine.

When confronted with such a choice of dishes, dispersed
through a menu which often contains one or two hundred
items (although many are variations on the same theme),
and bearing in mind the patterns of Chinese eating, and the
principles which should underlie the choice of dishes –
namely, the importance of variety and balance – what would
one choose, say, for a meal for four or five people at a
Cantonese restaurant? For the lover of seafoods and fish
(and if you are not a lover of fish and seafoods you should
not go to a Cantonese restaurant) I would make the following
choice of dishes:

MENU 1

Starter:
     Hot-Poached Prawns in Shells (2 portions – to be
        eaten with the fingers)
Soup:
     Won Ton Soup (2–3 portions only to be shared
        between the diners)
Main Course Dishes to be served with rice:
     Onion and Ginger Crab (1 portion)
     Steamed Fish (1 large portion Bream, Mullet or Bass)
     Chicken in Black Bean Sauce (1 portion)

Mixed Plate of *Roast Duck and Cantonese Cha Shao Roast Pork* (1 portion)
Quick-fried Heart of Greens (1 portion)

Onion and Ginger Crab can usually be used as a 'starter' to be eaten on its own, but as its sauce is superb to be mopped up with rice, it is grouped here to be served with rice. *Steamed Fish* is another excellent dish where the sauce or gravy is outstanding, and is, again, best eaten poured into the rice. When ordering the soup you should make it clear that you only want two (or three) portions, otherwise if you are served with as many portions as there are people, you will have too much soup, and it will probably become one of the most expensive single courses of the meal – unnecessarily.

MENU 2

Basically this menu is a variation of the previous one with slightly more emphasis on poultry and meat, giving slightly more weight to the latter part of the menu.

Starter:
    Crab in Black Bean Sauce (2 portions)
Soup:
    West Lake Beef Broth Soup (2–3 portions only)
Main Course Dishes to be served with Rice:
    Steamed Fish (1 large portion)
    Mixed Plate of Cha Shao Roast Pork and Crispy-Skin Pork
    Salt-Baked Chicken (1 portion)
    Sliced Beef in Black Bean Sauce (1 portion)
    Cantonese Roast Duck (1 portion)

If there are more than 5 people, say 6 or 7, the first menu can be increased by adding one dish of *Crispy-Skin Fried Chicken* and one of *Sliced Beef in Oyster Sauce* – or by just one of them; and the latter menu can be increased by adding

Quick-Fried Squid in Chilli and Black Bean Sauce and *Baked Chinese 'Salami' Sausages*.

Dining Cantonese Alone or in Pairs

When you are dining alone or in pairs, you will have to adopt an entirely different strategy in choosing your food. You will not be able to choose a whole selection of dishes, for the one reason that it would be too costly, and if you choose a whole selection of dishes, there will be too much food.

All Cantonese restaurants these days provide a selection of self-contained single-dish platters which are suitable for single diners who just want a snack-meal. The best of these to choose are:

Cantonese Roast Duck on Rice;
Mixed Roast Duck and Pork on Rice;
Mixed Roast Duck and Chicken on Rice;
Mixed Roast Pork and Crispy-Skin Pork on Rice (for those who enjoy the aromatic effect of crispy skin);
Braised Brisket of Beef on Rice.

All these 'meat on rice' self-contained dishes also provide for a small amount of lightly-cooked vegetables which are added to the meat-and-rice dish to restore somewhat the balance of meat and vegetables. For those whose appetite or hunger requires more appeasement these self-contained dishes could always be supplemented with an additional savoury dish chosen from the menu, or any single portion dish from Menu 1 or 2 given above. Hardly anyone would not be satisfied by such a two-dish combination.

If you are dining in pairs, the best idea would be to select one dish *each* from the above selection of 'self-contained' dishes, and then to choose another savoury dish from the menu to share between the two of you. This additional dish could be *Crystal Prawns, Prawns in Sauce* (tomato), *Cantonese Roast Duck, Black Bean Chicken, Mixed Plate of Roast*

Duck and White Cut Chicken, Beef in Oyster Sauce, Braised Brisket of Beef in Small Cantonese Casserole (Pao Chai). In all these cases where you start from a self-contained meat-on-rice dish, whether you are supplementing it with an additional dish or not, you are probably dining on a budget, and your outlay should be quite limited. Indeed, this might be one of the best ways of dining out, if you are embarking on a course of prolonged courting, or if you wish to have a break from the unrelieved matrimonial drudgery of always cooking and eating at home.

When you are not feeling well

When you do not feel quite up to the mark there is a selection of dishes called *Congees* (or soft-rice) in Cantonese restaurants, which we Chinese always resort to when not feeling a hundred per cent. These are self-contained dishes of mildly flavoured soft-rice with small additions of meat, fish or seafoods. The best of these are:

> *Sampan Congee* (with seafoods and fish);
> *Sliced Fish Congee* (fresh fish Congee);
> *Assorted Meats Congee*;
> *Duck and Chicken Congee*;
> *Brisket of Beef Congee*.

All these Congee dishes are easily digestible. When you have consumed a bowl you will feel a sensation of warmth pervading the body. Although the average westerner may not take to Congee immediately, because of its mildness in flavour, 'a taste for Congee' is something worth cultivating. It is a kind of food which gives the body and system a chance to heal and restore themselves.

When you want to Bulk Up

When you are in a party of three or four or more, and you wish to bulk up the weight of your meal (perhaps because you have several hearty eaters among you) one of the best dishes to choose is *Singapore Rice-Stick Noodles*. This is a dish of 'Chow Mein', which, being of rice-stick noodles, has borrowed from the cooking of Fukien, and, having a touch of curry flavour, is influenced by the cooking of Malaysia (but being Chinese we have no inhibition about absorbing anything from anywhere with or without acknowledgement!). It is a better dish to choose than any of the other Chow Meins, as Cantonese Chow Meins all tend to be over oily or greasy, due to the excess use of fat employed to fry the noodles in order to make the bottom parts slightly crispy, an achievement which no northern Chinese appreciates. *Singapore Rice-Stick Noodles*, apart from being hot and extremely savoury, has the added advantage of being absorbent, which enables it to readily absorb the flavours of other dishes. The left-over sauces from the dishes on the table – be they fish, crab, poultry, or meat – can all be poured over these noodles and make the latter even more appealing and satisfying. As a supplementary dish a double portion should satisfy any small party.

DIM SUMS

Dim Sums can be defined as Chinese *Tea House Snacks*. As a type of eating it is getting to be better known and increasingly popular with western people who are genuinely interested in Chinese food. As we have no pubs or bars in China, drinking is done in tea houses, when you do not wish to repair to restaurants for full-scale meals. By the way, restaurants are often styled 'Chiu Chia' (or 'Wine Pavilions') in China where wines are often consumed during meals, but the wines being all grain-wines – or nearly all – are not as much as a fad as in the West, as we do not have as great a range and variety as you have.

Dim Sums are small items of food (mostly meats and prawns) which are usually steamed for their soft-succulence, or deep-fried for their crispness, which makes them eminently suitable for accompanying drinks. When steamed they are normally first of all wrapped in jackets of thin dough-skin. Those which are designated with the word *Pao* (pronounced 'pow') are meat stuffings steamed and encased in a thick casing of slightly sweetened, raised dough. They are about the size of buns, and are perhaps best called 'steamed buns', but being steamed rather than baked, they are white in colour. These *Paos* are quite filling, and you would not need more than one or two of them to fill you up. Those which consist of prawns wrapped in thin dough-skins are called *Kows*. They are comparatively small items, of which anybody can consume up to ten or twelve. Both the *Paos* and *Kows* are brought to the table hot in the bamboo-baskets in which they are steamed. The collection of steaming basket-work on the table makes them doubly attractive and picturesque – intriguing objects to westerners. The deep-fried crispy items are more conventionally served, but there are one or two of them which are slightly out of the ordinary. One of them is called *Wo Kwok* which consists of meat or shrimps wrapped in a casing of mashed yam (which has a similar texture to mashed potato and the appearance of Scotch-Egg, but infinitely more satisfying to eat). The other is *Paper-Wrapped Prawns*, which consist of prawns wrapped in edible paper, and deep-fried. The third item which is not fried but steamed is called *Cheung-Fun*. This consists of minced beef, prawns or roast pork wrapped in a large sheet (about $12 \cdot 5 \times 15 \mathrm{cm} \, (5 \times 6 \, \mathrm{in})$) of snow-white open-ended rice-flour dough, which has been steamed on a plate, and doused with hot soya sauce and oil. Many people wonder what they are; they are eaten by being broken into smaller pieces with chopsticks, and then given a turn in the sauce at the bottom of the plate.

Dim Sums, being 'tea house' foods, are normally served and consumed only in the day time. They are, as you can imagine, very labour intensive to make, and few restaurants can afford another shift of chefs to continue to serve them in the evenings since they are provided merely as a means to bring Chinese customers to their doors, particularly the Cantonese who have got so used to having them at home in Hong Kong or South China.

ITEMS OF DIM SUMS

For the sake of easy reference I am listing below a selection of the most popular *Dim Sum* items which should be available in any Cantonese restaurant where *Dim Sums* are served. However, probably no more than one in four Cantonese restaurants are serving *Dim Sums* due to the costliness of skilled labour. One has to go to chinatown for them, as they hardly exist in the suburbs or provinces.

Har Kow: prawn dumplings wrapped in very thin dough-skin steamed and served in basket-steamers.

Shiu-Mai: open-top meat-stuffed dumplings wrapped in very thin dough-skin, steamed and served in basket-steamers.

Cha Shao Pao: steamed 'buns' of Cha Shao roast-pork encased in a thick wrapping of slightly sweetened raised dough, steamed and served in basket-steamers.

Gai Pao: a steamed 'bun' similar to the above, except the stuffing is of braised chicken.

Gai Chub: chicken and mushroom seasoned and wrapped together with chicken skin, and steamed and served in a basket-steamer.

Cheung-Fun: soft, white-coloured, rice-flour rolls, steamed with prawns, minced beef or pork stuffing wrapped inside. Usually served hot in an oval dish, sitting in a dark gravy-like sauce, which really consists of no more than soya sauce and oil.

Ngor Mai Faahn: lotus-leaf-wrapped savoury rice, which consists of about $\frac{1}{2}$–$\frac{3}{4}$ bowl of glutinous rice, which has been flavoured with roast pork or soya-braised chicken, steamed and wrapped in a large piece of lotus leaf, and served on a dish, which has been steamed inside a basket-steamer.

Crispy Pancake: when served in the context of other *Dim Sum* items, these pancakes are usually quite small, and sometimes cut into three or four crispy sections.

Hong Kong Prawn-Toast: miniature pieces of toast topped with a prawn – the two being fried together, they make for a very crispy combination.

Paper-Wrapped Prawns: prawns wrapped in edible paper, and deep-fried.

Wo-Kwok: deep-fried mashed yam, stuffed with minced meat, made into olive-shaped 7·5cm (3 in) long pieces. Has a particular appeal to the western palate due to its similarity to good minced meat and mashed potato.

Steamed Beef-Ball: seasoned beef-balls sitting on a small quantity of spinach or watercress on a tiny plate. Served steamed in a basket-steamer.

Steamed Spare Ribs: these are miniature pork spare ribs – chopped into about 2·5cm (1 in) sections – which have been seasoned and steamed and served in basket-steamers.

Custard Egg-Tart: this looks just like a very ordinary egg-tart but it is extremely light and of high quality – it 'melts' in the mouth.

A good soup to accompany these *Dim Sum* items is *Won Ton Soup*. One portion should be sufficient for two persons, especially if you have ordered a portion or two of *Chow Mein* to supplement the *Dim Sums*, which the Chinese often do.

EATING PEKINGESE

Unlike Cantonese eating establishments which were originally founded in seaports and cities (such as in San Francisco, New York, London, Liverpool, Cardiff) where there were natural growing Chinese communities which had to be fed, the Pekingese restaurants in the West were created only during the past couple of decades through the enterprise of some Chinese who wished deliberately to introduce the northern style of Chinese cuisine to the western public. They felt that the westerners should be introduced to Peking cooking, the haute cuisine of China, which should appeal to the western palate as much as the Cantonese cuisine. They therefore came in with a sense of pride and mission, and the majority of their earliest efforts were met with instant success. In point of fact, although Cantonese cooking can be termed as the 'cuisine bourgeoise' of China, Peking or North China is not necessarily all Imperial and haute cuisine. Much of the best of Peking cooking (such as noodles and dumplings) belonged to the lower strata of the society and was derived from the 'cuisine paysanne' of the provinces of Hopei and Shan tung. The majority of the truly haute cuisine dishes required too much refinement and cultivated eating to catch on: many of its top-line dishes are 'status dishes' (e.g. *Shark's Fins, Birds' Nests, Bêche de Mer, Fish Lips, Fish Maw,* etc.,) which are meant to lend weight and status to an official Mandarin banquet rather than for straightforward daily enjoyment and satisfaction.

What appeals to the western (and Chinese) palate in Peking and North China cooking are the roasts, barbecued meats, the hotpot dishes, the smoked dishes, the stir-fried thin-sliced or shredded meats where the yellow-bean paste is used, the lamb dishes (whether short-poached, quick-fried or barbecued), the braised dishes of meat, fish or vegetables, the noodles, steamed buns, and the light egg-white fu yung dishes, and curiously one or two sweet (dessert) dishes such as *Peking Glazed Apple* (sometimes misnamed 'Toffee Apple'), *Sweet Bean-Paste-Stuffed Meringue* (Kao Li Tao Sa), and *Peking Ice-Mountain Fruit Salad.* However, because of the formal background and official nature of Peking food it is less easy to adapt it to casual eating than Cantonese food. There is not a whole series of dishes which can be used or treated as 'self-contained' dishes for individual eating, as there are in Cantonese food. It is for party entertainment and official dinners that Peking food really comes into its own. When the full array of dishes are spread out on the table they can be very impressive.

As a rule the average Peking restaurants in the West are somewhat better furnished and attuned to the western idea of what a restaurant should be than their Cantonese counterparts, since they were originally meant to cater for westerners. However, very few of these Peking restaurants are thronging with Chinese customers as Cantonese restaurants often are, mainly because there are simply not many northern Chinese living abroad these days (probably less than five per cent of the Chinese abroad are northerners – the majority of the Cantonese are from Hong Kong, and come to the West on their British or Hong Kong passports). If some of the Peking restaurants appear to be thronging with orientals they are probably Japanese tourists who appear in them in droves. The Japanese love Pekingese food, as Japan is nearer to North China (and Canton used to be more within the influence of the British). As the Japanese are the wealthier tourists these days they are one of the influences which help to keep Peking food from veering away from the authentic, apart from the restaurateurs' own pride in the authenticity of their cuisine. In any case the western palate for Chinese food is growing rapidly more sophisticated and therefore more discriminating. As an observer it is interesting to note that the Chinese restaurateurs, especially the successful ones, are getting acutely aware that for any Chinese to be successful in the catering business their cooking must be not only of a high quality but authentic – and what the successful ones believe in quickly rubs off on the less successful ones. Hence there is now a great shortage of good Chinese chefs everywhere throughout Japan and the whole western world; they are in such high demand.

What should one order in Peking restaurants? When confronted with a Pekingese menu, with its usual one to two hundred dishes, one should again recall to mind the need for *variety* and *balance*, the over-riding principle in making up a Chinese meal, as well as the general pattern in the serving of dishes at a Chinese meal.

With these thoughts in mind I would make the following choice of dishes for a meal for four or five people in a typical Pekingese restaurant, purporting to serve authentic Pekingese dishes:

MENU 1

Starters:
> Smoked Fish (1 portion)
> Toasted Sesame Prawns (Chi ma Hsia)

First Main Dish 'Combination':
> 1 portion *Cha Chiang Mein Noodles* (freshly made noodles with meat sauce and shredded vegetables) served with 1 portion *Crispy Seaweeds* to be worked into the noodles.

Main Course Dishes to be Served with Rice (one portion of each):
> Shredded or Sliced Beef Quick-Fried with Spring Onion and Garlic
> Soft Sliced Fish in Peking Wine Sauce (Liu Yu Pien)
> Quick-Fried Diced Chicken Cubes in Yellow-Bean Sauce
> Plain Quick-Fried Tientsin Cabbage (Kai Yang Pai Tsai)

MENU 2

Starters:
> Phoenix-Tail Crispy Prawns
> Sliced Sole in Wine-Lee Sauce (Liu Yu Pieu)

Supplementary Starter:
> 10–15 *Peking Kuo Tieh Dumplings* (to be consumed after dipping in an *Aromatic Vinegar* and *Soya Sauce Dip*)

Independent Main Course:
> Half *Aromatic and Crispy Duck* (to be consumed with

pancakes, Peking Duck Sauce, and shredded
vegetables)

Soup:

Sliced Mutton and Cucumber Soup and Shredded
Vegetables

Main Course Dishes to be served with Rice:

Quick-Fried Diced Meats and Seafoods (Chao Chuen
Ting)

Plain Quick-Fried French Beans in Garlic Sauce

MENU FOR A PEKING BANQUET

The cost of Chinese banquets is usually calculated and
charged on the basis of how much per table – seating approximately ten people (but the charge will be the same for
eight or twelve people) – and not on how much per head, as
many of the dishes can only be served for group consumption. The cost of the following menu should range between
£80 to £120 per table, at the time of writing, depending
upon the reputation and standing of the restaurant and the
quality of the food and the refinement of the dishes served.
Good Chinese food is by no means cheap these days, as some
people may have once believed. Indeed Chinese food can be
considerably more expensive than French food. The charge
for a top gastronomic dinner prepared by some of the most
famous French chefs, held in Los Angeles in 1978, was no
more than £150 for two. The cost of an Imperial/Manchu
banquet held in Hong Kong at about the same time came
to more than £3000 per table!

Starter:

The Imperial Hors-d'oeuvres (A beautifully arranged
dish displaying at least seven cold items, all ex-
quisitely sliced or cut – these usually include such
items as Smoked Fish, Cold Quick Soya-Braised

*Prawns in Shells, White-Cut Drunken Chicken,
Pungent Pickled Eggs, Smoked Soya-Braised Beef,
Asparagus tips,* plus a variety of Pickles, etc.)

Wine-Drinking Dishes:

*Crispy Seaweeds with Shredded Dried Scallops
Shangtung Oil-Splash-Fried Chicken* (Yiu Ling Chi)
Crispy Snow-Flower Prawn Balls (Hseuh-Hua Hsia
Chiu)

Big Dishes:

*Braised Sharks' Fins in large Earthen-Pot Casserole
with Whole Chicken*
The Peking Duck (served with pancakes brushed with
sweet and pungent sauce with Shredded Cucumber
and Spring Onion)

Soup:

Vinegar 'Pepper-Pot' Sliced Fish Soup

Main Course Dishes:

Soya-Braised Whole Fish (bream, bass, carp)
Lion's Head Meat-Balls (specially succulent giant
meat-balls)
*Quick-Fried Sweet and Sour Duck's Liver
Braised Chinese Cabbage with Crab-Eggs*

Dessert:

Chilled Almond Jelly with Fresh Fruits (served as a
fruit salad)

A menu such as above should satisfy anyone, Chinese or
western, whose prime interest is in the enjoyment of eating.

As mentioned earlier, Peking food is more attuned for
party meals and banquets rather than for catering to individuals in ones and twos. However, as there is a good range
of dishes in its repertoire it should be possible to select and
arrange two-dish combinations which should satisfy and
appeal to the requirements of the casual individual diner.

FOR ONE PERSON (with average appetite)
Yang-Chow Fried Rice or *Cha Chiang Mein* (freshly-made noodles with meat sauce and shredded vegetables) with one dish of *Quick-Fried Sliced Lamb*.

Yang-Chow Fried Rice or *Cha Chiang Mein* with one dish of *Diced Chicken Cubes Quick-Fried in Yellow-Bean Sauce*.

Yang-Chow Fried Rice or *Cha Chiang Mein* with one dish of *Sliced Fish in Wine-lee Sauce*.

Yang-Chow Fried Rice or *Cha Chiang Mein* with one dish of *Quick-Fried 3 diced Fresh Savouries* (Pao San Yang).

Yang-Chow Fried Rice or *Cha Chiang Mein* served with *Egg-battered Sliced Chicken in Garlic and Spring Onion Sauce* (Kuo-ta chi).

Yang-Chow Fried Rice or *Cha Chiang Mein* served with *Braised Sliced Duck with Chinese Mushrooms*.

FOR TWO PERSONS (or for one person with a big appetite)
For two people who just want to have a quick casual meal together, the above six 'two-dish combinations' should be suitable for them as well, except that the *Yang-Chow Fried Rice* and *Cha Chiang Mein* should both be ordered together rather than treating them as an alternative choice to be served with the third Supplementary Savoury Dish. In other words, the meal will become a 'three-dish combination' meal for two.

Kuo Tieh or *Peking Steamed and Griddle-Fried Dumplings*. These 'dumplings' are stuffed with meats and chopped leeks or onion and are generally served in platefuls of ten or a dozen pieces. They can be ordered as useful supplementary items to add on to the foregoing two-or three-dish combinations', if these 'combinations' are found to be slightly short in weight for the requirements of the diners. These *Kuo Tieh Dumplings* convey a distinctive Peking flavour and atmosphere when consumed after having been dipped in Chinese Aromatic Vinegar, and some good quality soya sauce.

EATING CHOPSUEY

It seems that *Chopsueys* are somewhat out of fashion these days. When a westerner who has had some eating experience of Chinese food hears the word *Chopsuey* he or she will invariably turn his or her nose up. When a Chinese hears the word *Chopsuey* he will appear slightly amused and inscrutable, as *Chopsuey* is supposed to be something Chinese which he should know something about, and yet he doesn't: he has hardly ever ordered it in a restaurant, nor does he know a recipe for it (in fact there is hardly a definitive recipe for any Chinese dish – let alone *Chopsuey*!) It seems that *Chopsuey* originated in the Rocky Mountains about a hundred years ago. At that time they were building the transcontinental railways across the breadth of America. The Chinese labourers were building it eastwards from San Francisco, and the Irish were building it westwards from Chicago. When the lines met in the Rocky Mountains, the Irish found the Chinese eating some delicious, delectable stew. On inquiring what it was the Chinese said 'chopsuey', which in Cantonese meant 'mixed hash'. The Irish greatly enjoyed this dish, which in its most authentic form is really a Chinese Irish Stew! As one of the world's first great international dishes, in its original purest form, it should be fairly light in colour (like Irish Stew) as there could not have been a great supply of soya sauce in the Rockies in those early days. Over the decades it has been bastardized by the Chinese restaurants and take-away shops by the addition of an excess of monosodium-glutamate and soya sauce (which makes it much too brown in colour) and over-thickening with cornflour. To be authentic it should also be seasoned with only salt and pepper, with several varieties of vegetables added. Starting with onion, it should contain cabbage, and one or two other vegetables, such as celery, broccoli, cauliflower, or any other vegetables you can lay your hands on. It should be cooked in a rich meat broth (there being much meat and bone in the Wild West) which has been amply seasoned, and with bones all removed. The sliced meat should first be quick-fried (with sliced onion) in a small amount of oil, and the vegetables and stock added (the harder vegetables added first, and the softer vegetables last), to be simmered for about fifteen minutes longer. At its best it should resemble the French 'Pot-au-Feu'!

Seeing it in its true light and perspective, one should hardly turn one's nose up at a dish which has such a romantic background, and which with its 'family' of dishes still accounts for 75 per cent of the total turnover of Chinese food in the western world, which nowadays amounts to not much less than one billion US dollars per annum. If the dollar is All Mighty, *Chopsuey* is power. When properly cooked, *Chopsuey* is an excellent dish to consume together with *Spare-ribs* and *Fried Rice*. If you wish to be really economical, order a portion of plain boiled rice to go with the two savoury dishes. If you are dining in twos, order a dish of *Sweet and Sour Pork* to go with the *Chopsuey*, and *Spare-ribs* (plus rice).

The three dishes and rice (or Fried Rice) can be further supplemented with a *Chow Mein*. These four dishes can be termed the 'Chopsuey Classic' – when eaten together they should be sufficient to appease any two reasonable appetites. Besides, they represent a good variety of substance and flavours: the *Chopsuey* which is a 'semi-soup' dish provides the vegetables, the *Spare-ribs* is a comparatively dry and meaty dish, the *Sweet and Sour Pork* is entirely different in taste, and the *Fried Rice* is a bulk food, which is yet sufficiently savoury to be appealing to the average western palate. The main thing is that these dishes should be freshly-cooked, and not too greasy.

The other dishes of this 'chopsuey family' are:
Pancake Rolls;
Chicken Mushrooms;
Chicken with Almonds;
Fried Pacific Prawns;

Crispy Prawn Balls;
Quick-fried Prawns in Sauce (mostly tomato);
Sliced Beef with Mushrooms;
Shredded Beef with Onions;
Sliced Beef with Peppers;
Cha Shao Roast Pork;
Crispy Meat-Balls;
Quick-fried Sliced Pork with Greens;
Other *Chow Meins* (with prawns, chicken, beef or pork);
Braised Sliced Duck with Mushrooms.

Since in eating *Chopsuey* one is not launching on a gastronomic adventure, after having chosen the basic dishes, one can throw in any one of the above dishes, or several of them, to augment the meal. I do not mean that one can be indiscriminate; one has still to bear in mind the need for *balance*, and *variety*.

There are however a few *taboos*:

Taboo One
Do not order the same dish for each one of the diners at the table. If several people are dining together order a double portion of the dish which everybody likes and knows about, and make up the number of dishes (to at least one more than the number of people at the table) with other contrasting dishes. Repeat on the dishes which are the most popular. If only two people are dining together, order three dishes, and later repeat on the one which is the most appreciated. If there is no preference, and if you have appetite for more, select a fourth dish, which is different from the other three.

Taboo Two
Do not order a number of dishes which are all cooked in the same way, with the same sauces, and all the same colour. If you have a saucy dish, have another which is crisp and deep-fried. If you have two dry dishes, order one which is soupy, or have a soup (or two soups) which can be shared between the diners. If you already have two meat dishes, with one or

two mixed dishes (Fried Rice or Chow Mein), order a pure vegetable dish such as, Quick-fried Spinach, Quick-fried French Beans, or Quick-fried Bean Sprouts (never forget the vegetables, they are often the best dish on the menu). To order dishes all of the same colour, and cooked the same way is tantamount to having several ladies all appearing at the same party in the same dress!

Taboo Three
Do not pile all the food which can be gathered from the shared dishes on to your own plate, and wolf them down together. Place your share of the bulk food (rice, fried rice, or noodles) on your own plate first, add the other dishes, one variety at a time. In this way, you can taste the flavour and quality of each dish. If you pile them all on your plate in one great conglomeration, and stir them up together you will not know what each dish tastes like at all. Human beings should not try to out-do the canine species for indiscrimination!

HAVING A PARTY

If you wished to have a party, it would be best for you to go to a Pekingese or Cantonese restaurant. If there are none of these within convenient distance, and the only one from which you can obtain Chinese food is a chopsuey establishment, the best thing to do is to speak to the proprietors of the establishment first. Inform them of how much you are prepared to pay (£2–£5 per head, but always mention and emphasize the total sum – it sounds more impressive!), and ask them to prepare some of the dishes which they would recommend, on top of the dishes which you would like to have.

Apart from the basic dishes, such as *Spare-ribs* and one or two bulk dishes (there must always be one or two 'bulk dishes', such as *Noodles*, and *Fried Rice* for a party, as you cannot live off prawns alone without running up an astronomical bill), you should stipulate that you would like to have a couple of dishes where the foods are cooked whole: whole duck, whole chicken, whole fish, or whole chunks or large-sized pieces of meat which can be further divided when served. Only in this way can you have some large impressive dishes, instead of being always served with only stir-fried chopped-up foods, which are not the style in which we Chinese serve ourselves anyway – certainly not at a party. If you give the proprietors such a briefing, you may get a good display and selection of dishes even without going to chinatown, or to one of the Pekingese or Cantonese establishments. For the majority of Chinese caterers – even the ordinary take-away shops – are usually quite capable of producing some good-quality impressive dishes if given the direction and incentive to do so.

SZECHUAN AND HUNAN COOKING

The cuisine of the far western provinces of Szechuan and Hunan suddenly became popular in New York a few years ago. Every American who knows his onions about Chinese food would demand Szechuan and Hunan dishes. In point of fact hardly any Chinese would have a whole meal or banquet which consists of nothing but Szechuan and Hunan dishes. The effect would be dishes which are too hot and spicy and which, in the end, would defeat their own purpose. The style of food in China today and in the Far East is generally to make up a menu in which these hot-spicy dishes from Szechuan and Hunan are inserted and interspersed into a background of dishes from the other regions. What we aim for is balance and variety. All Pekingese restaurants are capable of producing a few Szechuan and Hunan dishes. Ask them to provide you with a Pekingese dinner with a couple of items of Szechuan (or Hunan) items thrown in: such as, *Tea and Camphor-Wood Smoked Duck*, *Kung-Po Diced Chicken Cubes in Yellow Bean Sauce*, *Dry-fried Chewy Shredded Beef*, *Bang-Bang Chicken*, *Mixed*

Shredded Duck with Shredded Ginger, and Hot Mustard Dressing, Quick-fried Kidneys in Sesame and Red-Oil Sauce, Whole Fish (steamed or fried) in Hot Black Bean Dressing, etc. The Szechuan dishes will provide a balance to the dishes from the other region or regions.

What to Drink with Chinese Food

Although wine has been very much a part of the Chinese scene from time immemorial, Chinese drinking habits have been characterized by little refinement.

Chinese wine is not made from grapes, but from glutinous rice; water is added to the rice, with a small amount of yeast, to induce fermentation, and some Kaoliang, which is a spirit distilled from sorghum seeds, to act as a catalyst. The wine is usually kept in large earthenware jars (like those Phoenician ones) and ladled out with a long ladle made from a section of bamboo. The taste is rather like dry sherry and it is often taken warm; at Chinese banquets it is served in pewter pots, which are stood in hot water in a porcelain bowl. The best known of these rice wines – or yellow wine, as it is called in China – are the *Shiao Hsing* and the *Hua Tiao*, but what is confusing to the westerner is that no distinction is made in China between spirit, wine and beer: all are called *Ch'iu*. The spirit wines which are also drunk in large quantities at a Chinese dinner are stronger than vodka so, if you are offered a tumbler of 'wine' at a Chinese banquet, beware!

If, however, you prefer to drink a wine made from grapes with your Chinese meal, here are some suggestions which may be of help. It is probably true that the stronger, full-bodied wines are more suitable than the weaker, white wines, because there are more rich and highly-flavoured dishes than lighter, plain ones.

Since many Chinese dinners these days commence with an assortment of hors-d'oeuvres, which include items ranging from *Thousand-Year-Old Eggs* to *Crystal-Boiled Chicken*, and since it would not be possible to have a wine with a character to match them all, it might be best to start the meal with a sparkling wine, or champagne, or sherry.

The hors-d'oeuvres are usually followed by a number of quick-fried dishes, some of which may be plain and natural-flavoured, such as *Crystal-Fried Prawns* or *Fu-Yung Chicken*, or strongly flavoured, such as *Quick-Fried Chicken with Black Bean and Chilli* or *Dry-Fried Shredded Beef* or *Diced Cubes of Pork in Soya Paste Sauce*, so perhaps it is best to serve two wines during this second series of dishes: a dry, white unassertive wine such as a Graves, to go with the lighter dishes, and a young red wine, such as a Beaujolais, to go with the stronger tasting dishes.

After the quick-fried dishes you come to the main big dishes of which there are generally three or four. To meet the size and succulence of these, you will need to bring out your 'big guns' – the bolder and heavier red wines, such as young Bordeaux or Rhône wine.

It has always been a problem to find a wine to go with *Sweet and Sour* dishes; one with any sharpness may clash with the sauce, but a soft, warm wine, with a slight edge to it, might be able to embrace, as well as offset, what sharpness there is in the sauce. Connoisseurs are up against the same problem when they try to find a matching wine for *Peking Duck*; the plummy sauce served with the duck has a sweet and sour quality, while the roast duck itself, which is rich and aromatic, and the pancake, may require something which is both full-bodied and settling to go with it. Since it is not possible to cater for both of them at the same time, it is best to compromise by serving the warm Chinese yellow wine, which has a soothing, sherry-like quality about it.

The marriage of western wines to Chinese dishes should afford plenty of scope for explorations of the highest sophistication. But I give here the menu for a banquet which the Chinese Gourmet Club held in conjunction with a wine club called *Les Amis du Vin*, during which a wine was selected to match every Chinese dish served:

Chinese Dishes	*Wines Served*
Deep-fried Crispy Scallop and Seaweeds	Candido, Very Very Dry Fino
Shanghai Crystal Prawns	Mori Dry 1971 (Hungary)
Sliced Fish in Peking Wine Sauce	Tsing Tao Dry White Wine (People's Republic of China)
Shanghai Miniature Pork Chops	Chardonnay Blanc de Blancs de Haut-Poitou
Quick-Fried Diced Chicken Cubes with Almonds	Crozes-Hermitage Blanc, Tête de Cuveé 1973
Quick-Fried Mange Tout	Californian Zinfandel
Quick-Fried Sliced Lamb with Spring Onions	Malbeck, Grave del Friuli 1972 (Italy)
Braised Stuffed Mushrooms	Lirac, Château St Roch 1971
Pot-Roasted Boneless Duck	McWilliams Cabernet Sauvignon 1971 (Australia)
Fresh Fruits	Lychee Wine (Taiwan)

China Tea

Tea is drunk in China for its flavour and fragrance, for its refreshment, and for the promotion of conversation and sociability, whereas in Britain it seems to be taken for its warming and reviving effect.

The different attitudes are probably explained by the difference in climate. With Britain's long murky winter and damp chilly spring, it is essential to have a drink to revive the sagging spirit; the tea for such occasions should naturally be hot, strong, dark and full of body.

China is a hot country during the summer, and as we do not drink beer, or iced-drinks, tea is our main thirst-quencher, and the chief source of the body's liquid replacement. Apart from these primary functions, tea also takes the place of the western cocktails and cigarettes; it is passed around whenever there is a visitor or a social gathering. In contrast to English tea, China tea should be the colour of whisky or brandy; pale, yellow and golden.

Tea is usually made and served in individual cups, which are fitted with lids, to keep the floating tea-leaves from the drinker's lips; when the lid is opened it releases a momentary fragrance. Tea is sipped from these cups, just as one takes puffs from a cigarette in the West, during pauses in conversation. In more intimate companies, between close friends, tea is made in small pots, enough for four small cups; in both instances, a second infusion is allowed, but a third is not permissible.

In the family, on shop counters, in police stations, and government offices, tea is usually made in a large pot, which is placed inside a padded or upholstered basket-work bucket, to keep it hot, and is drunk continually throughout the day.

Perfect China tea should be made in a small pot, and from a small kettle of boiling water, so that for each infusion a new lot of water is boiled; for the best effect an earthenware kettle should be used. The Chinese believe that tea should be made from water which still contains fresh life-giving air (oxygen); the infusion should therefore be made immediately the water comes to a full boil. An earthenware kettle is preferred because it is porous and will be able, it is believed, to hold more fresh air in the water; besides it would be less likely to make the water taste metallic.

As for the types of water which we Chinese use for making tea, we prefer them in the following order, which takes into account their air content as well as their purity: deep spring water, well water, rain water, river water, taken from the middle of the river (not from the sides, where it is bound to be polluted).

From the foregoing it would seem almost impossible to make good China tea in the average kitchen in the West without going to immense trouble. The best that can be done is to make small pots of tea from small kettles, and to serve the tea as though it were a precious liquid, in small cups, as one does brandy.

When sipping tea the connoisseurs always wait to savour the so-called 'return flavour' which is that certain pleasant sweetness which comes to the mouth when one is able to sip tea leisurely. Again, the Chinese attitude towards tea is like the western attitude towards brandy; you smell and inhale its fragrance, and then you sip for its flavour and its 'return-flavour' before you enjoy the warmth and satisfaction of gulping it down.

Chinese tea-drinking should be a contemplative experience; it should be like the enjoyment of the full moon, the first snow of winter, or the first blossoms in spring – an experience to be enjoyed with people of similar tastes, and in the right mood.

In China it is said that tea is best enjoyed with a few friends, and not in a crowd as is beer-drinking; when engaged in pleasant conversation deep into the night; in quiet secluded temples by famous springs; in studios with lighted incense. Tea-drinking and preparations are, therefore, as much an artistic and philosophical discipline as a sensual experience. If you can evoke the contemplative mood, holiday spirit, and organize the few prerequisites, you should be able to enjoy China tea to the utmost – or as much as the Chinese themselves have made and enjoyed this 'golden nectar'.

There was no tea in England during the time of Shakespeare. He did not mention it in his plays or sonnets. Nor did any of Chaucer's characters appear to drink tea during their long pilgrimage to Canterbury. Indeed, tea was first mentioned in European literature in 1559, in the *Voyage & Travels of Giovannita Ramusio*, a Venetian author; he called it *Chai Cata* (Tea of China). The first recorded mention of the beverage in the English language occurred in a letter written by an agent of the East India Company in Japan to a fellow agent in Macao. He wrote on 27 January 1615, 'I pray you buy for me a pot of the best Chaw.' Tea only began to make itself felt in Europe towards the middle of the seventeenth century: in France it made its first appearance in 1636, in Russia in 1638, and in England in 1650.

Tea drinking soon became the vogue in England; it cost just under £1 a lb, which makes it one of the very few commodities not to have increased much in price in three and a half centuries! Dr Johnson drew his own portrait as 'a hardened and shameless tea-drinker'. For twenty years, he said, he drank tea with all his meals; and it was with tea he amused his evenings, with tea solaced the midnight, and with tea welcomed the morning.

In China, except in the provinces of Kwangtung and Fukien, we do not drink tea at mealtimes, we drink soup. We drink tea before the meal and afterwards, but it is not our habit to drink it during the meal. On the other hand, there is no reason why it should not be drunk during the meal, especially on occasions when there is no soup, or when there are not enough wines for the number of dishes served. Tea undoubtedly seems to possess an ability to cleanse and dissolve grease; its astringent quality seems to have a decongesting effect. Since the majority of Chinese dishes are stir-fried and, in many Chinese dishes, pork fat and skin are consumed in quantity and enjoyed, the drinking of copious amounts of tea must have a beneficial influence on the digestive tract. In view of this I would recommend that tea should be drunk during meals if no soup is served; and even if soup is served, one or two small cups of tea should be drunk, as if they were liqueurs, to conclude the meal.

Fortunately some of the best China teas are still available in this country. The following are some of the best known:

Dragon Well (green tea from Chekiang)
Lu An (green tea from Anhui)
Water Nymph (green tea from Kwangtung)
Gunpowder (north China)
Oolong Leaf Bud (very expensive semi-fermented tea from Formosa)
Iron Goddess of Mercy (black tea from Fukien)
Keemun (black tea from Anhui)
Pu-trh (black tea from Yunnan)
Jasmine Tea (Jasmine with *oolong* from Fukien)
Chrysanthemum Tea (green tea with dried chrysanthemums)
Rose Tea (black tea with dried rosebuds)
Lychee Tea (black tea with lychee flavouring)
Lapsang Souchong (smoked black tea from Hunan)

There you have your choice. Treat China tea like wine if you drink it during a meal; make it stronger, and treat it as a liqueur, if you drink it to conclude a meal. You will enjoy it more if you treat it with greater reverence – and it will then probably reward you by being more beneficial and uplifting to you.

The Act of Eating – The Chinese Way

When you have a distinctive cuisine you naturally have a distinctive style in consuming it. Although the Chinese mouth differs only marginally from the western mouth it is capable of functioning in several ways which the average western mouth would require very specialized training to achieve! These special capabilities of the Chinese teeth and mouth have arisen purely from the traditional items which the mouth and teeth have been made to eat.

For instance, all properly brought up Chinese mouths and teeth are capable of extracting the kernel from a hard, flat, dried melon seed at the rate of five to six seeds a minute. Hence, in the past, the floor of every cinema or theatre was practically carpeted with the husks of melon seeds. Now the extraction of the white nutty kernel from the husk of the seed is by no means easy. It requires the cracking of the tip of the flat seed with a front tooth, which causes the husk to split, and the moment this split occurs, the teeth fasten on to the kernel of the seed like a pincer and extract it. The kernel is then chewed or ground up with nutty satisfaction by the molars. The process is then immediately repeated, often several times a minute, always automatically without any thought at all given to any part of the process. The result is that there is often a tiny rut worn in the Chinese front teeth for fitting in the melon seed. I had a very distinctive rut in one of my front teeth until the tooth itself got lost in chewing a crab! Eating shrimps and prawns with shells is another specialized process, although not quite as difficult as extracting melon seed kernel from husks. We Chinese believe that shrimps and prawns can taste better if cooked (usually dry-fried) with their shells on, although often with their heads removed. The correct way to remove the shell and get at the meat is to place the meaty end of the shrimp or prawn (usually the end where the head has been removed) pointing towards the back of the mouth, and then proceed to bite gently the outside of the shell from the tail-end of the shrimp in quick, short nibbles, in the direction of the back of the mouth; the meat of the shrimp is then squeezed out. The Chinese also enjoy chewing the sauce-laden shells.

The Chinese way of eating spare ribs is again very different from the western way. The Chinese eat their small chops of spare ribs by putting the whole thing into their mouths and by biting the meat on either side of the bone. The meat is soon stripped from the bone and finally, by pushing the bone from the mouth with the tip of the tongue, the last severing of the meat from the bone is achieved by snapping together the front teeth, and pulling or taking away the bone with the aid of chopsticks. This is a less messy way of eating them than handling with the fingers from the beginning. Most Chinese are aghast at the large size of the spare ribs in the West!

The eating of rice from the bowl, as you will know, is not done with spoons, but by lifting the rice-bowl to the mouth, and shovel-eating with chopsticks. This is a very satisfying process, when you get the habit of making the right mixture of meat, gravy, rice and vegetables. In China the whole process of eating a meal with many dishes on the table always consists of picking from the dishes and placing the various morsels of your choice on top of your own rice and 'watering' the arrangement with just the right amount of gravy or soup, and then 'shovelling' them into the mouth. The repetition of this process, in changing the pattern and composition of the food on top of the rice, adds to the gastronomic and aesthetic delight. To pile all the food which you intend to eat during the whole meal all at once on to your rice, is to deny yourself this pleasure.

The use of a slight sucking action is more usual in Chinese eating than in western eating, which seems to be noiseless. Sucking, or breathing inwards, is a necessary part of 'shovel-eating' rice or when you are drinking very hot soup from a porcelain spoon (the inward breathing seems to help in ruffling and cooling the surface of the soup, which we like very hot). This latter habit seems to spread to the eating of all kinds of very hot food. Since, in many stir-fried dishes heat is an integral part of the flavour, a great deal of mild sucking goes on all around the table when several hot dishes are brought in steaming from the kitchen. Polite Chinese eating admits of making some noise while eating, but not of making any exaggerated noise. Belching, which is said to be prevalent in Japan, is positively discouraged in China, except amongst the senile.

When eating crab and fish-heads a good deal of sucking action is required to detach the meat from the bones or shells, for here the meat seldom occurs in large chunks or pieces, but more often in strips and small bits, which can only be separated from the shells and bones by a general gnawing and chewing, rather than cutting and biting. Hence the mouth, tongue and teeth have to act as a kind of combined flexible sieve, which separates the meat from the bone and shell, the edible from the inedible. The sieve-like function is again another special capacity of the Chinese mouth. On a Chinese dinner-table there is a side-plate beside the rice-bowl, on which bones and other inedibles, which are bound to accumulate during a Chinese meal, can be piled. The side-plate, which is about the size of a saucer, is also where the spoon is placed, and against which the chopsticks are leant during a meal. A small chopstick rest, made from porcelain or metal, is only provided at a party dinner or banquet, except in the most fashionable, pretentious or elegant households.

Soups, as I have often explained, are drunk at intervals throughout the meal, but are seldom taken when eating a mouthful of crispy food. The joy of eating crispy food is partly derived from cracking the crispness in the mouth as you eat, which releases the full aromatic flavour; therefore the food should remain crisp until it is swallowed.

The consumption of so much food, which is cooked with shells or chopped through the bone, the need to strip and detach the meat from the bones and shells, makes the use of toothpicks imperative after a Chinese meal. When picking their teeth, the Chinese always raise their unoccupied hand to screen this operation. It is interesting to note that, as the western sensibility drifts away from Edwardian stuffiness, the use of toothpicks has been growing everywhere during the past couple of decades.

The eating of noodles is a function which combines the process of sucking, sipping, gulping and biting all at once. The soup is sipped from the edge of the bowl, the noodles are partly sucked in and are bitten by the front teeth, so that the uneaten part is eased gently back into the bowl for the next mouthful. If the soup is hot it is blown on first, at the edge of the bowl, and sipped into the mouth while outgoing breath furrows the top of the soup, cooling it somewhat as it streams gently over the lip into the mouth.

Chopsticks

The use of chopsticks is of course basic to Chinese eating, but the method of holding them is often described in the most complicated way. I shall endeavour to describe it here as simply as possible: hold the top chopstick between the index finger, middle finger and thumb; the stick should pass under the index finger, slightly on top of the tip of the longer finger, and be held in position by the thumb. Test this chopstick by moving it up and down. The lower chopstick is inserted below, through the junction between the index finger and the thumb; this chopstick is held in position by firmly crooking the fourth finger and is held firm and static. Objects are picked up by pressing the top chopstick on to the lower one so that the tips of the two chopsticks come together.

Quite a few westerners learn to use chopsticks at the first trial, and become quite adept by the end of the meal. The most important thing is to try to relax while using them. Most artistic people, who have learned to concentrate and relax at the same time, can generally use chopsticks readily. I taught Sir Malcolm Sargent in Liverpool during the war in just one minute. One should not practise by trying to pick up rice from a flat plate, as this is discouraging and it is not the way the Chinese eat rice anyway. We only use the chopsticks to pick up rice when a quantity of grains have become stuck together in a lump. Most Chinese food has either been cut into suitable bite-size pieces, which are easy to pick up with chopsticks, or it has been cooked lengthily to such a degree of tenderness that it can be taken apart with chopsticks easily. At Chinese meals, therefore, everything is eaten with chopsticks, except the soup, which is drunk with a porcelain spoon. We consider porcelain spoons superior to metal spoons because they do not take on heat from hot soup; as we are in the habit of serving food as hot as possible, directly from the pan, this is important. But, also, porcelain can be made more decorative than metal, being capable of variation in colour as well as shape.

Table arrangement

In the past, in China, the diners at a table took spoonfuls of soup direct from the communal bowl, so no separate soup-bowl was required for each person at the table. For the individual, the only bowl needed was the rice-bowl, which sometimes doubled for the soup-bowl when, at the end of the meal, some soup was poured into the bowl and drunk with any remaining rice. Apart from the side-plate, that was all there was; nowadays, as a concession to hygiene, a separate soup-bowl is provided for each diner for the soup to be transferred to from the large communal bowl which is done with a specially large porcelain spoon. Nowadays too, several pairs of communal chopsticks are often provided to transfer food from the communal dishes to the individual bowl. Most Chinese regard these new arrangements with disfavour, as all this transferring tends to cool the food, which we prefer very hot; and the use of double sets of chopsticks and spoons, to separate people from people, reduces the feeling of togetherness and communal spirit of a Chinese meal, where there should be complete participation. Besides, the use of additional equipment simply makes more washing-up, and, anyway, has it ever been proved that the use of communal chopsticks and spoons causes people to fall ill? Perhaps a few bacteria will help to build up resistance to infection. Many Chinese indulge in these latterday practices only as a show – to impress the westerners – and in the end, either through forgetfulness, or frustration, half of the personal spoons and chopsticks will have gone into the communal bowl. In any case, we seem none the worse for it (you do not live longer by keeping apart!).

Chinese dining tables are generally round, especially the large party tables (occasionally there are square tables but that should not disturb the scheme of things on the table), and the dishes of food are arranged at the centre. The communal soup, contained in a large bowl or tureen, is placed at the very centre; if there are other types of food in bowls, casseroles or tureens, they should also be placed in the centre, behind a 'rampart' formed by the flat dishes. This is a logical arrangement, because situated as they are, everybody is at an equal distance from the food, and the foods which are contained in higher dishes or bowls, are behind the lower, flatter dishes, which makes them all equally visible and easily reached. The diners sitting round the table take 'pot shots' at the food, or make occasional charges or sallies into the centre. At a properly organized Chinese dinner there are always reinforcements, waiting to be brought in; not to do this would be to lose face, which is not permissible. At a polite Chinese dinner, dignity must be maintained at all costs, so if you have any doubt about how far you can stretch the food, cook more rice or noodles; and, in preparing the savoury meat dishes, add fractionally more soya sauce or pickles or dried food. These have the effect of concentrating the flavours and making savoury foods stronger tasting; stronger flavoured and more pungent foods always go further. It is also a Chinese convention that, to be polite, you must eat everything in your own bowl, and certainly not leave even a grain of rice in the bottom.

Table manners and etiquette

At a formal Chinese dinner the guest of honour is placed with his back to the north, facing the host, who sits opposite him with his back to the south, as if he were a subject facing the sovereign, who always sits facing south in the throne room. At the beginning of the dinner everyone fights to avoid the seat of honour; even the obvious guest of honour places himself in the second or third place of honour, but he will eventually be pushed into the proper seat by the host. After the first two or three honoured guests have been seated the rest will fill in the places between the guest of honour and the host. When everybody is seated, the host proceeds on his round of drinks, which means he moves around the table and drinks to the health of everybody, starting with the guest of honour. When this procedure has been completed, the host will point his chopsticks at the cold dishes or hors-d'oeuvres in the centre of the table and invite the guests to proceed. At this signal, which is not unlike the signal for the 'charge of the Light Brigade', all the diners at the table will rise slightly, push forward their own chopsticks, like so many sabres, and take pot-shots at the juicy bits on the dishes at the centre of the table.

The main dishes are served in courses, one after another, and since the earlier courses generally consist of the lighter quick-fried food and are comparatively small dishes, they are demolished by the diners, who acquire fresh appetites in next to no time. At the beginning of each course the host invites everybody to a fresh round of drinks before he signals to them to 'attack' again. Some remark will be made by him, or by one of the others at the table about how seasonal the food is, that it has only just come on to the market, or something concerning the special technique of the chef, or that such a dish has not been eaten or even seen for some length of time; or the host might say how meagre his provision of food is. But by this time, after a few rounds of drinks and several courses, a spirit of easy conviviality and relaxation will have taken over and there will be less formality. Between the guests themselves there will be invitations to drink and certainly more than one guest will rise to propose the health of the host and to thank him for his hospitality. Occasionally the guests will begin to play the finger-game in pairs, shouting loudly at one another at the next seat, or across the full width of the table (the finger-game consists of shouting the right number of fingers extended simultaneously by two people, and the loser is obliged to 'dry cup', or drink a full measure in his own cup). By this time the party will have been carried away on its own momentum, and there will be no formality left at all, and everyone will be slapping everyone else's back and all talking at once.

As a matter of fact there is not as much etiquette or manners to a Chinese dinner as western people would like to imagine – after all we are no longer living in the Manchu Dynasty, any more than you are in Edwardian times – the main thing is not to make an obvious pig of yourself at the dining table or go and sit in the seat of honour without invitation. For, if you take more than your share of the choicer bits, several people will have made a mental note of the fact. In the old days if you did that too often you would not be invited to any more parties, and these were most important to material and spiritual health. In present day China, where the whole morality is aimed at the common good, you would not be dining off the fat of the land in any case, and if you did and you ate like a pig you may soon be obliged to write a 10,000 word confession on why you are such a pig, or to answer 200 questions put to you by your peers at a very formal meeting, none of which are likely to be very flattering!

In these days of Revolution and unprecedented Reconstruction the Chinese mind is not bent entirely on food – although Chinese cuisine is certainly one of China's great cultural heritages. As for the westerners eating Chinese food, so long as they are polite, considerate, and have good manners in the western sense, they will hardly go wrong, or be considered ill-mannered in a Chinese sense. Politeness and good manners are universal, and consideration for others, indivisible.

A Selection of Chinese Dishes

The dishes in this selection will be divided into the following categories: Soups, Chicken, Duck, Pork, Beef, Lamb, Fish and Crustaceans, Rice, Egg Dishes, Noodles, Breads, Vegetables, Hotpots, Sweet Dishes, Dim Sums, Chopsueys.

The names of each dish will be given in both Mandarin and English, as well as in Cantonese, since most Chinese restaurants and waiters abroad are from Canton or the province of Kwangtung; if a dish has strong regional connotations the name of the province, town, or area, will be added in brackets to distinguish it from the majority of dishes, which are common throughout China.

SOUPS

Primary Stock

Mandarin: *Gāo Tāng*
Cantonese: *Gòu Tòng*

This stock is in constant use in the Chinese kitchen both for making soups and for adding to braised or stir-fried dishes to augment the gravy. It is normally made by boiling and simmering together meat bones and poultry carcasses. When made purely with bones and carcasses, it is sometimes called *Err Tang* or *Secondary Stock*. For stocks of somewhat superior quality a proportion of lean pork, and ham (only a small quantity of it, or ham bone) are added. The result is a clear broth, which is often served free of charge in restaurants in China, and very occasionally in chinatown restaurants abroad.

Chicken Stock

Mandarin: *Ji Tang*
Cantonese: *Gāi Toṅg*

This is a variation of the *Primary Stock*, where a whole chicken (usually an old bird or cockerel) is added; the result is clear stock with a strong chicken flavour.

Meat-Ball Spinach Soup

Mandarin: *Rou Wan Bo Cai Tang*
Cantonese: *Yuhk Yùhn Boi Choi Toṅg*

The meat-balls here are made of minced meat which has been seasoned with chopped onion, ginger and soya sauce, and have a diameter of about 18mm (¾ in). There should be at least one meat-ball to each diner at the table. They should be simmered for not much more than 4–5 minutes so that when they are bitten into one can savour the fresh meaty taste. About 100g (4 oz) of chopped spinach is usually added to an average bowl of soup. Its distinctive flavour, and greenness in colour provide a contrast to the meat-balls in the soup.

Sliced Meat and Cucumber Soup

Mandarin: *Roù Piān Huang Gūa*
Cantonese: *Yuhk Pin Wohṅg Gẁa Toṅg*

Both the meat and the cucumber (including skin) are simmered in the stock for a very short time in order to retain their freshness.

Dried Scallop, Sliced Meat and Asparagus Soup

Mandarin: *Gan Bèi Ròu Piān Lóng Xu Cai Tang*
Cantonese: *Gòn Bui Yukh Pin Luhng Sòu Choi Tong*

The dried scallops which are used for flavouring in China are not the whole scallop, but just the piece of muscle which connects the body to its shell; this muscle is cut into disc-shaped pieces, and has a very delicate savoury flavour. It is used only for the more refined dishes in which a mild background flavour is required to vary a soup or sauce which is already savoury. In this soup the distinctive flavour of asparagus is given more body with the sliced pork, and sometimes varied with a background flavour of dried shrimps. The dried scallop has to be simmered for a good length of time; the asparagus would require about thirty minutes, while the sliced meat would require no more than a few minutes of simmering before serving.

Abalone and Sliced Chicken Soup

Mandarin: *Bao Yǔ Jì Piān Tāng*
Cantonese: *Bauh Yùh Gāi Pin Tong*

Abalone is used in almost precisely the same manner as dried scallop – for flavouring – though it needs only a short cooking time.

The Triple Fresh Flavour Soup

Mandarin: *Sān Xiān Tāng*
Cantonese: *Saàm Sín Tong*

The three fresh ingredients used in making this soup usually consist of shrimps, meat (chicken or pork) and bamboo-shoots. The difference between this soup and a soup known as *Triple-Sliced Soup* is that, in the latter soup, the ingredients used may already have been cooked, while in this soup all the ingredients added must be fresh and raw.

Sliced Fish Soup

Mandarin: *Yú Piān Tang*
Cantonese: *Yuh Pin Tong*

In western cooking fish is usually cooked in fish stock; the Chinese on the other hand, true to their principle of blending flavours, cook fish more frequently in chicken stock or primary stock. Often a small amount of ginger, wine or vinegar is added to the soup to help eliminate its fishiness. The fish is sliced into 2·5 × 4cm (1 × 1½ in) pieces and often given a thin coating of egg-white and cornflour before being simmered, for not more than 4–5 minutes. Not infrequently, dried mushrooms are added to increase the subtlety of flavour. This very appealing soup is suitable for serving at party meals.

Hot and Sour Soup (Peking and north China)

Mandarin: *Suān Là Tang*
Cantonese: *Syūn Laaht Tong*

This is one of the few Chinese thick soups. It is made hot and sour by the addition of vinegar and freshly-ground pepper to a highly-savoury soup, made of shredded chicken, shrimps, dried shrimps, dried mushrooms, 'golden needles' (lily-bud stems), and diced bean-curd. The soup is dark in colour and thickened with cornflour. It is a peppery soup with plenty of body which makes it most suitable for the Peking winter.

Clear Whole Chicken Soup

Mandarin: *Ching Dun Ji Tāng*
Cantonese: *Ching Deuhn Gāi Tong*

This is one of the big soups, where a whole chicken (preferably an old hen) is cooked in a big pot over low heat in a double-boiler for 2½ hours, with only some seasonings of salt, ginger, spring onion, and yellow wine added. The important point about this soup is that it must be clear, which is the essential quality of a good consommé. The chicken meat is eaten by dipping pieces of it into good-quality soya sauce, after the diners have drunk the liquid.

Clear Whole Duck Soup

> Mandarin: *Chīng Dùn Ya Tāng*
> Cantonese: *Ching Deuhn Ấp Tòng*

This is very much the same kind of soup as the *Clear Whole Chicken Soup*, except the duck, usually being more fatty than chicken, requires more skimming of fat during the first hour of cooking. A whole piece of ham and several slices of bamboo-shoot are also added. After 2½–3 hours of slow cooking (either in a steamer or double-boiler) the duck-meat should be tender enough to take apart with a pair of chopsticks.

Pork Tripe and Green Pea Soup (Szechuan)

> Mandarin: *Féi Cháng Dòu Shà Tāng*
> Cantonese: *Feìh Cheùhng Dauh Sà Tòng*

For six portions over 400g (1 lb) of tripe, and 300g (12 oz) green peas should be used. The peas should be minced; the tripe cut into square or triangular pieces and steamed for 3 hours with onion, garlic, ginger, yellow wine or sherry and salt. Then both tripe and peas are combined in a chicken stock; this is a connoisseur's dish.

Shark's Fin Soup

> Mandarin: *Yú Chi Tāng*
> Cantonese: *Yùh Chi Tòng*

Shark's fin soup is a classic banquet dish and is capable of many variations: it can be prepared with shredded chicken and beaten egg-white, with crab meat, with shredded ham and abalone. The shark's fin, which comes dried, is extremely tough, like a rhinoceros horn, and requires several stages of lengthy soaking and simmering before it is ready for cooking. What we Chinese enjoy about *Shark's Fin Soup* is partly the knowledge of the time and care which have gone into the preparation, and the excellence of the quality of all the ingredients employed. It is an amalgam of carefully orchestrated flavours enhanced by the texture of the shark's fin itself, which should now be soothing, sticky, and tender.

Won Ton Soup (Canton) (see recipe on page 196)

Mandarin: *Hún Tàn Tāng*
Cantonese: *Wàhn Tàn Tong*

To be authentic, the soup, which is a consommé, should not be too savoury, nor should it be too chickeny in flavour. The thin-skinned ravioli, with long flapping tails, should float in the soup like so many 'lost souls' or like 'floating clouds'. The stuffing should consist of finely chopped meat (chopped, not exactly minced) with spring onion and, occasionally, shrimps. Although delicate, this is a dish of the people, which is served in tea-shops and ordinary eating-places in China, rather than first-class restaurants. In the West (especially America) the skin of the dough packets is usually too thick (more like the authentic Italian), which causes the *Won Ton* to lose its 'lost soul' effect.

Chicken Noodle Soup

Mandarin: *Jī Sī Tāng Miàn*
Cantonese: *Gāi Sī Tong Mihn*

This is one of the most popular and common soups served in Chinese restaurants, probably because it is so easy to make, and also because westerners know exactly what they are eating. In China this soup is often served as a kind of tea on occasions marking an anniversary in a family, when every visitor is given a small bowl as soon as he arrives. It is a very welcome 'small dish' to have as soon as one steps indoors, in anticipation of the occasion and all the friends and relatives one is about to meet.

Bird's Nest Soup (see recipe on page 197)

Mandarin: *Yán Wo Tāng*
Cantonese: *Yin wò Tong*

'*Yán Wō*' means swallow-nest: the edible bird's nest is made by special sea-swallows which nest in the South China Seas where they gather and eat small fish and seafoods and re-gurgitate them to form the nests. These are cup-shaped and have to be prepared before being cooked with other in-gredients into a dish which is either savoury or sweet. Since nests which retain their whole cup-shape are very scarce (they can sometimes fetch over £100 a lb) the bulk of them are marketed in dry, porous, broken, brittle cakes contained in small boxes. After preparing them, which means sim-mering at a slow boil for an hour or so, when the pieces will separate into strips or shreds, they are ready to be cooked with other ingredients such as top-quality chicken stock, shredded ham, and chicken, occasionally with beaten egg-white added. Like shark's fin, bird's nest soup has only a faint taste of its own; its flavour is mainly an orchestrated one, produced by the various ingredients which are carefully in-corporated into the soup. Also like shark's fin, bird's nest soup is translucent, but it has a slightly firmer and rougher texture. It is largely a pretentious soup; part of the pleasure of eating it is derived from the knowledge of its cost and scarcity and the amount of time that has been expended in its preparation; it is very much part of a Chinese 'Mandarin official banquet'.

CHICKEN

Red-Cooked Chicken

Mandarin: *Hóng Shāo Jī*
Cantonese: *Hùhng Sìu Gāi*

One of the most common and popular ways of preparing
meat or poultry is to red-cook (or soya braise) it. The
chicken is cooked either whole, or chopped through the
bones into large bite-size pieces, with the addition of soya
sauce, some water and a small amount of sugar, wine and
ginger. The technique is to cook it slowly over low heat for
1½ hours, and the result is felicitous: the meat should by this
time be very tender and easily detachable from the bones,
and there should be ample gravy, which can be poured on
rice, or used for dipping steamed buns into. The chicken can
be browned first by frying in oil, or chicken fat, and drained
before the soya sauce and water are added, but it is not
essential, as with the amount of soya sauce added (about 5–7
tablespoons for an average-size bird) the bird should become
quite brown in any case. Soya sauce enriches all meats and
poultry and the addition of a small amount of sugar and
wine further enhances the flavour. A couple of slices of
root-ginger give the dish a background piquancy which
helps to eliminate any rawness or chemical taste which
might be present in the bird (especially if it is a factory-
produced one).

Red-Cooked Chicken is often varied by adding chestnuts
(which have been boiled for 1½–2 hours) during the last
15–30 minutes of cooking.

Cantonese Liquid-Filled Roast Chicken

> Mandarin: *Guǎng Dōng Shao Jī*
> Cantonese: *Gwong Dùng Sìu Gāi*

When the Cantonese roast duck or chicken they fill it with a liquid mixture and rub the skin with soya sauce, honey and oil, thus making the bird look as if it is lacquered. The filling liquid generally consists of soya sauce, stock, bean paste and sugar, seasoned with minced dried tangerine peel, and this is used as a sauce to pour over the chicken after the latter is chopped into bite-size pieces. Chicken roasted in this manner has a moister meat which carries a slight herbal flavour due to the tangerine peel. The special appeal of the Chinese roast chicken is its crisp, salty outer skin contrasting with the meat underneath.

White Cut Chicken (see recipe on page 215)

> Mandarin: *Bai Zhǎn Jī*
> Cantonese: *Baahk Jám Gāi*

This dish is in direct contrast to *Red-Cooked Chicken* in that no soya sauce at all is used in its cooking. Instead it is crystal-boiled and the meat of the bird is completely white. Crystal-boiling involves placing a chicken in a pan of boiling water to which a few slices of root-ginger and some salt have been added and leaving for a few minutes. Then the pan is removed from the heat and the chicken is allowed to continue cooking in the remaining heat under cover for a further $\frac{1}{2}$–1 hour, before it is drained and chopped into bite-size pieces, which are served with dips. At least one of these should contain some sesame or salad oil, to give the meat a feeling of smoothness, mixed in with one or other of the usual ingredients such as: 'sherry-and-soya', 'soya-and-chopped-garlic', 'soya-and-chopped-chives', 'soya-and-chilli'.

Fried Chicken

Mandarin: *Zhà Jī Kùai*
Cantonese: *Ja Gāi Faai*

Although officially this dish is called *Deep-Fried Eight-Piece Chicken*, the chicken is often chopped into many more than eight pieces. The pieces are usually marinated for a couple of hours with salt, sugar, soya sauce, sherry, and chopped onion or spring onion. They are then floured and deep-fried or semi-deep-fried (shallow frying with 125–250ml ($\frac{1}{4}$–$\frac{1}{2}$ pint) oil, and turning the chicken over continually) for 4–5 minutes, and served with dips. The dips may include any of those used with the preceding dish. Another favourite for this dish is the 'aromatic salt and pepper mix'.

Oil-Basted Chicken

Mandarin: *Yú Lín Jī*
Cantonese: *Yaùh Làhm Gai*

This is considered a more refined fried chicken than the previous one. Here the chicken is neither dipped in batter nor immersed in oil during cooking. It is split into two halves and placed on a wire range or filter immediately over a pan of boiling oil. The oil is ladled and poured carefully over the chicken halves. This process is continued for 10 minutes, or until the chicken is well-browned and cooked. Since each time a ladleful of oil is poured it immediately drains away, a chicken so cooked is less greasy than when it is fried.

Salt-Baked Chicken *(south-west China)*

Mandarin: *Yan Guo Jī*
Cantonese: *Yìhm Wò Gai*

A whole chicken is buried in hot salt (in a casserole) and baked for 40–60 minutes in an oven. The chicken has usually been hung up to dry for a few hours or overnight. The result of this double-drying – drying by hanging, and drying by being buried in hot salt – produces a chicken which is cooked in its own juice, which is crisp and well-seasoned outside and juicy and full of flavour inside. Although buried wholly in salt, the saltiness does not penetrate much more than the skin of the chicken, and once the cooking is complete, the salt can be easily brushed off the chicken, which is then chopped into bite-size pieces and served.

Eight-Treasure Chicken

Mandarin: *Bá Bǎo Jī*
Cantonese: *Baat Bóu Gāi*

Eight-Treasure Chicken is a chicken which has been stuffed with eight different ingredients after its bones have been removed. The items used for the stuffing usually consist of: ham, dried mushrooms, bamboo-shoots, sliced lotus-root, chicken liver and kidney, barley, lotus seeds. Most of these items are usually parboiled in water first, drained and then turned in salt, yellow wine, and flavour powder (monosodium glutamate) before being inserted into the cavity of the bird, which is then sewn up. The bird is placed on a heatproof dish and steamed for 2–2½ hours. The juice or gravy collected in the dish is then blended with some wine, sugar, seasonings, and thickened with some cornflour (and occasionally a red colouring agent) and poured over the chicken as a sauce. By this time the chicken meat will have attained a degree of tenderness, which should enable it to be taken to pieces with a pair of chopsticks. It is served together with the stuffing.

Barbecued Chicken (Chinese Muslim)

Mandarin: *Chā Shāo Jī*
Cantonese: *Cha Sìu Gāi*

This is a way of eating chicken in the same way as the *Peking Duck*. The chicken is first of all encouraged to dry by having a large kettle of boiling water poured over it, then it is rubbed down with absorbent paper and hung up to dry for several hours or overnight. But before being hung, the cavity of the bird is stuffed with ingredients such as shredded fat pork, onion, shredded ginger, peppercorns, chilli pepper, bean sprouts, soya sauce, soya paste, which have been quickly stir-fried.

The bird is then skewered and turned under a grill or over a fire until well-browned and cooked through. The meat and skin of the bird are then sliced off and served on different plates. The diners will then put the crisp chicken skin and meat in buns, with spring onion and cucumber which have been brushed with sweetened soya paste sauce. The crispness of chicken skin, contrasting with the tenderness of the meat, and the crunchiness of the shredded raw vegetables, picked up with a strong sauce, feature a 'sandwich' which can offer as much gastronomic pleasure as the more renowned *Peking Duck*.

Tangerine Chicken (Szechuan)

Mandarin: *Chén Pí Jī*
Cantonese: *Chàhn Peih Gāi*

The chicken is boned and its meat cut into bite-size pieces, and it is marinated for an hour or two in salt, soya sauce, ginger, and onion. It is then quickly deep-fried (or shallow-fried) over high heat and drained. Before serving, a small quantity of the following ingredients – chilli pepper, peppercorns, and dried tangerine peel – are fried in a small quantity of oil. When the oil has been flavoured, the chicken is returned to the pan for a quick fry and a small quantity of sweet and sour sauce is added.

Fu Yung Sliced Chicken (Peking)

Mandarin: *Fu Róng Jī Piān*
Cantonese: *Fu Yùhng Gāi Pin*

This is in fact the only authentic way the term *Fu Yung* should be used. *Fu Yung* indicates a mixture of minced chicken meat with egg-white with some cornflour added. In this dish the *Fu Yung* mixture is cooked by floating it in separate spoonfuls on top of hot oil or fat. As the spoonfuls or lumps of mixture spread out and flatten in the hot oil they become slices. After no more than 10–15 seconds' cooking, and turning over once, they are lifted out with a perforated spoon. They are then given a very short turn, cooking in a sauce made of chicken broth, white wine, salt, and monosodium glutamate thickened with a little cornflour. This is a very delicate and completely satisfying dish, which is typically Pekingese.

The Royal Concubine Chicken

Mandarin: *Guì Fēi Jī*
Cantonese: *Gwai Fei Gāi*

The distinctive feature of this dish (said to have been invented in Shanghai) is that it is made slightly 'drunken' by the addition of a small glass of grape wine, and a tablespoon or two of yellow rice wine just before it is dished out. Otherwise the chicken, which is chopped, is simply quickly shallow-fried and braised together with winter mushrooms, bamboo-shoots, onion, ginger and some sugar.

Chicken in Black Bean Sauce (Canton)

Mandarin: *Dou Gǔ Jī*
Cantonese: *Dauh Gú Gāi*

Although salted black beans are used throughout China, they are especially typical with chicken in Canton. The chicken is chopped into bite-size pieces and the black beans are soaked until soft. The chicken is first shallow-fried and drained. The black beans are fried together with onion, ginger, garlic, tangerine peel, with some soya sauce, sugar and wine added. Finally, all the ingredients are combined in the pan, and stir-fried together over high heat.

The Gold Coin Chicken

Mandarin: *Jīn Pái Yoú Jī*
Cantonese: *Gam Chin Gāi*

This dish involves simmering a young chicken in a strong
'Master Sauce', which colours the chicken deep brown, for a
matter of 15–20 minutes. The chicken meat is drained with
the skin attached and then sliced with a sharp knife into thin
round pieces like gold coins and laid out nicely on the serving dish. The salty savouriness of the skin is especially good
with the tenderness of the chicken meat which has been
cooked only briefly.

Chicken Rolls (or Balls) in Tomato Sauce (Hunan)

Mandarin: *Fan Qié Jī Qíu*
Cantonese: *Fàn Kèh Gāi Kaùh*

Small slices of chicken-breast meat are cut to a depth of
16mm ($\frac{2}{3}$ in), at close intervals of about 6mm ($\frac{1}{4}$ in), which
causes the slices to roll up when deep-fried, having been
seasoned with salt, egg-white and cornflour. They are then
drained, and added to a sauce made from chicken stock,
yellow wine or sherry, tomato purée, and given a quick fry
over high heat for a matter of 15–30 seconds. During this
latter stage of cooking 3–4 tablespoons of green peas are
added which help to make the dish a little more colourful.

Paper-Wrapped Chicken (see recipe on page 219)

Mandarin: *Zhǐ Bǎo Jī*
Cantonese: *Jī Beàu Gāi*

Slices of raw chicken are wrapped into a parcel with some
shredded spring onion, ginger and mushrooms, along with
small amounts of wine, soya sauce and sugar. The parcels,

which should be bite-size, are then deep-fried for 2½ minutes and served, drained, but not unwrapped. Usually a dozen or more 'parcels' are piled up on a serving dish for the diners themselves to unwrap with chopsticks. Since the foods are cooked in an enclosed packet, much of the original flavour of the ingredients is retained or intensified. *Paper-Wrapped Chicken* is a favourite for party dinners.

Drunken Chicken

Mandarin: *Zuì Jī*
Cantonese: *Jeui Gāi*

This is useful for a summer dish or for serving as an hors-d'oeuvres. Its preparation consists of 'crystal boiling' a chicken which has been flavoured with cinnamon bark, fennel, ginger and chives. The chicken is then chopped in eight pieces which are rubbed with salt and left to season for three hours. Finally, 125ml (¼ pint) (for a whole chicken) of the best yellow wine, or dry sherry, is poured over it; the chicken pieces should be turned in the wine several times to ensure that every piece is well-soaked. The chicken is left to marinate in the wine in a refrigerator overnight. It is chopped into bite-size pieces just before serving.

Smoked Chicken

Mandarin: *Xūn Jī*
Cantonese: *Fàn Gāi*

In China, smoked chicken is usually prepared by first simmering it for about 30 minutes in a wine and soya solution in which meat has been previously cooked. The bird is then quartered, placed on a wire-rack and smoked by burning some tea, sugar, camphor wood, or dried pine needles underneath it, generally for no more than ten minutes. The smoking is only meant to flavour it. It is then painted or rubbed over with sesame oil, chopped into bite-size pieces and served.

Combining Two Types of Chicken Meats

Mandarin: *Hùi Liăng Jī Sī*
Cantonese: *Wuih Leúhng Gāi Sì*

It is one of the Chinese culinary concepts to bring together
into the same dish the same basic material, which has been
prepared or cooked in two or more different ways, and
therefore possesses entirely different flavours. In this case
two types of shredded chicken (smoked and freshly shredded
to thread-size) are assembled in the same dish. The shredded
fresh raw chicken is first quickly shallow-fried and drained,
added to the shredded smoked chicken, and given a turn
and toss together in some chicken stock and chicken fat.
The dish conveys elements of the chicken in two different
colours (brown of the smoked, and white of the freshly-
cooked) and an amalgam of two quite different flavours.

DUCK

Although duck is a very common fowl in China there are far
fewer duck dishes than chicken ones; this is probably due
to the fact that the flavour of duck, as I have mentioned, is
less neutral than that of chicken and therefore cannot be
used as frequently to combine and cross-cook with other
food materials. However, duck has such a distinctive flavour
that all its dishes are notable.

Onion-Simmered Duck

Mandarin: *Cōng Shao Yā*
Cantonese: *Chung Sìu Àp*

Onion-Simmered Duck is a slightly lighter-coloured dish than
Red-Cooked Duck which is dark brown in colour; 1½–2
teaspoons salt are added in place of the soya sauce. The

duck is stuffed with sliced onion or spring onions – often 3–4 medium size onions are used, and three or four stalks of spring onions are added just a few minutes before the duck is ready. 1½ teaspoons of sugar and 250ml (½ pint) of yellow or white wine may be added during the second hour of cooking which will help to enrich the dish. The duck, although served whole in a large bowl or tureen, should be tender enough to be taken to pieces with a pair of chopsticks. Such a duck is usually served as a family party dish.

Eight-Treasure Duck

Mandarin: *Bá Bǎo Yā*
Cantonese: *Boat Bóu Àp*

In contrast to the previous dish, this one is always served at a party dinner or banquet. The duck is stuffed with eight ingredients and long-braised. The eight ingredients usually include: rice, barley, gingko nuts, lotus seeds, chestnuts, raisins, dates and fresh ginger. The flavourings used for the cooking usually consist of soya sauce, sugar, yellow wine and spring onions. The braising is conducted at a slow pace – for 2½–3 hours – in a heavy pot casserole. When brought to the table the shape of the duck should still be intact. Since no rice is served at a banquet, the stuffing becomes an essential complement to balance the richness and succulence of the bird.

Slow-Cooked Crispy Duck

Mandarin: *Guo Shāo Yā*
Cantonese: *Wò Sìu Àp*

This is another party dish, which differs from the previous two duck dishes in that here the pieces of duck are crisp rather than just tender. The duck is first marinated and seasoned; it is then steamed or slow-cooked for 1½–2 hours, when the bones are removed. The duck meat is then divided into a dozen portions, each of which is then floured and

briefly deep-fried until quite crisp. The pieces are finally
reassembled into the shape of the bird and served. Being a
dry dish it should be served with various dips (such as plum
sauce, soya sauce blended with chilli, mustard, tomato) and
mixes (such as the aromatic salt-and-pepper mix).

Peking Duck

Mandarin: *Běi Jing Kǎo Yā*
Cantonese: *Baāk Ging Háau Àp*

This is essentially a roast duck but it is prepared and cooked
with some refinement. First, the skin of the duck is made
loose and separate from the meat by pumping air in between
them (this can be done with a pair of bellows); a kettle of
boiling water is poured slowly over the bird which is then
wiped with a towel and hung up to dry overnight in an airy
spot. When it is dry the bird is painted with a light mixture
of soya sauce and sugar water, then placed on a wire-rack
in a preheated oven at about 200°C (400°F) to roast for
1–1¼ hours, when the skin should be quite brown and crisp
and the meat well-cooked. The distinctive feature of this
dish is the style in which it is eaten: it is inserted into a
pancake which the diner will first have brushed with a
strong, fruity sauce made of yellow bean-paste blended with
some sugar and sesame oil; he will then place one or two
pieces of crisp skin and a slice or two of duck meat on the
pancake and add a strip or two of shredded cucumber and
segments of spring onion. He will roll all these together
inside the pancake and eat it with his hands after turning
the bottom of the pancake up so that nothing will drop out.
Most people who have eaten the dish, properly prepared
and cooked, have considered it a memorable experience.

Aromatic and Crispy Duck (north China and Szechuan)

Mandarin: *Xiāng Cuì Yā*
Cantonese: *Heùng Chui Āp*

This dish is quite often passed off as *Peking Duck* in Chinese restaurants abroad. It is eaten in the same way, but it is either first simmered for an hour in a strongly-flavoured herb sauce, or long-marinated in Five Spice Powder blended with soya paste and soya sauce, and then steamed for 1½–2 hours. Just before serving, the cooked duck is deep-fried for 9–10 minutes, the flesh scraped from the carcass and packed inside a pancake. It is an easier version for restaurants to serve because the duck can be already steamed or cooked and, when the customer orders, it can be deep-fried and served almost immediately.

Camphor Wood and Tea-Smoked Duck

Mandarin: *Zhāng Cha Xun Yā*
Cantonese: *Jeùng Chàh Fàn Gāi*

Chinese smoked dishes are generally only lightly-smoked – smoking is only one phase of the cooking and flavouring. Here the duck is rubbed with a mixture of salt, crushed peppercorns, and bicarbonate of soda, and left to season overnight; on the following day it is hung up in an airy spot to dry again overnight. It is then placed on top of a perforated or wire-range platform with dried tea and camphorwood sawdust burning underneath in an enclosed box to provide the smoke, for 10–15 minutes. It is then steamed for two hours, which incidentally washes the duck of any excess smoke. Just before serving, the duck is given 6–7 minutes of deep-frying until quite brown. It is then chopped into large bite-size pieces, reassembled on a dish and served. Its distinctive smoky taste gives the dish an exceptional flavour and interest and the steaming makes it extremely tender.

Stir-Fried Shredded Ginger with Shredded Duck

Mandarin: *Zǐ Jiāng Chǎo Yā Sī*
Cantonese: *Jī Geùng Cháau Àp Sì*

The duck meat is shredded fresh and marinated in soya
sauce, sherry, and spring onion before being quickly stir-
fried with ginger for just one minute, over very high heat.
Then shredded root-ginger is added, and both are stir-fried
together for another 2 minutes. The dish should be eaten
hot, immediately it comes out of the pan.

Ducks' Feet in Mustard Sauce

Mandarin: *Jiè Mó Yā Zhǎng*
Cantonese: *Gaai uuht àp Jeúng*

This is a cold dish, often served to accompany wine. It is
made simply by simmering 5–6 pairs of ducks' feet in water
for 1½–1¾ hours, or until tender. After removal of the bones
and the tougher tendons, they are cut with a sharp knife into
shreds. The sauce is prepared by mixing 1 tablespoon mustard powder, 1½ tablespoons meat stock, 1 tablespoon soya
sauce, 2 teaspoons wine vinegar, ¼ teaspoon flavour powder
(monosodium glutamate), 3 teaspoons yellow wine or dry
sherry, and 3 teaspoons sesame oil. They are mixed together
until well-blended and the mixture is poured evenly over the
plain, boiled and shredded ducks' feet. Although this is a
dish of cultivated taste it can be easily appreciated by many.

Sweet and Sour Sliced Duck (Kwangtung East River)

Mandarin: *Tián suān Yā*
Cantonese: *Tìhm syūn Àp*

The duck is first of all browned by frying it in oil and then
cooked in a casserole in stock until tender (about 1 hour).

The bones of the bird are then removed and its meat cut into 5 × 2·5cm (2 × 1 in) slices. These slices are then coated with beaten duck egg and floured and shallow-fried until crisp. A sweet and sour sauce, made by heating together sugar, vinegar, tomato purée, and cornflour blended with water, is poured over the crispy pieces of duck and served.

PORK

Pork is the most widely consumed meat in China. Because we are an economical race, we naturally make the fullest use of all different parts of the animal and allow nothing to go to waste; so we have many dishes which are made from the various parts of the pig, such as tripe, pig's trotters, liver, kidney, etc.

Basic Red-Cooked Pork

Mandarin: *Hóng Shāo Zhu Ròu*
Cantonese: *Huhn Sìu Jyu Yuhk*

This dish is best eaten with plain rice. Its rich gravy makes rice so succulent that some people appreciate the mixture more than the meat itself. This dish is usually prepared with belly of pork, which is called the 'five-flower' pork (perhaps because this cut often contains five layers: skin, fat, and lean, followed by two more layers of fat and lean). In this dish the skin and fat are as important as the lean; indeed the dish cannot be cooked properly with lean meat alone. The pork skin here lends a sticky thickness to the gravy and a rich brown colour to the whole dish; the fat provides most of the succulent richness of the dish. If lean meat alone were cooked in this manner it would be too dry and fibrous. The 'five-flower' belly of pork provides just the right combination of pork meat and skin for the purpose. It is usually cut through the skin into 4 × 2·5 × 4cm (1½ × 1 × 2½ in) pieces, and simmered in a mixture of soya sauce, water, sugar, and wine for 1½ hours. The key to its success is low heat and long-cooking. This is one of the very basic dishes of Chinese home-cooking.

Red-Cooked Pork with Winter Bamboo-Shoots

Mandarin: *Dōng Sun Shāo Roù*
Cantonese: *Dùng Sèun Sìu Jyù*

This is another traditional dish. The bamboo-shoots, which are cut diagonally into triangular shapes, can be added to the pork to cook from the beginning, or after the meat has been cooking for one hour. The bamboo-shoots give a different texture, but in the end it is the overall richness and succulence of the dish which count.

Red-Cooked Pork with Abalone and Salted Fish

Mandarin: *Bào Xían Yú Shāo Ròu*
Cantonese: *Bauh Hàahm Yùh Siù Yuhk*

The salted fish (in small quantities) is added to the pork to cook together from the beginning, but the abalone, which is cut into slices, should be added only 3–4 minutes before the dish is ready to be served. The use of salt fish with pork adds a strong salty, smoky background flavour to the dish; and this flavour is brought out and made more savoury by the addition of abalone towards the last stages of the cooking. Although the dish is not heavily spiced, it is certainly one of the most savoury dishes of the whole culinary world. This is a dish of the southern coast and can be brought to the table to add a regional flavour.

Red-Cooked Pork with Eggs

Mandarin: *Yuán Bao Roù*
Cantonese: *Yuhn Bóu Yuhk*

When red-cooked pork is cooked with hard-boiled eggs the dish is called *Pork of Original Preciousness*, probably because the egg is the origin of life. The eggs are first hard-boiled and then immersed in the gravy during the last 20 minutes of cooking. This should cause the eggs to be coloured completely brown. Often they are cut into halves and used as decoration around the pork – but they are a highly edible decoration.

Marinated Roast Fillet of Pork (Cantonese)

Mandarin: *Chā Shāo Roù*
Cantonese: *Chā Siù Yuak*

This is one of the favourite Cantonese pork dishes. Here the pork is thoroughly marinated in long strips (the natural shape of fillet of pork) and then quickly roasted in a hot oven (for 15–20 minutes). When well-cooked the flavour of the encrusted marinade on the outside of the pork contrasts with the fresh juiciness inside each piece of pork. After cooking, the pork is sliced across the grain into 6mm ($\frac{1}{4}$ in) thick pieces. The marinade usually consists of honey, soya sauce, soya paste, soya cheese, yellow wine, and red colouring. Hence, on the serving dish, one sees a pile of pinkish-white sliced pork surrounded with reddish-brown borders.

White Cut Pork (see recipe on page 204)

Mandarin: *Pái Piān Roù*
Cantonese: *Baahk Pin Yuhk*

This dish features the pork in its true native state and flavour. Nothing more is done to the pork other than plain slow-simmering. The cut usually used is the 'five-flower' pork, or belly of pork. It should be cooked in ample water (enough to cover it completely), and slow-simmered for 1–1¼ hours, until well-cooked through; the fat should be jellifying, but not so over-cooked as to fall to pieces. Indeed, each slice of pork about 6mm (¼ in) thick, cut in a whole piece through the skin to about 5×7·5cm (2×3 in) pieces, should be quite firm. About 18–20 pieces should be laid out on the serving dish in fish-scale fashion. In contrast to *Chā Shāo Ròu, Pái Piān Ròu* should always be served with dips, the favourite ones for this dish being: 'soya-garlic', 'vinegar-garlic', 'soya-ginger', 'soya-chilli', 'soya-mustard', 'soya-tomato'. The range of dips on the table gives a great variety of flavour to a single dish of plain-cooked pork and is very much an aspect of the Chinese gastronomic tradition.

Double-Cooked Pork (Szechuan)

Mandarin: *Húi Gūo Ròu*
Cantonese: *Wùih Wò Yuhk*

When the pork of the previous dish is given a turn of short-cooking in a thick sauce made of crushed garlic, root-ginger, soya sauce, soya paste, chilli sauce, sugar, chopped chives (or spring onions) and oil or fat, the result is *Double-Cooked Pork*, which is a popular and renowned dish of west China. Here, in effect, the flavouring ingredients of the dips in the previous dish are used, with one or two additions, to cook with the meat during the last stages. This is an excellent dish to eat with plain boiled rice.

Crispy Pork 'Sandwich' (Peking)

Mandarin: *Gūo Tēi Lǐ Jī*
Cantonese: *Wò Tip Leíh Jik*

This is an unusual dish of lean slices of pork which are sandwiched between two thin slices of pork fat, and deep-fried until crisp. The lean pork is first seasoned with salt, soya sauce, chopped ginger and chives, and rice wine, and inserted in between two slices of pork fat. The edge of the 'sandwich' is sealed with thick batter. After a process of deep-frying for 3 minutes over high heat, and 2 minutes over remaining heat (after the deep-fryer has been removed from the top of the fire), the pork is returned for 1 minute of final frying over a high heat. The result is a crispy pork 'sandwich', which is cut into smaller bite-size pieces, and served with various dips, including the salt-and-pepper mix and 'soya-tomato' dip. The dish has a palace background and is said to have been derived from the once extensive royal kitchens.

Quick-Fried Sliced Pork with Red Peppers (Peking)

Mandarin: *Shēng Bào Jiān Ròu*
Cantonese: *Sàng Bau Yìhm Jìn Yuhk*

This differs from *Double-Cooked Pork* in that fresh rather than cooked pork is used. The pork is cut into 6 × 5cm (2½ × 2 in) thin slices. They are first shallow-fried for 2 minutes in ample oil over a very high heat. The excess oil is then drained away, and flavourings of sugar, salt, soya sauce, black beans, rice wine, chilli pepper, red sweet pepper, soya paste added. The fried sliced pork is turned quickly and mixed with the other ingredients over a high heat for no more than 1–1½ minutes, and the dish is ready. This is regarded as an excellent dish for a home-cooked dinner.

Roast Suckling Pig (Canton)

Mandarin: *Piān Pí Shāo Rǔ Zhū*
Cantonese: *Pin Peìh Sìu Yúh Jyu*

Roast suckling pig is barbecue-roasted. Its skin is made crisp by first of all dousing it several times with boiling water. When it has been aired and dried, the skin is rubbed with malt sugar and vinegar; and the inside cavity-walls are rubbed and pasted with a mixture of salt, sugar, Five Spice Powder, sesame paste, chopped garlic, hoisin (made with vegetables and soya) sauce, and rice wine. The pig is then cooked on a spit long enough for the skin to attain maximum crispness, and for the whole pig to be well cooked. It is eaten in three stages: first its crispy skin is cut off in square slices and inserted in steamed buns with hoisin sauce, shredded spring onions, and some sugar. In the second stage some meat and the various parts of the pig, such as the cheek, tongue, ears are cut off and sliced into suitable bite-size pieces and served. Finally, the meat is cut off the body in slices, quickly cooked with green vegetables and served as a separate dish. This is usually a party or banquet dish.

White-Cooked Pork in Sandpot Casserole (Peking)

Mandarin: *Shà Gūo Bai Ròu*
Cantonese: *Sà Wò Baahk Yuhk*

This is another dish which derives from the palace kitchen. Large chunks of pork are first cooked in water and then long-simmered over very low heat for 3–4 hours until extremely tender. They are then cut into bite-size slices, and placed in a casserole with some of the original stock which is now full of flavour and very rich, and some wine, sliced bamboo-shoots, reconstituted dried mushrooms, a small heart of Chinese cabbage, a few stalks of spring onion and a couple of slices of root-ginger. They are brought to the boil, left to simmer for 20–25 minutes and then served in the casserole. When the pork is eaten it should practically melt in the mouth. The soup in the casserole is a harmonized blending of the rich with the fresh. The dish is a feature of a well-known establishment in Peking called 'Home of the Sandpot Casserole'.

Steamed Pork with Ground Rice (see recipe on page 205)

Mandarin: *Mǐ Fěn Zheng Ròu*
Cantonese: *Maíh Fan Jing Yuhk*

Here the steamed pork is made aromatic by adding a small amount of Five Spice Powder mixed with ground rice; but, prior to steaming, the pork is seasoned and marinated with cinnamon bark, salt, soya sauce, star anise, peppercorns, soya cheese, sugar, and rice wine, for a matter of 2–3 hours. The pork is cut through the skin into 7·5×5×1cm (3×2×½ in) pieces, coated with aromatic ground rice, and arranged on a bed of potato, or yam, or sliced lotus roots, and placed in a steamer to steam for 2–2½ hours; it is served on the original dish.

Chinese Pork Pudding

Mandarin: *Kòu Ròu*
Cantonese: *Kau Yuhk*

Belly of pork is cut through the skin into 9×4cm (3½×1½ in) pieces and fried for 2 minutes, then placed in a heatproof basin with skin side down, interleaving the layers with pickles, onion, ginger, garlic, soya sauce, soya paste, wine, potatoes and/or turnips. The basin is then placed in a steamer and steamed for 1½ hours. When ready the contents of the basin are turned out like a pudding in a serving dish. This is another excellent pork dish for a family meal.

Sweet and Sour Pork (see recipe on page 208)

Mandarin: *Tang Cu Gu Luo Ròu*
Cantonese: *Tòhng Chòu Gù Lòu Yuhk*

Although a fairly common dish in China, it seems to have become even better known abroad. The sauce should be light and translucent, and the pieces of pork should be hot, fresh and tasty. In China belly of pork is normally used; it is cut into large olive-shaped pieces. It is seasoned in salt and left about an hour, then coated with beaten egg and sprinkled lightly with flour. The pork is then deep-fried, or semi-deep-fried until crisp and brown, drained and put aside. The sauce is made of a small amount of chopped garlic, onion, 1 sweet pepper and 1 chilli pepper; (these last two are cut into strips and shallow-fried in a couple of tablespoons of oil for 30 seconds). Vinegar, sugar and blended cornflour are added and after stirring the sauce over medium heat for 30 seconds it should begin to thicken and become translucent. At this point the fried pieces of pork are added to the pan for a couple of turns in the sauce, over increased heat, and the dish should be ready to serve. This is the authentic method of preparation by the Metropolitan People's Service Department of Canton.

Red-Sugar Pork Pudding

Mandarin: *Táng Zhēng Ròu*
Cantonese: *Tohng Jing Yuhk*

Although this sounds like a sweet dish it is really a savoury dish (from the Wuhan City Catering Department). The pork (800g or 2 lb) is first seasoned in salt and then marinated in soya sauce, chopped onion, garlic, pepper, rice wine, and 1½ tablespoons of brown sugar. It is then put, skin side down, into a heatproof basin and steamed vigorously for 1 hour. Thereupon a further 2 teaspoons of brown sugar are dissolved in 3 tablespoons of water and stirred into the basin to mix evenly with the pork. The pork is then subjected to ½ hour more vigorous steaming, before it is turned out on a dish and served. Red-sugar is really brown sugar, just as most Chinese red-cooked dishes, which are cooked with soya sauce, are rich brown.

Braised Pork-Balls

Mandarin: *Nán Jiān Wán Zĭ*
Cantonese: *Naàhm Jīn Yùhn Jí*

The minced pork is mixed with beaten egg, yellow bean paste, soya sauce, cornflour, rice wine and a small amount of finely-chopped onion and ginger. This is made into balls and shallow-fried in oil until brown; the excess oil is then poured away and a cup of water or stock is added to the pan, together with some shredded ginger and a few stalks of spring onion cut into 2·5cm (1 in) segments. The contents are then simmered over a low heat until the liquid has been reduced by half, and it is thickened with cornflour blended in water. A useful dish to serve for a workaday family meal or in a community dining-room.

Braised Lions' Heads with Pea-starch Noodles

Mandarin: *Shì Zĭ Tóu Hùi Fĕn Si*
Cantonese: *Si Jí Taùh Wuih Fáu Si*

A Lion's Head is just a large meat-ball, made with minced belly of pork which is only one third lean. Such proportions of fat and lean make the balls, which should be cooked for a good length of time, extremely tender, smooth and succulent. A small proportion of other ingredients may be added, such as water chestnuts, chestnuts or yam. The usual flavourings are also incorporated, such as salt, soya sauce, sugar, cornflour, rice wine, and egg to help to bind them together. The Lions' Heads are first browned on all sides, then stock, soya sauce, wine, flavour powder (monosodium glutamate) and sugar are added. The meat-balls are cooked in the sauce for 10 minutes on either side. They are then placed in the oven to keep hot, while the pea-starch transparent noodles, which should have been soaked in warm water, are cooked in the gravy with some additional

stock for 5–6 minutes, by which time they will have ab-
sorbed at least three-quarters of the liquid. They are then
poured over the Lions' Heads, and should look like the
lion's mane, or so the Chinese think.

Shredded Pork Stir-Fried with Chinese Fried-Egg

Mandarin: *Mù Shū Ròu*
Cantonese: *Muhk Seùi Yuhk*

This is a favourite dish in Peking, very evocative of the
ordinary households of north China. It is quite simple and
can be very quickly made. About 75g (3 oz) of pork meat is
shredded into threads and 2–3 eggs beaten lightly. The pork
is stir-fried in oil or lard with some shredded bamboo-shoots
and a few stalks of spring onion and a tablespoon of 'wood
ears' for a matter of 2–3 minutes. In a separate pan, the
beaten egg is fried in oil until set. The egg is then broken up
and added to the contents of the other pan with some stock,
rice wine, and sesame oil; after turning them over a few
times they are dished out and served. The black 'wood ears',
green spring onions, and yellow eggs give the dish three
distinct colours and the blending of wine, eggs, and sesame
oil endows it with a distinctive and appealing aroma.

Bean Sprouts Stir-Fried with Shredded Pork

Mandarin: *Dòu Yá Chǎo Ròu Sī*
Cantonese: *Dauh Ngáh Cháau Yuhk Sī*

All kinds of vegetables can be stir-fried with shredded pork,
but they should be shredded into the same fine shreds. In
this case the bean sprouts, which are already of the correct
size and shape, require no further shredding. They are
combined with the pork in a frying-pan over a high heat, subjected to vigorous stir-frying, with some of the usual seasonings and flavourings, such as salt, pepper, soya sauce, sugar,

flavour powder (monosodium glutamate). Occasionally some shredded mushrooms are added to provide interest.

Red-Cooked Spare Ribs

Mandarin: *Hóng Shāo Pái Kŭ*
Cantonese: *Hùhng Siu Paaih Gwat*

The spare ribs can be prepared either dry or with sauce. If prepared with sauce the ribs will need to be braised for an hour in a casserole with some onion, garlic, ginger, and an appropriate amount of soya sauce, sugar, stock and yellow rice wine (or sherry) for approximately 1 hour to 1 hour and 20 minutes, turning the ribs over in the sauce once every 20 minutes. The ribs can then be served in the casserole. Some people prefer to have the ribs dry, so that they can handle them with their fingers: all that needs to be done is to bake the ribs in a hot oven uncovered for 10–15 minutes. The remains of the gravy in the casserole can be made into a sauce by adding some additional stock, wine or sherry and cornflour. In China spare ribs are normally chopped into 2·5×3cm (1–1½ in) pieces and eaten by putting the whole piece into the mouth, pulling out only the bone. Most Chinese can perform this operation with great dexterity through years of practice, taking only 5–10 seconds to strip the rib of its meat.

Sweet and Sour Spare Ribs (see recipe on page 207)

Mandarin: *Tan Chu Pai Ku*
Cantonese: *Tohǹg Chòu Paaih Gwat*

These are prepared and cooked in precisely the same way as in the previous recipe, except that the sauce is made separately and poured over the ribs when the latter are ready. Both kinds of spare ribs make excellent starters for a main meal, or a substantial item in a buffet dinner.

Sweet and Sour Pig's-Trotters

Mandarin: *Táng Cù Zhū Tǐ*
Cantonese: *Tòhng Chòu Jỳu Taìh*

The trotters can be prepared in the same way as the spare ribs, though they may take somewhat longer to cook. To ensure that they get the right amount of cooking it is a useful practice to parboil the trotters for 15–20 minutes first before subjecting them to the same cooking time as for spare ribs.

Red-Cooked Tripe

Mandarin: *Hóng Sháo Zhū Dù*
Cantonese: *Huhǹg Siu Jỳu Toúh*

One of the attractions of the tripe is its texture: when it is well cooked it has a firm squashy layer as well as its jelly-like layer. In some sophisticated quarters, where tripe is eaten as one of the high delicacies, the pig is specially nurtured for its tripe. In such instances, the jelly-like layers in the tripe would be of double or triple the usual thickness. It should be cooked slowly over a low heat for a couple of hours with other ingredients such as wine, soya sauce, sugar, ginger, garlic and a touch of Five Spice Powder. The pieces should be cut into strips, or triangular or diamond shapes, and biting into a piece should be like biting into a savoury jelly-cake, with one side firm yet spongy.

Onion-Smothered Sliced Liver

Mandarin: *Cōng Mǐ Gān Piān*
Cantonese: *Chùng Maíh Gōn Pin*

The liver is seasoned and cut into large bite-size slices, then given a quick turn in hot oil or lard and drained. Two medium onions are sliced thinly and stir-fried in the oil until soft, when the liver is returned into the pan with vinegar, pepper, sugar, soya sauce, soya paste, and a small quantity of stock and rice wine. The liver should be turned in this mixture of ingredients over a high heat for no more than 1–1½ minutes. This is a highly satisfying dish to consume with rice, and is sometimes promoted to the banquet table.

The Kung Po Hot-Fried Sliced Kidney (Szechuan)

Mandarin: *Gōng Bǎo Yāo Kuài*
Cantonese: *Gùng Bóu Yiù Faai*

The kidney is cut into large slices, given criss-cross cuts of two thirds of the depth right across the whole surface, and cut into 1 × 2·5cm (½ × 2 in) strips. These are then seasoned in salt, rice wine and cornflour and cooked very rapidly in hot oil or lard, and taken out. Meanwhile, a mixture of soya sauce, sugar, vinegar, good stock and flavour powder (monosodium glutamate) is made ready in a bowl. A small amount of red chilli pepper, garlic, ginger and paprika is fried in the fat for 30 seconds and then the kidney and contents of the bowl are poured back into the pan for a rapid quick-fry together. Result: hot, crisp kidney strips.

BEEF

Most meat dishes are cooked in much the same way: the main difference between pork and beef dishes is that while long-cooked beef dishes require longer cooking than pork, quick-cooked beef dishes should be cooked even more quickly than pork.

In the matter of flavouring, the Chinese are inclined to use more spices and herbs with beef than pork, and the vegetables selected to cook with beef are usually of the stronger-tasting varieties, such as leek, onion, scallion, turnip, tomato. We have far fewer beef than pork dishes; perhaps this was because the ox was a beast of burden in China, and the slaughter of it was a more serious undertaking than the slaughtering of a pig; perhaps it is also because beef is a less versatile meat than pork, and cannot be combined as successfully with other food materials.

Red-Cooked Beef

Mandarin: *Hóng Shāo Níu Ròu*
Cantonese: *Hùng Siù Ngauh Yuhk*

The beef is usually cut into 2·5–4cm (1–1½ in) cubes and cooked with the same ingredients as those used in cooking *Red-Cooked Pork*, with the addition of some of the 'five spices', either in powder form or in pieces (cinnamon bark, star anise, cloves, fennel, anise pepper).

Turnips are often added during the last 1–1½ hours; they should be cut into triangular pieces about the same size as the beef; carrots are sometimes substituted for turnips. *Red-Cooked Beef* is usually served in bowls or tureens and is particularly good with rice or noodles.

Beef Braised with Tomato (Tientsin-Peking)

Mandarin: *Xī Hóng Shi Huáng Mèn Níu Ròu*
Cantonese: *Saì Hung Chīh Wohng Huhn Ngāuh Yuhk*

This dish is really a variation of *Red-Cooked Beef*. When the beef is three-quarters done it should be fried in a small amount of oil, adding to it roughly half its own weight of skinned tomatoes and stirring for 4–5 minutes. A teaspoon of chilli sauce is added to the gravy, along with a tablespoon of lard, and the liquid rapidly reduced by a third over a high heat, and then poured over the beef and tomatoes. This dish, though a product of the Peking–Tientsin area, where there is an abundance of tomatoes in the summer, has a Muslim–Mongolian flavour.

Long-Simmered Beef

> Mandarin: *Shŭi Zĥu Sū Nív Ròv*
> Cantonese: *Seúi Jȳu Sōu Ngàu Yuhk*

This dish involves simmering a leg of beef in ample water for no less than six hours with small amounts of onion, ginger, cinnamon bark, and sugar; the beef is then cut into slices or bite-size pieces and a tablespoon or two of a mixture of sesame oil, chilli sauce, soya sauce, and chopped spring onion is poured evenly over it just before serving. A delectable dish which can be eaten and enjoyed time and again.

Sliced Beef in Oyster Sauce (see recipe on page 212)

> Mandarin: *Háo Yóu Níu Ròu*
> Cantonese: *Hoùh Yaùh Ngaùh Yuhk*

The special feature of this dish is its extreme savouriness and tenderness. The meat can be made exceptionally tender by marinating it in a very small amount of bicarbonate of soda blended with soya sauce, rice wine and sugar. A couple of slices of root-ginger and onion are first turned in hot oil for 5–6 seconds. Once the oil is flavoured, the beef is spread out in the pan and stirred over a high heat (a high heat should be maintained from the beginning) for 40–50 seconds. The oyster sauce, which is frequently used in Cantonese cooking, is blended with some stock, soya sauce, additional wine, and cornflour, and poured into the pan. After a few turns the slices of beef should be shining, succulent and extremely tender and ready to serve. A highly recommended dish either for accompanying wine or for eating with rice.

Dry-Fried Shredded Beef with Shredded Celery (Szechuan)

> Mandarin: *Gan Biān Nív Ròu Sí*
> Cantonese: *Gòn Bin Ngaùh Yuhk*

In this dish both the beef and celery are cut into matchstick shreds, and the root-ginger is cut into threads about a quarter the size. The shredded beef is stir-fried first over a high heat with some salt; after 4–5 minutes, the beef should become quite dry. At this point the following ingredients are added: soya paste, soya sauce, ground chilli pepper, sugar, rice wine, celery and flavour powder (monosodium glutamate). The stir-frying is continued at high heat for one more minute and the dish is ready to serve. In this dish the beef is meant to be firm and chewy, and the celery somewhat sweet and savoury. It is a traditional dish to accompany wines.

Quick-Fried Shredded Beef with Onions

Mandarin: *Níu Ròu Sī Chǎo Yáng Cong*
Cantonese: *Ngàuh Yuhk Sī Chǎau Yeuhng Chung*

In this dish the usual role of the beef is reversed: the onion, which should be thinly sliced, is put into the pan to fry first for a minute or two to soften, and then pushed to one side of the pan. The previously-marinated beef is then stir-fried in the pan for just 1 minute; the onion and the beef are then combined, and some wine and cornflour, blended with water and a pinch of flavour powder (monosodium glutamate), are poured over the beef and onion. Within seconds the sauce thickens and the beef appears almost shiny. In this dish the beef is featured as extremely tender and just cooked, and the onion which has taken on something of the beef and soya flavour is sweet and savoury. An excellent dish both for eating with rice or for accompanying wine.

Clear-Simmered Beef (Szechuan)

Mandarin: *Chǐñg Dùn Níu Ròu*
Cantonese: *Chǐñg Deuhn Ngaùh Yuhk*

This dish is not often seen on the Chinese dinner-table. It has a Muslim–Mongolian origin, but it became well-known when produced and served with regularity in a restaurant in

Chungking, which specialized in beef dishes. The dish is usually produced on some scale. Over 5kg (10 lb) of beef (cuts such as shin, shank, brisket, ribs, leg) and one chicken are boiled together in an enormous pot with ample water. After the first 20 minutes it is skimmed thoroughly for impurities. The heat is then reduced, and a second skimming is made after 40 minutes' cooking. From then on the heat is maintained at a mere simmer, and the only ingredients added are salt, root-ginger and some peppercorns. The slow simmering should be allowed to continue for four hours and the contents turned over every 20 minutes. When ready the beef should be sliced into finger-shaped and -sized pieces. They should be given one turn in hot fat just before serving. They should be served with strips of cucumber and carrot, sprinkled with salt, soya sauce, chilli sauce, mustard, vinegar, flavour powder (monosodium glutamate), chopped chives, garlic and ginger at the table. Each person should be provided with a cup or bowl of the incomparable beef broth (the chicken is there only for the flavour, and should be removed and used for some other dish). Beef so simply cooked often possesses a flavour and appeal which is more down-to-earth and compelling than many elaborately produced dishes.

Deep-Fried Fillet of Beef (Kiangsi)

Mandarin: *Zha Níu Lì Jì*
Cantonese: *Ja Ngaùh Leíh Jìk*

To western people this must be an unusual way of serving fillet of beef, which in the West is normally only grilled. Here the beef is first sliced into $2 \cdot 5 \times 1 \times 0 \cdot 5$cm ($1 \times \frac{1}{2} \times \frac{1}{4}$ in) slices, seasoned with chopped chives, ginger, some salt and rice wine, and left for an hour, then it is lightly coated with a batter (made of beaten egg, flour, cornflour and water), and deep-fried in hot oil for 3 minutes – 1 minute over high heat, then the pan is removed from the heat for 1 minute, finally it is returned again to a high heat for another minute. Fillet of beef cooked in this way should be served sprinkled with sesame oil and with the salt-and-pepper-mix.

Red-Cooked Beef Tripe

Mandarin: *Hóng Shāo Ngíu Du*
Cantonese: *Huhng Siù Ngauh Toúh*

This is cooked in much the same way as other red-cooked dishes, but the tripe should first be soaked in brine for an hour, and then boiled and simmered in fresh water for one hour before being cut into strips of about 1 × 5cm (½ × 2 in). It is then cooked over a low heat in a casserole with some spring onion, shredded root-ginger, soya sauce, lard and rice wine, for 2 hours, stirring every 30 minutes. The tripe should then be tender and very enjoyable to eat with rice or noodles or steamed buns.

Stir-Fried Calf's Feet with Fresh Vegetables (Muslim-Mongolian)

Mandarin: *Shāo Tí Jīn*
Cantonese: *Siù Ngàuh Taìh Gaǹ*

This is a conventional way of cooking unconventional materials. The calf's feet are first of all boiled and simmered for 2 hours, and then cut into 6mm × 5cm (¼ × 2 in) strips. These strips can then be stir-fried quickly with sliced vegetables, such as heart of cabbage, French beans, asparagus tips. What is appealing to the Chinese about this dish is the firm jelly-like texture of the calf's feet within a conventional combination of other materials and ingredients.

Tangerine-Flavoured Long-Simmered Ox Penis

Mandarin: *Gou Qǐ Níu Biān Tañg*
Cantonese: *Gáu Géi Ngàuh Bìn Tong*

As this dish keeps cropping up in Chinese restaurants, to the embarrassment or amusement of some western customers, and it occurs only in good authentic Chinese establishments, we might as well be clear as to what it is meant to be, and how it is prepared. The foreskin of the ox penis, which in the whole piece weighs about 1–1·5kg (2–3 lbs), is first removed and the penis sliced into two halves. It is then soaked in fresh water for 2 hours, drained, placed in a pot, covered in water and brought to the boil. After 20 minutes the surface should be skimmed for impurities and about a quarter of the liquid is poured away. A further skimming and pouring away of a quarter of the soup takes place after another 20 minutes. At this point a whole chicken is added together with root-ginger, tangerine peel, peppercorns, rice wine, salt, soya sauce. The contents are brought back to the boil, and the simmering continues for a further 3 hours over a very low heat. The chicken is then removed for other use. The penis is taken out, cut into 6mm × 5cm ($\frac{1}{4}$ × 2 in) strips, given a quick turn in hot oil and drained. The pieces are sprinkled with salt, flavour powder (monosodium glutamate) and lard before serving. All the conventional dips used for beef dishes, such as mustard, chilli sauce, and soya sauce, can be used for this dish. As you can see, the dish is a delicacy, and the inclusion of a whole chicken makes it quite an expensive dish. The soup is drunk in separate cups or bowls, like beef tea.

LAMB

Lamb is more a food of north China than of the Yangtze River valley and the south. Indeed, some southerners regard lamb with as much horror as a westerner would regard dog

meat. But, in the Peking area and the majority of the northern provinces, lamb is nearly as popular as pork. This is
principally because the northern provinces are nearer the
frontier regions of Inner Mongolia, Manchuria, and Sing-
kiang, the grasslands of China, where there are great herds
of sheep and cattle. In the south, where there are hardly any
spare lands for grazing, animals are only kept in very small
numbers, almost as pets. Except for pigs, which are reared
exclusively for food, they are seldom slaughtered for meat.
There are probably more lamb or mutton dishes than beef,
because sheep are hardly ever used as beasts of burden.
Lamb is generally regarded as a strong-tasting meat (compared with the neutral flavour of pork and chicken), and
therefore it is usually cross-cooked with strong-tasting
vegetables, or accompanied by strong-tasting dips and
mixes, or when it is long-cooked it is frequently cooked in
ample wine. Most beef dishes can be reproduced with lamb,
using practically the same ingredients except for those beef
dishes where the beef is dry-fried into firm chewy strips, and
eaten partly for its texture.

Red-Cooked Lamb

Mandarin: *Hong Shāo Yang Ròu*
Cantonese: *Hùhng Siv Yeùhng Yuhk*

Lamb, when red-cooked like pork or beef, is cooked in a
soya sauce with some sugar and rice wine added. Some Five
Spice is added whether in powder form or in pieces and the
cooking time is about $1\frac{1}{4}$–$1\frac{1}{2}$ hours over a very low heat.
Lamb is usually cut into 2×4cm ($1\times1\frac{1}{2}$ in) cubes or oblong
pieces when red-cooked. There is hardly anything tastier or
more savoury than red-cooked lamb or mutton.

Quick-Fried Sliced Lamb

Mandarin: *Yáng Ròu Pian* or *Dì Sī Mǐ*
Cantonese: *Deih Sī Maht*

This dish is quite simply prepared and very quickly cooked (no more than 30 seconds for every 400g (1 lb) of lamb). A leg of lamb is cut into thin 4×4cm ($1\frac{1}{2}$×$1\frac{1}{2}$ in) slices, seasoned with a small quantity of cornflour, salt and sweetened bean-paste. Additionally, some cornflour is mixed in a bowl with vinegar, sugar, soya sauce, finely-chopped ginger and rice wine into a cooking sauce. 125 ml ($\frac{1}{4}$ pint) vegetable oil is heated in a large frying-pan and when it is very hot the lamb is added. The pieces are turned and stirred for 15–20 seconds and then lifted out with a perforated spoon and drained. The oil is poured away leaving only a couple of tablespoons in the pan. The cooking sauce mixture is poured into the pan and as soon as it is boiling, the once-fried lamb slices are returned to the pan. It is stir-fried quickly for 15–20 seconds when this typically northern dish is ready to serve. Its heat counteracts the freezing wind and swirling dust of a typical Peking winter; the lamb should almost melt in the mouth.

Tung-Po Lamb

Mandarin: *Dōng Pō Yáng Ròu*
Cantonese: *Dùng Pò Yeuhng Yuhk*

Soo Tung-Po was a famous Chinese poet of the Sung Dynasty to whom the invention of this dish is attributed, although I am not aware of any attempt at historical authentication. The dish is in essence one of stewed lamb with potatoes and carrots. The lamb is cut into 4×1cm ($1\frac{1}{2}$×$\frac{1}{2}$ in) oblong pieces, and the potatoes and carrots are cut into somewhat smaller, triangular pieces. They are all given a short period of frying in oil and then drained. The lamb pieces are placed in a casserole, where they are joined by onion, ginger, garlic, peppercorn, sugar and rice wine. They are simmered together for 1¾ hours, and then the carrots and potatoes are added to cook together for the last 25 minutes. The dish should be served in a soup bowl or tureen. This would appear to be much more a mother's dish for feeding a hungry family than a poet's dish to enliven his imagination!

Quick-Cooked Three Items of Lamb

Mandarin: *Dū Sān Yáng*
Cantonese: *Dōu Saàm Yeuhng*

There is no such dish in a southern restaurant, so do not ask for it! In the north the dish falls in line with the Chinese inclination to use up every bit of the animal: in this case the lamb's eyes, marrow and brain. The eyes should be cut into thin slices, the brain into somewhat thicker slices and the marrow into 2·5cm (1 in) strips. The other ingredients are: ginger, garlic, onion. These are first fried until they are about to turn brown; 125ml (¼ pint) of good stock should then be added along with rice wine. When the liquid boils, the onion, ginger and garlic are lifted out and the 'three items of lamb', soya sauce, brown sugar, and flavour powder (monosodium glutamate) are added. After cooking for 5–6 minutes some cornflour blended with water is added to thicken the sauce which is made aromatic by sprinkling with a couple of teaspoons of sesame oil. This is definitely an acquired local taste!

Quick-Fried Lamb with Spring Onion

Mandarin: *Coñg Bào Yáng Ròu Pīan*
Cantonese: *Chūnng Baau Yeùhng Yuhk*

This is a universal dish in China compared with the previous ones, although it is rarely served in Cantonese restaurants. It should be on the menu of any restaurant which has any pretension to being Pekingese. The dish consists simply of sliced lamb, which has been seasoned in soya paste, soya sauce, sugar and rice wine, and quickly stir-fried in hot oil in which some ginger and garlic have been fried for a short period, which need not exceed 1 minute per 400g (1 lb) of lamb. Finally, about 200g (½ lb) spring onions cut into 5cm (2 in) segments are added and cross-cooked together over a high heat for a further minute. Then the dish is ready to serve. Although simple, the dish is very down-to-earth and appealing, and very much a favourite in Peking. When eating it, one is reminded of the smell of frying onion and garlic sprinkled with rice wine when one pushed one's head through the padded curtain of a Peking transport café in the winter.

Fish Eats Lamb

Mandarin: *Yú Yäo Yańg*
Cantonese: *Yùh Ngaúm Yeuhǹg*

This is quite an unusual dish from the town of Ho Fei, in which the northern taste for lamb appears to have met the fresh-water product of the Yangtze. A good weight of lamb (about the weight of the fish) is stuffed into the stomach of the fish (a small carp), which should weigh about 600g (1½ lb). The fish is then wrapped in a piece of suet. The parcel is fried until quite brown. After draining, it is placed in a casserole and 500ml (1 pint) of chicken stock is added along with some anise, peppercorns, ginger, onion, soya sauce and sugar. The contents are brought to the boil and then simmered for 1½ hours. The ginger, anise, onion and suet are removed and a pinch of coriander leaves and a tablespoon of vinegar are sprinkled over the soup.

Deep-Fried Crispy Lamb (Anhui Province)

Mandarin: *Jiāo Zhà Yáng Ròu*
Cantonese: *Jiù Ja Yeuhng Yuhk*

This is a crisp dish of lamb, not very often seen in other parts of China; it is a useful contrast to the many stewed or soft-dried lamb dishes. Here the lamb is first braised for 45 minutes and then marinated in chopped ginger, spring onion and peppercorns, flavour powder (monosodium glutamate) and sesame oil. The sliced lamb is then coated with a batter and deep-fried until brown. Just before serving, the pieces are cut into 5×2·5cm (2×1 in) pieces and sprinkled with freshly-milled pepper. The dish should be served with sweetened bean-paste as a dip, accompanied with spring onions cut into short segments.

Jellied Lamb (Peking)

Mandarin: *Yǎng Gāo*
Cantonese: *Yeūhng Gòu*

This is a dish for accompanying wine. It is made simply by cooking lamb – especially those cuts near the joints and bones – with the bones for some length of time. When the lamb is tender, all the meat is scraped off the bones and cooked for a short while in its own juice with some wine, flavour powder (monosodium glutamate) and chopped spring onions added (a small amount of gelatine may be added to encourage jellifying). The contents are then poured into a rectangular container and placed in the refrigerator until set (all the meat must be covered by liquid), when it is cut into small bite-size rectangular pieces and served. Apart from accompanying wine, the dish is excellent eaten with hot rice Congee or noodles.

Peking Sliced Lamb Hotpot

Mandarin: *Shuan Yáng Ròu*
Cantonese: *Saan Yeuhng Yuhk*

This is a self-cooked dish, where a charcoal-burning hotpot is placed at the centre of the table, surrounded by plates of thinly-sliced lamb, supported by plates of other ingredients, such as pea-starch transparent noodles, and selected leaves of cabbage. When the stock in the hotpot is brought to a rolling boil, the diners plunge individual pieces of sliced lamb into the boiling liquid to cook for a matter of a minute. The lamb is then retrieved and dipped into one of the various dips placed on the table. Sometimes a personal dip is prepared by the diner in a small bowl where he mixes various dips. In the end the stock in the hotpot becomes extremely rich and tasty. When all or most of the lamb has been consumed (there should be at least 10–12 plates of meat to start with), the diners will put all the other ingredients on the table into the hotpot. A few minutes are allowed for this final mixture to cook, and then each diner will fill up his own personal bowl (often the one containing his dip). What greater comfort could there be in a Peking winter?

FISH

The Chinese have no more than half a dozen established ways of cooking fish, but they are all outstandingly successful. The ingredients which they use belong to four main categories: strong tasting vegetables, such as ginger, garlic, onion; pickled, dried, smoked and salted foods, such as black beans, pickled greens, dried mushrooms, dried shrimps; animal fat and meat stock; soya sauce, vinegar, rice wine and other seasoning ingredients. These factors combine to form a completely new concept of fish cookery from which the West probably has a great deal to learn. We would never use a sauce which is derived from another fish or from seafood, as this makes fish doubly fishy. Nor would we marinate a fish or seafood in any kind of wine or alcohol for any length of time before cooking, as this makes the flesh limp (though such ingredients are highly recommended for addition during cooking). Finally, when presenting a fish that has been cooked whole, the Chinese believe that the fish should appear almost as if it is still in its natural, watery-weedy habitat; the fish is therefore often dressed heavily in

four or five different coloured, shredded vegetables (hence
Five Willow Fish), so that it looks fresh and almost alive!

Steamed Fish *(see recipes on pages 231 and 232)*

Mandarin: *Chīng Zsēng Yú*
Cantonese: *Chìng Jing Yùh*

Most fish can be steamed successfully if fresh. It should first
be rubbed and seasoned inside and out with salt and minced
root-ginger, left for a period, and then doused with a mixture of soya sauce, sugar and wine just before cooking. The
whole fish is then dressed with various shredded vegetables,
such as spring onion, dried mushrooms (previously soaked
and shredded), shredded pork fat or bacon, salted pickles
and any other vegetables which would add colour or savoury
appeal. It is then inserted into a steamer and steamed for
15–30 minutes (but no longer) depending upon the size and
thickness of the fish. A fish which is less than 800g (2 lb) in
weight, and 2·5cm (1 in) in thickness should not require
more than 15 minutes' vigorous steaming. (Fish should
always be steamed vigorously.) Although this is a comparatively simple way of cooking fish (there are no sauces to
make, and all the ingredients used are generally present in a
Chinese kitchen), Chinese *Steamed Fish* can be one of the
best fish dishes on any menu.

Steaming is also suitable for cooking fish in slices, which
are usually seasoned in the same way as when the fish is
cooked whole, but the pieces should also be rubbed with
some oil or fat so that they do not stick to one another when
cooked.

Steamed Fish is one of the dishes which one should always
order when dining in a Cantonese restaurant. Indeed, Cantonese restaurants which have no *Steamed Fish* on the menu
are generally best avoided. It means that either they are too
lax to send anybody daily to the market to pick up the
freshest fish or that their business is too sluggish for them to
use up all their fresh foods immediately, which results in

their serving up several days later what can only be served up very fresh for one day. With *Steamed Fish* you cannot camouflage any lack of freshness.

Red-Cooked Fish

Mandarin: *Hong Shāo Yú*
Cantonese: *Huhǹg Sìu Tuhk*

The method is practically the same as for red-cooking meat. After the fish has been seasoned and shallow-fried for 4–5 minutes, the fat or oil should be drained away completely. In its place a cooking-sauce consisting of a mixture of soya sauce, sugar, rice wine (sherry), and chopped spring onions (in 2·5cm (1 in) segments) is poured over the fish, which should be turned once or twice in the sauce and left to cook gently in it for 10 minutes. The approximate quantity of sauce used should be roughly 3–4 tablespoons to every 400g (1 lb) of fish.

Sweet and Sour Fish

Mandarin: *Táng Cū Yú*
Cantonese: *Tohng Chou Yùh*

The most famous of the *Sweet and Sour Fish* dishes is *Yellow River Carp*. The fish is first seasoned with salt and ginger, and then fried until crisp; the sweet and sour sauce is bright and translucent and sometimes enhanced by the introduction of some chilli pepper. Its visual appeal is improved by dressing the fish with some shredded coloured vegetables. *Sweet and Sour Fish* is more of a party dish, because of this visual attraction. Taken all in all, for sheer eating pleasure, *Red-Cooked Fish* is more earthy and basic in its appeal.

Five Willow Fish

Mandarin: *Wŭ Lĭu Yú*
Cantonese: *Ńgh Laùh Yùh*

This is in fact a sweet and sour dish, which is given a more detailed and planned dressing (with five types of shredded vegetables) and the sauce is generally piquant. The fish need not necessarily be fried to crispness; it can be poached or steamed, and the sauce poured over it after it has been drained. The shredded ingredients which are used for the dressing include Chinese pickles (often sold in jars and usually consisting of ginger, cucumber, turnips) and fresh vegetables, such as spring onions, sweet peppers, some dried chilli pepper and mushrooms. The appeal here is the contrast between the hot sharpness of the sauce (hot from the chilli, and sharp from the sweet and sour sauce) and the freshness of the fish. The dish usually appears on the table at party dinners.

Fish Balls in Soup

Mandarin: *Chīng Yú Wàn*
Cantonese: *Waht Yùh Yuhn*

The usual way of making fish balls in China is to pound the fish with the back of a chopper and then chop it for about 10–15 minutes. A lightly beaten egg-white and a small amount of cornflour, some salt and flavour powder (monosodium glutamate) are then kneaded into the minced fish for another 6–8 minutes. By then the fish paste should be in a state when it no longer sticks to the fingers; it is then ready to be formed into balls (of about 18mm (¾ in) in diameter), which are immersed in a barely simmering stock for 5–6 minutes. When the fish balls are drained they are cooked again in 250ml (½ pint) of chicken stock with a small amount of reconstituted Chinese dried mushrooms which have been quickly fried in lard, and simmered for 15 minutes. The dish is served as a semi-soup dish with a strong mushroom flavour to which some wine and chopped chives might also be added to vary the flavour and increase the appeal.

Smoked Fish

Mandarin: *Xūn Yú*
Cantonese: *Fàn Yùh*

As mentioned elsewhere, most Chinese smoking is a quick process used purely for flavouring the food, and the food is cooked in some other way. Fish is usually smoked in China by placing it on a perforated dish, or a wire range, and burning sugar, tea, sawdust (camphor wood) underneath it. The smoking needs to last for no more than 8–10 minutes. The fish is then red-cooked; that is, it is first fried and drained of oil, and a mixture of soya sauce, rice wine, sugar and chopped chives added. The fish is cooked and turned in the sauce until the latter is almost dry, when it is ready to serve. Fish so cooked has a very distinct smoky flavour; it can be served either as a whole fish or, more often, in slices or bite-size pieces.

CRUSTACEANS

Seafood is almost as widely consumed in China as fish, which is probably due to its great savouriness and the fact that it occurs mostly in small sizes or units which makes it both easy and convenient to combine and cross-cook with other ingredients, thus resulting in the production of a vast number of dishes. The most popular seafoods in China are prawns, crabs, scallops, clams, squids, sharks' fins, abalone and lobsters.

Dry-Fried Splashed Prawns

Mandarin: *Gān Chǎo Xiā Dùan*
Cantonese: *Gòn Cháau Hà Dyuhn*

Prawns used for this dish are not shelled. They are simply washed and their heads and tails removed. The prawns are stir-fried in lard or oil over a high heat for a matter of 1–1½ minutes and removed. Into the same pan and remaining oil are stirred soya sauce, chopped ginger, garlic and spring onion (about 1½ teaspoons each of ginger and garlic, and 1 tablespoon of onion), sherry and 3 teaspoons of sugar (to about 600g (1½ lb) of prawns). The prawns are then returned to the pan for 1–1½ minutes. By this time most of the liquid in the pan will have dried and the sauce will have formed a crust on the shells of the prawns. The Chinese delight in biting through the hot, strong-tasting shells into the freshness of the prawn meat underneath, and we are all experts in squeezing the meat out of the shell.

Stir-Fried Fresh Prawns

Mandarin: *Ching Chǎo Xīa Rén*
Cantonese: *Ching Cháau Hà Yàhn*

The prawns used in this are shelled, and the cooking can be done very quickly. The prawns are first of all seasoned in salt, cornflour, chopped ginger, spring onion, garlic and some rice wine. They are then stir-fried in oil or fat over a high heat for 1–2 minutes. Since no soya sauce is used, the prawns appear pinkish-white. They are extremely tasty and very easy to eat. It is an extremely popular dish for both family meals and on the banquet table. When the prawns are very fresh and well-cooked, the meat of the prawns should feel almost crisp.

Phoenix-Tail Prawns

Mandarin: *Fèng Wĕi Xīa*
Cantonese: *Fuhn Méih Hà*

The prawns are shelled but the tails are left on. The body is then coated with seasoned batter, which should be a mixture of egg, flour, water and salt. After 2–3 minutes of frying in oil (either by deep-fry or semi-deep-fry) the tail will turn quite red, which is one of the features of the dish. This dish of prawns is usually served with dips such as salt-and-pepper mix, and 'chilli-and-soya sauce,' or 'tomato-and-soya sauce'.

Stir-Fried Prawns with Snow Pickles

Mandarin: *Xŭe Cài Chăo Xīā Rén*
Cantonese: *Syut Choi Cháau Hà Yahn*

This is another uncomplicated way of cooking prawns. All that needs to be done is, first, to fry a small amount of chopped ginger and garlic in a couple of tablespoons of oil over a high heat. A couple of tablespoons of chopped pickles (which are salty and slightly sour) are then added; the mixture is turned and stirred in the pan over a high heat for 2½–3 minutes when the dish should be ready to serve.

All the prawn dishes can be reproduced with scallops, if the latter are cut into the same sized pieces as the prawns. Very often in China scallops are used dried as a flavouring (particularly for soups), and only a small quantity of them are used at a time. The part of the scallop used for this purpose is usually the main muscle which connects the body to the shell, which is cut into disc-shaped pieces. Few people recognize these as scallops. The current price is over £10 per 400g (1 lb) for these disc-shaped dried scallop muscles.

Next to prawns and shrimps, crabs are probably the most popular seafood (or fresh-water crustaceans) in China.

Although crab meat can be combined with other ingredients to produce numerous dishes, they are best cooked in their shells and eaten on their own. When cooked and eaten from their shells, there are only a few ways in which they are prepared and cooked.

Onion and Ginger Crab

Mandarin: *Cōng Jiāng Gūo Da Xiè*
Cantonese: *Geùng Chūng Wò Daaih*

When cooking this crab, the main shell is lifted from the body and the body is chopped into half a dozen pieces, each with a leg attached. The claws are cracked but not chopped. Some chopped onion, garlic, ginger and minced pork are first of all stir-fried in a few tablespoons of oil over a high heat for about a minute. The sectioned crabs are then added to turn and fry together for 3–4 minutes. When the contents of the pan are all sizzling and very hot, a cup or two of good stock (or chicken broth) and rice wine are poured into the pan (almost causing an explosion); a heavy lid is immediately placed over the pan to keep the spluttering down. It is during this period of boiling and spluttering that the wine-onion-ginger-garlic flavoured oil and stock are shot through the cracks of the crab shells to flavour the crab meat. After 3–4 minutes' cooking over high heat, a beaten egg is poured in a thin stream over the crab and sauce, which is also sprinkled with a tablespoon of chopped chives. The result is that when the diner picks up a piece of crab to suck and chew, he has plenty of other things to suck and eat apart from the crab meat: namely, the plentiful sauce, minced pork and egg with chives in the sauce, all flavoured by the crab. There is hardly a dish which is more delicious in the whole gastronomic world.

Deep-Fried Crab

Mandarin: *Zhà Xiè*
Cantonese: *Ja Háaih*

Crab, when deep-fried, is usually given a short period of steaming and chopped into sections with legs attached. Only the chopped open part of the body is dipped into seasoned batter (egg, flour, minced ginger, chives and garlic), and the pieces are then deep fried for 2–3 minutes. The diner picks up the pieces by holding on to the legs; the claws are well cracked first and then covered in batter, so that the shell can be removed quite easily. The crab eggs in the main shell can be scraped out and eaten with the seasoned batter. Because this is a dry dish, it should be eaten with at least one or two dips.

Lobsters are considered more special than crabs and not to be treated as roughly, but they can be cooked in almost the same manner, though the sauces and ingredients are inclined to be less overwhelming in strength than those customarily used with crabs.

Steamed Lobsters

Mandarin: *Zhēng Lóng Xià*
Cantonese: *Jìng Luhng Hà*

When lobsters are steamed they are sliced lengthwise into halves (with the shell on) and a mixture consisting of blended soya sauce, rice wine, finely chopped spring onion and ginger is applied to the meat of the lobster. Each piece of lobster is placed with the meat side up and shell side down on tiers inside a steamer, and they are steamed vigorously for 10–12 minutes. The halves are served on a well-heated dish accompanied by various seafood dips.

Lobster Cantonese

Mandarin: *Jiāng Cŏng Gūo Lóń Xiā*
Cantonese: *Geùng Chūng Wò Luhng Hà*

The term 'Lobster Cantonese' is usually applied to this dish abroad and especially in America. The lobster is prepared and cooked in the same way as *Onion and Ginger Crab*, except that slightly less of each of the ingredients is used, so that the native delicate flavour of the lobster is not overwhelmed.

Lobster Steamed with Egg

Mandarin: *Lóng Xiā Zheng Dàn*
Cantonese: *Tòhng Chou Luhng Hà*

This is a clean, light-coloured dish, a little unusual by European standards; the lobster is here served in a 'custard', which is made by blending beaten egg with good chicken stock and some small pieces of lobster and seasonings. This mixture is steamed until the top surface has set (about 10 minutes), whereupon sections of shelled lobster are arranged on top, and the bowl or basin is returned into the steamer for a further 6–8 minutes. This is a pleasant dish with the pink of the pieces of lobster contrasting with the yellow of the savoury egg-custard.

Squids are used either dried or salted for a flavour which is not unlike kipper. When served fresh it has little flavour of its own. It is an inexpensive, rough and ready fish, which has to be cooked with other tasty ingredients.

Stir-Fried Squids in Black Bean Sauce

Mandarin: *Dòu Gŭ Chăo Yú Yú*
Cantonese: *Dauh Gú Cháau Yaùh Yùh*

Here the squids are cut into approximately 5×2·5cm (2×1 in) pieces and stir-fried in oil in which black beans (previously soaked), ginger, onion, garlic, sugar, soya sauce and good stock have been mixed and stir-fried together; since the latter is a strongly-flavoured mixture, the pieces of squid soon acquire the flavour of the sauce. With the interesting texture and white, clean appearance of the squid, the dish is a popular one in Cantonese restaurants. Occasionally some minced pork is added to the stir-frying to make the sauce even richer and more savoury.

Stir-Fried Squids with Prawns and Diced Pork

Mandarin: *Chǎo Sān Xiān*
Cantonese: *Yaùh Yùh Cháau Hà Yahn Yuhk*

Here the squids are stir-fried not only with a tasty sauce, but prawns and pork as well. The pork is diced into 8mm ($\frac{1}{3}$ in) cubes and is fried first with some ginger, onion, garlic; some stock and rice wine are then added with seasonings, making a highly savoury mixture. This is about the most refined way of cooking squids and is frequently seen on party tables. Otherwise squid dishes are seen mostly in inexpensive eating places or on family dining tables.

In contrast to squids, abalone is considered a refined and expensive food. Fresh abalone is seldom seen in China: it is almost always used dried, or canned. When dried it is usually used as a flavouring, especially for soups. A few slices or shreds of abalone would give a distinct and added flavour to chicken soup (which is, after all, the basis for most Chinese soups). For instance abalone is used in a famous semi-soup banquet dish called *Chicken-Abalone-Shark's Fin-Ensemble*.

Braised Abalone with Red-Cooked Meat Sauce

Mandarin: *Hóng Shāo Bào Yú*
Cantonese: *Huhng Siù Baàu Yùh*

Fresh or canned abalone can only stand very short cooking, otherwise it will soon turn very tough. Hence the cooking time should seldom exceed more than 1½–2 minutes. The sauce from the red-cooked pork is used, but since abalone is seafood, some sliced or minced ginger is stir-fried first in a little oil before the red-cooked sauce and some abalone water are added to the pan. The mixture is thickened with cornflour and sliced abalone is introduced for only a minute or two's gentle cooking together. The slices of abalone are then laid out neatly on a serving dish, and the sauce from the pan poured over them. It is a dish for an occasion rather than for hungry mouths at a family dinner table.

Braised Abalone with Winter Mushrooms and Bamboo-Shoots

Mandarin: *Bào Yú Shuāng Dōng*
Cantonese: *Bàau Yùh Wuih Seùng Dùng*

Here the bamboo shoots are introduced to add a clear new dimension in texture (crunchy as opposed to soft rubberiness), and the mushrooms (Chinese dried) for a distinct variation in flavour. The same sauce and other ingredients are used as in the previous dish, and occasionally some oyster sauce is also added to further strengthen the already high savouriness of the dish (this is one of the few occasions where a seafood sauce is actually added to a seafood dish). Once again this is a dish for occasions rather than family meals.

Clam meat has a texture not unlike that of squid but, unlike squid, clam has a taste of its own; it is therefore mostly poached or steamed, and eaten dipped in mixes and sauces.

Steamed Clams

Mandarin: *Chĭng Zhēng Gé Lí*
Cantonese: *Chìng Tōng Càp Leih*

The clams are simply washed and scrubbed and steamed vigorously for 8–10 minutes. The clam meat, which requires cutting from the shells with a sharp knife, is dipped in mixes, such as 'soya-tomato sauce', 'soya-chilli sauce' and soya sauce mixed with chopped chives and ginger.

Poached Clams

Mandarin: *Chiñg Tañg Gé*
Cantonese: *Chìng Tòng Gāp Leìh*

The meat of the clams is removed from their shells when the shells are opened up after being dipped in boiling water. The clam meat is then cut out from the shells and placed in a heatproof dish with 250ml (½ pint) of very clear chicken consommé with 2 slices of ginger and 2 tablespoons of rice wine added. The dish is then placed in a steamer and steamed for 8–10 minutes. The dish is served as a semi-soup where the diner will enjoy the soup as well as the clam. A few re-constituted dried mushrooms might be added from the beginning to provide a background flavour to counteract the inevitable slight fishiness in seafoods.

Deep-Fried Stuffed Clams

Mandarin: *Zhà Gé Lì*
Cantonese: *Ja Gàp Leìh*

Here the clam meat is finely chopped and mixed with minced pork, ginger, chives, egg, soya sauce; the resultant paste is used to stuff the clam shells. They are then deep-fried for 3–4 minutes and either drained and served, or submerged in chicken stock and steamed vigorously for 7–8 minutes, and then served as a semi-soup.

Sharks' fins always come dried, and are as rough as rhinoceros horns. Before they can be made edible at all, they need to be soaked in two or three changes of water, then simmered first in ordinary bone-stock with a few slices of ginger and finally in the best stock for at least three separate sessions. All these soakings and simmerings involve several days' work, and it is the appreciation of this that makes shark's fin such a superior dish. Nearly all its flavour is derived from the top-quality ingredients which are cooked with it; and the memory of the great banquets of the past, when the dish was always an important item on the menu, is not an unimportant ingredient.

Red-Cooked Shark's Fin

Mandarin: *Hóng Shāo Yú Chǐ*
Cantonese: *Huhng Siù Yùh Chi*

After all the soaking and simmering, when the fins are considered to be sufficiently soft and savoury, they are placed in a pot with an equal amount of the best meat-stock and red-cooked meat (or chicken) gravy; an appropriate amount of the best grade of soya sauce and rice wine are added and the contents are allowed to simmer gently for 30 minutes; the liquid in the pot or casserole is then thickened with cornflour. To add to the general succulence and savouriness a small amount of chicken fat and flavour powder (monosodium glutamate) are stirred into the dish and a couple of tablespoons of very finely-shredded ham are placed on top as a garnish.

The sharks' fins are then either served in a large tureen or in small individual bowls; the diner sips and eats with the appropriate expressions of satisfaction, deference and gratitude.

Shark's Fin with Crab Meat and Crab Eggs

Mandarin: *Xiè Huáng Yú Chǐ*
Cantonese: *Háaih Wòhng Yùh Chi*

The early stages of the preparation of the sharks' fins are exactly the same as in the previous dish, but in the final half hour of cooking, an appropriate amount of crab meat, crab eggs, rice wine and lard are added. The lard increases the richness and succulence and the wine neutralizes what fishiness there may still be in the crab.

Casserole (Sand-Pot) Shark's Fin

Mandarin: *Shà Gūo Yú Chǐ*
Cantonese: *Sà Wò Yùh Chi*

Shark's fin cooked in a casserole enables a greater range of ingredients to be combined in the same pot. These include ham, bamboo-shoots, shredded dried mushrooms (soaked first), fish stomach, and sometimes the Muslim school adds ox tongue and ox brain. All these are placed together in the sand-pot (or earthenware) casserole, with top-grade chicken stock and some rice wine and flavour powder (monosodium glutamate) and simmered for 30–35 minutes. Some onion and ginger are fried for 1 minute in the pot, and then removed before the stock and other ingredients are added. The fins, which have been suitably softened, and a heart of celery-cabbage are added for the last 20 minutes of simmering.

EGGS

There are not many more ways of preparing eggs in China than in the West, but there seems to be a greater number of dishes which can be cooked with eggs. Even eggs which have not been shelled (which in the West are simply boiled) are prepared in a number of ways.

'Thousand-Year-Old' Eggs

Mandarin: *Pí Dàn*, or *Soñg Huā*
Cantonese: *Pèih Dáan* or *Chùhng Fā*

These are usually made with duck eggs, which are thickly coated with a mixture of lime, ashes and mud and placed in a jar to mature for 3–4 months. The mixture of lime, mud and ashes has the effect of pickling the egg. After the 100 days or so in the jar, the lime and wet mud generate a certain amount of heat, and the egg-white becomes firm and amber-coloured, while the yolk goes spinach-green and cheese-like. When they are placed in a large jar, thickly coated with lime, ash and mud, they are kept separate from one another by being rolled in chopped straw while they are still damp or wet. They need to be turned around a few times during their period of 'incubation'. When they are taken out of the jar they look as if they have been recovered from inside some ancient Phoenician jar, or excavated from under the Great Wall after years of burial with other mummified objects. But, once the mud and lime have been washed off under running water and the clean shells are removed, the green-amber egg inside can appear quite appetizing, except for the smell of ammonia, which originates from the changing state of sulphur in the yolk. If you can hold your nose, or allow the smell to evaporate, or simply pretend that it does not exist, the cheesey taste of egg can be quite palatable. They have all the appearance of being cooked, and are usually eaten with hot soft rice for breakfast or midnight supper; sometimes they are cut into neat segments and served as a part of an hors-d'oeuvres.

Marbled Tea-Eggs

Mandarin: *Chá Dàn*
Cantonese: *Chàh Dáan*

These eggs are more easily acceptable to the average Western palate than the pungent 'Thousand-Year-Old' variety. They are made simply by hard-boiling the eggs. When they have cooled the shells should be lightly cracked at 2–3 different points, and the eggs immersed in salted strong tea to boil for a further 15 minutes. The eggs are left in the tea for another hour or more (sometimes even overnight). When the shells are removed one is surprised to see that there is a pattern on the white of the egg, which resembles that of the pattern on marbles; they have a mild flavour which is interesting, and can be made even more interesting by the addition of some dried tangerine peel to the tea.

Salt Eggs

Mandarin: *Xián Dān*
Cantonese: *Haàhm Daan*

'Salt eggs' are usually duck eggs which have been immersed in brine for 30–40 days, which makes the egg-white quite salty and the yolk bright orange. They are prepared for eating by boiling them for about 10 minutes. Strangely, when served for breakfast, when they are most often eaten, they are normally cut through the shells into segments and the shells left on. Salt eggs are quite versatile. Although most often they are just eaten with plain rice or soft rice, they are often used to add flavour to other foods. They can be steamed with minced pork, added to beaten-egg dishes (stir-fried or steamed), or even used to flavour soups and vegetables.

Iron Pot Eggs (Grown Eggs)

Mandarin: *Tiě Gūo Dàn*
Cantonese: *Tit Wò Daan*

This is really the only Chinese version of the western soufflé. The eggs are thoroughly beaten and combined with minced pork, soya sauce and lard, and the mixture placed at the bottom of an iron pot (or oven-proof dish), large enough for the egg mixture to expand during cooking, which is done over a low flame. After about half an hour the mixture will have grown to 4 or 5 times its original volume and it will start to push against the lid of the pot. The ingredients can certainly be varied, but we do not bother very much about the variation as we seem to be quite content just to watch the eggs grow!

Stir-fried eggs are often loosely called *Egg Fu Yung* in Chinese restaurants in the West, which is a misnomer. *Fu Yung* should actually apply to egg-white cooked dishes, where the egg-whites have been well beaten and combined with minced breast of chicken or minced white fish.

Basic Steamed Eggs

Mandarin: *Zhēng Dàn*
Cantonese: *Jing Daan*

Steamed eggs is one of the most economical dishes, as only a very few eggs should be used. If more than about 3 eggs are used, the steamed egg (which is really a kind of savoury egg custard) becomes too firm and hard. A good steamed egg should be light. Usually not more than 2 eggs are beaten and blended with 375ml (¾ pint) of good stock to which a small amount of salt and sherry (1 tablespoon) are added. The mixture is then placed in a bowl and steamed for 20–25 minutes. By that time the surface of the mixture should have become quite firm, although underneath the mixture should still remain quite light and soft. A large pinch of chopped chives or spring onion and ¾ tablespoon of the best soya sauce are sprinkled on top of the egg. Although simple and economical, the dish is one of the most appealing accompaniments to plain cooked rice.

Basic Stir-Fried Eggs

Mandarin: *Chǎo Jī Dàn*
Cantonese: *Cháau Gāi Daan*

To describe stir-fried eggs as an omelette is a misnomer. The Chinese concept is to pour the beaten egg into the frying pan and stir and mix it gently with the ingredients which are already cooking in the pan; the gentle stirring should be done when the top of the egg is still slightly liquid but the bottom of the egg has distinctly set. The ideal is to have a mixture of well-set egg as well as almost liquid egg. The appeal is enhanced by sprinkling over the egg a small amount of rice-wine and chopped chives, which gives the dish a very appealing aroma. The only seasoning which needs to be added is a tablespoonful of soya sauce, which should be sprinkled over the dish at the last moment.

RICE

Rice is mostly consumed boiled or steamed, both of which are fairly dry, and eaten at midday and evening meals. At breakfast time 'soft rice' or *Congee* is usually eaten; this is Chinese porridge, or rice cooked with 3 to 4 times as much water as usual. It is often the only hot food eaten at breakfast time, the other dishes or accompaniments are usually salted, pickled foods, nuts, or cold soya-braised dishes, which go well as contrasts to the blandness of the rice. Fried rice, which is regarded as a snack, is hardly ever served at a meal where there are already a number of savoury dishes on the table, but it is often served in Chinese restaurants to foreigners who want everything savoury and tasty and are not aware of the function of rice which is the bulk food at mealtimes for cushioning the multiplicity of savoury dishes. When Congee is made savoury, which it often is in south China, it is eaten as a simple snack at teatime, or at midnight.

Boiled or Steamed Rice (see also page 175)

Mandarin: *Fàn*
Cantonese: *Faahn*

Although boiled rice is produced by simply boiling rice in water and steamed rice is also generally started by a short par-boiling in water, the end product should be quite dry, flaky and absorbent. Because of its blandness and bulk, rice gives meaning to the richer and more savoury dishes, which on their own would be too rich and savoury to consume in any quantity. Westerners who insist on Chinese food without rice have really missed the point, which is that a Chinese meal at its best should be a balanced one. It should not be all mouth-watering savouriness. At an ordinary Chinese family meal, rice is served automatically, one bowl for each person. The diner can replenish his bowl as often as he likes. It is normal to consume 2–3 bowls of rice (about 400g or 1 lb) per meal, and it is not unusual for the young, or manual workers, to consume 4 bowls. But when someone consumes more than 5 bowls per meal, he is immediately nick-named *Fan-Tun* which means 'rice-bucket'. In the West these days, when most people are overfed and have developed a carbohydrate complex, they have to be reminded that to eat a proper Chinese meal they need to eat a bowl of rice (or at the very least half a bowl) to go with all the various dishes on the table. But, to enjoy rice thoroughly, after eating it with several mouthfuls of rich savoury foods, one should also endeavour to eat a mouthful on its own. For it is only by eating rice on its own and feeling the individual grains in the mouth and tasting their sweetness, that one really gets to know and appreciate it.

Fried Rice *(see recipe on page 177)*

Mandarin: *Chǎo Fàn*
Cantonese: *Cháau Faahn*

Fried rice is a mixture of rice with chopped savoury foods and is therefore one degree away from the natural goodness and native quality of rice, but it can be a convenient and self-contained dish which can be served when there is only a soup or vegetable dish to go with the meal. An important ingredient is onion; all the other ingredients should contrast with the rice either in colour or in taste. Useful ingredients are bacon, and salted meats (salt beef, salt pork, soya-braised pork) which have been diced into small cubes; fresh vegetables, such as diced carrots, cucumber, green peas, or salted or pickled vegetables. Fresh meats (beef, lamb, turkey, chicken or pork) should all be diced into small pea-size pieces and stir-fried in some salt before adding to the fried rice.

Eggs are frequently used boiled and chopped or just beaten lightly and stir-fried, then broken up and added. Seafoods or chopped button mushrooms can also be added. A fair quantity of oil, fat or butter should be used, for besides the rice, all the other ingredients require a fair amount of lubrication to give the dish a feeling of smooth savouriness, which is acceptable and appealing to most palates. One frequently sees more than half a dozen fried rice dishes on a restaurant menu, such as *Chicken Fried Rice*, *Beef Fried Rice*, *Prawn Fried Rice*, *Egg Fried Rice*, *Pork Fried Rice*. But it is not a dish that is seen on a Chinese banquet table!

Vegetable Rice (Shanghai)

Mandarin: *Cài Fàn*
Cantonese: *Choi Faahn*

This is a simple way of combining and cooking vegetables and rice together at the same time; it involves stir-frying some chopped green vegetables at the bottom of a pan with some oil and salt, and then adding rice and water on top. The mixture is brought to the boil and left to simmer for ten minutes; finally the heat is turned off and the rice and vegetables are left to steam in their own heat for a quarter of an hour. During that time the vegetable flavour will have entered into the rice, which makes it an eminently suitable dish for eating with savoury and meaty foods.

Lotus-Leaf-Wrapped Rice

Mandarin: *Nùo Mǐ Fàn* or *Zōng*
Cantonese: *Ngoh Máih Faahn*

This is usually a savoury rice, with some roast pork or soya-braised chicken and gravy added, which is tightly wrapped in a sheet of lotus leaf (usually dried lotus leaf which has been softened by soaking) into a triangular-shaped

parcel. It is then steamed for about $\frac{1}{2}$–$\frac{3}{4}$ hour. Usually
dozens of these parcels are steamed together and hung up in
strings. When required, they can be given a final steaming
and served to the diners, who open up the parcel with chopsticks at the table. By this time the rice will have gained a
certain appealing vegetable aroma from the lotus leaf in
which it has been wrapped.

Soft Rice or Congee (see recipe on page 178)

Mandarin: *Zhōu*
Cantonese: *Jùk*

When served in this plain way, rice is extremely settling to
the stomach and is therefore given to invalids in China. The
taste for soft rice is a cultivated one, but to get to know it is
to acquire an important Chinese taste. It is sometimes
cooked with pork bones, carcass of chicken or roast duck,
or whole chicken and whole duck, or both. Some ingredients,
such as bones, whole birds or dried shrimps, are added
during the early stages of the cooking (and the cooking goes
on for a couple of hours), and some towards the very end
(such as sliced raw fish or fresh shrimps). The result is a large
bowl of easily digestible food which is both delicious and
nutritious.

NOODLES

Noodles rank with steamed buns and rice as the most important staple foods of China. Unlike steamed buns or rice,
which are usually served plain to be eaten with a host of
savoury dishes, noodles are usually cooked with the savoury
ingredients, and served as complete dishes. For this reason
they are useful for small meals or snacks. Hence many small
eating places in China are called Noodle Shops (*Mein Dian*).

Although there are hundreds of different noodles dishes,
in the main they are prepared and served in four different
ways: Fried Noodles or *Chow Mein*, Soup Noodles or *Tang
Mein*, Cooked Mixed Noodles in sauce, also called *Lu* (or

Lo or *Wo*) *Mein*, Tossed Noodles or *Pan Mein*, that is, noodles tossed with other ingredients either by the diners themselves, or just before serving.

I should like to reproduce in full a paragraph written by a fellow Chinese cookery-writer, Buwei Yang Chow, on how to eat noodles, from her book *How to Cook and Eat Chinese*:

Noodles should not be wound on your chopsticks as you would wind spaghetti on a fork. It is also not good manners to put a great thick bunch of noodles into your mouth at one time. You can lift a dozen noodles or so with your chopsticks and shove the lifted part into your mouth and bite off, so that the remainder will ease back into your bowl. Instead of biting off, it is also alright to suck in the remainder, if not too long, and the accompanying noise is considered permissible and gives the right atmosphere to noodle-eating occasions. Be careful of course that the loose ends will not flip any juice on to your neighbour, especially when it is hot.

Tossed Noodles with Meat Sauce and Shredded Vegetables (north China)

Mandarin: *Zhà Jiàng Miàn*
Cantonese: *Ja Jeung Mihn*

The dish bears some similarity to spaghetti Bolognaise in that a meat sauce is poured over boiled noodles. The only difference is that, in the Chinese version, the meat sauce is made by cooking soya paste (or soya jam) with minced meat rather than, as in the Italian version, tomato. But we have added a fresh dimension to the dish by serving an array of shredded vegetables which can be added to the noodles by the diners themselves; these may include shredded cucumber, carrots, radishes, and bean sprouts. In addition there may be a dish or two of sweet or salted pickles. One or two liquid condiments such as Chekiang vinegar, or soya sauce with mustard or chilli may also be served.

In the world of Chinese food *Chow Mein* can probably be equated with Fried Rice, as one of those dishes which can be prepared with all the titbits and pieces which happen to be lying around in the kitchen. The only difference is that in cooking fried rice all the ingredients which are cooked in with the rice are chopped or diced into pea-size pieces, whilst in the case of *Chow Mein* they are all shredded into matchstick-size strips. It is one of the principles in Chinese cutting that all ingredients employed in cooking should be cut more or less into the same shape as the main ingredient of the dish – which in this case are noodles. The cooked noodles are first of all made savoury by turning them in hot oil and gravy in the frying-pan in which the fairly substantial garnish has been cooked. The garnish, which usually consists of shredded meat and vegetables, is then given a second turn in the pan, and laid on top of the noodles.

Chicken Chow Mein

Mandarin: *Jiè Sī Chǎo Miàn*
Cantonese: *Gāi Sih Mihn*

This is one of the most frequently seen fried-noodle dishes on any Chinese restaurant menu, in which there are generally as many as six to a dozen *Chow Mein* dishes. Any one of the half-dozen types of Chinese noodles can be used for the purpose. Many of the Chinese egg noodles are precooked and therefore need no more than 6–7 minutes' cooking before being fried. Once they have been cooked they should be immediately drained and rinsed under running water so they keep separate.

When cooking 300g (12 oz) of dried noodles, which should attain at least double that weight when cooked, no more than 75–100g (3–4 oz) of shredded chicken (cooked or uncooked) is needed to produce a substantial dish of *Chow Mein*. The garnish is made more interesting and savoury by stir-frying a number of other ingredients together with the shredded chicken. These usually consist of shredded onions, or sectioned spring onions, shredded Chinese dried mush-rooms (soaked first), shredded celery (or spinach, cabbage, or any vegetable) with soya sauce, sugar and a little rice wine. In the Cantonese version, the noodles are fried until they are crisp at the bottom (or both on top and at the bottom) using a good deal more oil. But this version of half-crisp and half-soft noodles (soft in the inside portion) is not favoured by the Chinese in other parts of China; they prefer the noodles soft, and in the north they are in the habit of eating quantities of noodles, rather than just a snack.

Basic Wo Mein or Pot-cooked Noodles

Mandarin: *Wō Miàn*
Cantonese: *Wò Mihn*

The difference between this type of noodles and *Chow Mein* is that the noodles are not stir-fried, but placed in a sauce to cook for a short while after parboiling. The garnishes can be the same as for *Chow Mein*. Part of the garnish is used to generate the sauce, by stir-frying it first and removing half of it, and adding some stock to the half left in the pan and simmering for 6–7 minutes with some soya sauce before it is thickened with cornflour. This is the sauce in which the parboiled noodles are cooked for 5–15 minutes so that they can absorb some flavour before they are poured into a large bowl or tureen, where they are topped with the balance of the garnish which is shortly quick-fried. Because of the ample sauce in which the noodles are cooked, this is usually a larger and more substantial dish than a *Chow Mein*, and to the hungry perhaps more satisfying.

Soup Noodles (see also page 188)

Mandarin: *Tang Miàn*
Cantonese: *Tong Mihn*

Fish, which cannot be subjected to stir-frying without being broken into pieces, is a good garnish for soup noodles;

otherwise garnishes can be much the same as for other types of noodle. It is important not to overcook the noodles, as they then lose their textural interest. To the uninitiated it would seem that the richer and more varied the garnishes, the better the soup noodles. But in point of fact some of the most prized soup noodles, with the most regional character, consist of nothing but an ounce or two of shredded pork with shredded pickles which have been stir-fried together and placed on top as a garnish. The addition of any further ingredients would be considered damaging to the character and purity of the dish.

It would be a mistake to regard soup noodles as just a soup. We certainly do not. We regard it as a meal on its own – although not a large one – but it can be a substantial meal if contained in a bowl as large as a tureen. For the dish may contain as much as 375ml (¾ pint) of soup, 300g (12 oz) of noodles, a leg of chicken or a chunk of red-cooked meat, a poached egg, assorted vegetables, a few dried shrimps, some shredded meat, fish balls, or sliced chicken kidney and liver. The idea of having so many ingredients in one dish is to make it a well-balanced meal. There certainly does not seem to be the tradition of such a soup in the West, where a soup is usually meant to be a starter. Chinese soup noodles can be the beginning and the end of the meal. On the other hand there are some soup noodles which are meant to be just light snacks. A typical instance is the Chinese version of the plain *Shredded Chicken Noodle Soup*. This is normally served on occasions when guests or relatives come to pay a courtesy call; the moment he or she enters the reception room he or she will be given a small bowl of this soup which will contain no more than 50–75g (2–3 oz) of noodles in a small bowl of clear chicken consommé, with a few shreds of white-cooked chicken meat (occasionally also with a few shreds of ham) placed on top. Although small, such a bowl of *Shredded Chicken Noodle Soup* can be quite welcoming both because of its warmth and its flavour. It is meant to express welcome and promote sociability.

BREADS

We have the *Chiaotze, Hsiao Mai, Paotze, Man Tou* and *Choon Juen*. The *Paotze* and *Man Tou* are the steamed buns of China (since not many Chinese kitchens have ovens, the majority of buns are steamed rather than baked).

Man Tou (Màah Taùh)

The *Man Tou* is the solid steamed bun which has no stuffing; they are served regularly at mealtimes in north China together with, or instead of, rice. They are about half the size of tennis balls and creamy-white in colour. Since they are steamed and not baked there is no crust; they are soft outside and quite solid inside. A couple of them are equivalent to a heaped bowl of rice. They rank with rice as one of the two staple foods of north China, but are hardly ever served in the south. Hence one seldom sees them in Chinese restaurants abroad, except in Pekingese restaurants.

Paotze or Baozi (Báu Jí) (see recipe on page 252)

Paotze, or stuffed steamed buns, are altogether daintier. They are seldom served at mealtimes, but usually consumed as snacks. They vary in size: some come the size of a tennis ball, but the majority are about the same size as *Man Tou*. The stuffings vary from chicken, Cantonese *Cha Shao* roast pork, cabbage, to sweetened bean paste or a mixture of sugar, sesame-paste/seeds, and pork fat. In a way *Paotze* can be said to be the Chinese sandwiches, which are often eaten in teashops at tea-time, or can be taken on picnics or travels. The cabbage-stuffed *paotze* are prized because they are so useful for eating with savoury meat dishes. There is always some sugar mixed into the dough mixture, which makes them somewhat sweet. This makes it extremely easy for westerners to take to them; *Man Tou* on the other hand, is bland and unadorned.

Chiaotze (Jiǎo Zǐ) (see recipe on page 254)

These are consumed more widely in the north than in the south; they are, like *Won Tons*, made with meat or prawn stuffings and wrapped in a thin dough-skin, but they are 4–5 times the size of *Won Tons*, and much fatter and squatter. They are about 6cm (2½ in) long and are kidney-bean shaped. They can be served steamed, boiled, or in soups. The seasoned meat and vegetable stuffings encased in the thin dough-skin are voluptuous to taste, and the mouthful is made piquant by being dipped into a tangy mixture of vinegar and soya sauce. It is a sensation which the palate is drawn to try and repeat time and again.

Hsiao Mai (Sìu Maai)

This is another type of stuffing in a dough-skin, which is left open on one side and often topped with a small mushroom or a single prawn. They are served mostly in Cantonese restaurants and tea-houses, where they are consumed as snacks, and never in large quantities for a meal like *Chiaotze*.

Chūn Juǎn (Chēun Gyun)

These are known as 'spring rolls' in the West, and are prepared and served in China early in the spring to mark the advent of the season; on such occasions the pancakes are left open for the diners to wrap round their own stuffings. These stuffings usually consist of several dishes of hot, quickly stir-fried vegetables. One of them will be a vegetable called *Chin T'sai*, which is not unlike bean sprouts, but has the taste of shredded young leeks. It is an occasion for fun and celebration.

The spring roll has undergone a change with migration. It is no longer a do-it-yourself affair, but a deep-fried pancake roll, with stuffing inside and a crisp pancake skin outside. Admittedly, the crispness of the skin and the fullness of the stuffings inside are appealing to the western palate, but it is no longer the original thing.

VEGETABLES

Vegetables occupy an important area of Chinese cuisine. Yet not many Chinese vegetable dishes seem to appear on the menu of Chinese restaurants abroad. This could be due partly to the fact that not all Chinese vegetables are available in the West (even the basic Chinese cabbage only became available in Britain very recently), and partly to the fact that many Chinese seem to think that the majority of westerners are carnivorous, and that it would be a waste of effort to create the more intricate vegetable dishes which are often very time-consuming. In any case, many of the Chinese vegetables contain bean curd, and the derivatives of bean curd (such as bean-curd skin, bean-curd stick, and bean-curd cheese), which are not easily appreciated by the average westerner without prolonged cultivation. Hence the majority of Chinese vegetable dishes served in Chinese restaurants abroad seem to fall into the quick-cooked varieties.

The general technique employed by the Chinese in cooking their quick-fried vegetable dishes usually consists of first frying some small amount of the strong vegetables such as garlic, onion and ginger in 2–3 tablespoons of oil for 15–30 seconds in order to flavour the oil. The flavoured oil is then used to cook the main vegetable which is turned and stirred in the hot oil for a matter of a minute or two. It is only then that the liquid flavourings such as soya sauce, concentrated chicken stock, some sugar and perhaps some rice wine and flavour powder (monosodium glutamate) are added. In the last stage of the cooking, a tablespoon or so of fat, lard, butter or sesame oil is added to give the final gloss, which certainly adds to the appeal.

Any vegetable dishes can be made Sweet and Sour, either

by cooking them in the *sweet and sour sauce* for a very short while (15–30 seconds) or by pouring the sauce over the vegetables in the serving dishes. The important thing is that both the vegetable and sauce should be freshly cooked, and the sauce should appear bright, translucent, colourful, and fruity. Sweet and sour vegetables can be served either hot or cold.

Fu Yung sauce can also be applied to almost any vegetable dish except cold ones; but vegetable dishes to which the *Fu Yung* sauce is applied should be seasoned with salt or light-coloured soya (not the dark variety, as this would discolour the white sauce). The vegetables – usually cauliflower, courgettes and cabbage – to which the sauce is applied are cooked until they are somewhat softer than usual.

White-braising in vegetable cookery means braising in good stock or chicken broth; red-cooking means braising in soya sauce (with a smaller amount of stock added). In either case the liquid added should not be more than, say, a quarter of the weight of the vegetable. Other ingredients used are a small amount of dried shrimps (especially in white-braising) and dried mushrooms and a liberal amount of oil, fat or butter. The technique of braising is slow-simmering, which should generally last about 15–20 minutes, which is a sufficient length of cooking to make most medium-hard vegetables tender. For rice-eaters, these are some of the most favoured ways of serving vegetables. They seem to make the rice more succulent.

Mixed-vegetable dishes can be excellent if the richness of slow-cooked vegetables combines with the crispness of stir-fried vegetables; or where quick deep-fried vegetables are cross-cooked or stir-fried with freshly blanched vegetables to bring out their respective qualities. But unfortunately too many restaurants are in the habit of throwing vegetables together quite indiscriminately with some soya sauce; or cooking a pot of them and leaving it to stand until it is required, which denies the vegetables their inherent quality of freshness.

Sub-Gum Vegetable

Mandarin: *Sù Shí Jǐn*
Cantonese: *Sou Sahp Gám*

This usually consists of a mixed, stir-fried dish of Chinese mushrooms (soaked first), sliced or shredded carrots, bamboo-shoots, with greens or cabbage, wood ears, cucumber, bean sprouts. The first three vegetables are usually put in to fry first, or are deep-fried, and combined in a frying-pan with the last four which are quick-fried. In the latter process some soya sauce, sugar, chicken stock and rice wine are often added and the heat turned very high. The contents are then dished out to be served and eaten whilst still sizzling hot.

Buddhist's Vegetable Ensemble

Mandarin: *Lúo Hàn Cài*
Cantonese: *Lòh Hon Choi*

This is really just an elaborate dish of mixed vegetables with a grandiose name, which consists of a number of specific ingredients which are stewed together, some of which are initially quick deep-fried. The following are the ingredients: hair vegetable (or black hair-like seaweeds), lily-bud stems (also called golden needles), pea-starch transparent noodles, gingko nuts, dried mushrooms, bean-curd skin, bamboo-shoots, green peas, cabbage and deep-fried, small puffy cakes of bean-curd. The bean-curd cakes and cabbages are first of all deep-fried, and then added to the other ingredients in a pot. 500ml (1 pint) of water is added with the appropriate amount of soya sauce, and other flavouring ingredients, including some sesame oil. The contents are brought to the boil, and left to simmer for 30 minutes. This pot of vegetables is often served as a main dish on meatless days. In restaurants they often add chicken stock instead of water for the cooking, which spoils the essential vegetarian nature of the dish but adds to its general savouriness and flavour.

All stuffed-vegetable dishes are refined dishes, which are elaborately produced. They generally take a great deal of time in preparation. The vegetables which are most often stuffed are mushrooms, peppers, tomatoes and marrows. The stuffings are usually made up of a mixture of meat or seafoods with vegetables. In cases where the vegetables are small, the cooking can usually be done by shallow-frying and braising. But where the vegetable is large, such as the marrow, it is usually steamed. Stuffings can consist of a great variety of ingredients, ranging from seafoods to fungi, giblets and smoked ham. These large, steamed vegetable pots are often termed 'bells' in China.

Stuffed Mushrooms

Mandarin: *Niàng Dōng Gu*
Cantonese: *Neùhng Dùng Gù*

The mushrooms used in these recipes, as in most Chinese cooking, are the large black Chinese mushrooms, which require about 20 minutes' soaking before using. The stuffing used usually consists of minced pork with chopped onion, garlic, beaten egg and water chestnuts. The ingredients are mixed into a paste, and this is then spread firmly and thickly on the underside of the mushrooms from which the stem has already been removed. The mushroom is placed paste-side down in a frying-pan which has been greased with a suitable amount of oil. After 2–3 minutes of cooking over medium heat, the mushrooms are turned over, and some liquid flavourings (soya sauce, mushroom water, stock and rice wine) are sprinkled into the pan, and the heat lowered to a simmer. A lid is then placed over the pan, and the contents allowed to braise and simmer for 7–8 minutes. The stuffed mushrooms are then lifted out from the pan and neatly arranged on a serving dish. What gravy there is left in the pan can then be enhanced by the addition of more stock and wine; and this is poured over the mushrooms in the dish. A pinch of chopped parsley is often sprinkled over the mushrooms.

Melon Chicken

Mandarin: *Xī Gūa Jī*
Cantonese: *Sài Gw̄a Gāi*

Melon and marrow can both be served stuffed with a variety of stuffings. Since, with melons or marrow, we are cooking on a large scale, much of the stuffing material should be cooked or partly cooked beforehand. In this case a whole chicken is used, with ham, bamboo-shoots, dried mushrooms, lotus seeds, ginger, and some of the melon or marrow itself neatly cut up. All these should be cooked together in ample water for an hour before they are used to fill the cavity of the melon or marrow. Indeed, the idea is to make the inside of the melon or marrow look like a natural pond, when it is filled up with the chicken and all the other materials and the lid is replaced (the lid is the top fifth of the marrow or melon which has been sliced off) and held in position with tooth-picks. The whole or sphere is stood in a heatproof bowl and steamed for 40–45 minutes. Frogs, which in China are called 'field chickens' are often used for stuffing the melon or marrow.

Tou Fu

Although *tou fu* or bean-curd, which is made from soya beans, is now very much an in-thing with people who are inclined towards health foods because it is an excellent source of natural protein, its appreciation is not one of those things which comes easily to the average westerner. First of all, it is bland and comparatively tasteless. Secondly, its texture is uninteresting – being neither custard nor jelly. It is in fact a junket, which is slightly firmer than yogurt, and tastes something like unflavoured yogurt, which is exactly what the average Anglo-Saxon, brought up to appreciate steak-and-kidney pudding, and fish and chips, feels good food should not taste like!

The Chinese and Japanese have come to appreciate *tou fu* and will take a long taxi-ride to a place where it is on the menu. Its importance in Chinese culinary art is shown by the fact that in a recently published cookbook produced in China by the Light Industries Publishing Co., there are 32 *tou fu* recipes on their list. Besides, over half of all Chinese vegetarian banquet dishes are *tou fu*-based.

HOTPOTS (OR CHAFING-DISH COOKING)

Chafing-dish cooking is characteristic of a good Chinese home-cooked meal in the winter. The three principal types of hotpots follow.

Sliced Lamb Hotpot

Mandarin: *Shuàn Yáng Ròu*
Cantonese: *Saan Yeùhng Yuhk*

This is the typical Peking version of the hotpot, with strong Mongolian/Muslim overtones. The contents of the pot are contained in a 'moat' surrounding a fat, squat-based funnel at the centre, into which hot charcoal is packed. This funnel rises about 10cm (4 in) above the circular lid of the pot. Its overall height is about 30cm (1 ft), but it can sometimes be lengthened by slotting on an additional funnel extension to provide the extra draw. In any case the firing-power of the pot is impressive and is able to keep the soup and other materials in the 'moat' (which holds 1·5–2 litres (3–4) pints of liquid) at a constant rolling boil. Pieces of sliced lamb are laid out in sheets of one layer on medium-size plates for four or five people. The diner picks up a piece or two at a time with his chopsticks and dips it into the broth boiling in the 'moat' of the hotpot. These thin slices of lamb do not require much more than $1\frac{1}{2}$–2 minutes of cooking, after which they are retrieved by the diner, dipped lightly in his own dip bowl and eaten. The dips usually contain the following ingredients: coriander leaves, vinegar, shrimp sauce, sesame jam, chilli oil, mashed bean-curd cheese, soya sauce.

The soup becomes more tasty as the cooking proceeds. There are only two ingredients, apart from the liquid, in the pot: Chinese cabbage or spinach, and pea-starch transparent noodles. In the end, each person fills his own bowl from the hotpot to wash down the meal, which brings beads of perspiration to everyone's forehead – a fitting conclusion to a hearty meal in the chill of winter.

As you can see, this Peking version of *Sliced Lamb Hotpot* is very limited in its use of ingredients – to some fussy southerners almost too simple and straightforward in its concept – but it must not be confused with the so-called *Steamboats* of Singapore and the South Seas, which seems to be an illegitimate dish of ill-defined origins. When properly served the true Peking version is almost barbaric in its splendour.

First-Rank Hotpot

Mandarin: *Yī Pǐn Gūo*
Cantonese: *Yāt Bán Wò*

The pot is the same funnelled affair used for the *Peking Hotpot*, but the ingredients are infinitely more varied; they are mostly pre-cooked as well as being simmered for about ½ hour in the clear broth in the pot before they are brought on to the table, when they are packed separately into different sections of the pot. They include: chicken, duck, uncooked ham, fried bean-curd, fish balls, egg-wraplings (egg-skin stuffed with minced meat), abalone, Chinese celery-cabbage, pea-starch noodles, dried mushrooms, hard-boiled eggs. From time to time the liquid in the pot is replenished. The hotpot is served along with many other dishes, but it forms the centrepiece of the dinner.

Chrysanthemum Hotpot

Mandarin: *Jú Hūa Gūo*
Cantonese: *Gūk Fā Wò*

This hotpot differs from the previous two in that it is a flat-bottomed chafing-pot without a funnel, and is fired with methylated spirit instead of charcoal. It takes its name from the cylindrical metalwork which holds the pot up, and which is cut to such a design that the bouquet of licking flames, which envelops the pot, resembles the petals of an enormous chrysanthemum. It is the Chinese imagination at work! After the ingredients have been piled into the pot, the petals of a large white chrysanthemum are sprinkled over them by the hostess. As this flower begins to bloom in October or November perhaps this hotpot signals the arrival of autumn, a season which requires something hot on the table. The ingredients are usually Chinese cabbage, pea-starch noodles, spinach, sliced pork tenderloin, sliced breast of chicken, fresh shrimps, chicken, duck, and sliced pig's liver and kidney and oysters. After the spirit has been lit, a large, circular lid is placed over the pot, and the contents allowed to boil under cover for 5–6 minutes before the lid is removed and the diners begin to help themselves. Unlike the previous hotpot, in which the different ingredients are packed into the 'moat' of the hotpot in vertically divided sections, here the ingredients are laid in horizontal layers, the cabbage and noodles at the bottom, and the meats and seafoods on top. A cup of rice wine and the petals of a chrysanthemum are sprinkled over the contents last. After 5–6 minutes of boiling most of the ingredients are ready to eat, but, as time goes on the soup becomes further enriched, and is sometimes used for poaching an egg, either in the diner's own bowl, or in the main pot itself.

SWEETS

There is a general impression in the West that there is only a very small range of sweets in China, which is not quite true. There are in fact many scores of Chinese sweet dishes, but the majority of restaurateurs regard sweets as not being quite in their sphere. They belong to the confectioners' world, and the restaurateurs feel that that is where they should stay. We Chinese do not eat sweets at meal-times; at most we would take some sweet soups to provide a change in taste and texture, or use a few sweet things to nibble; but they should not be confused with main courses. Savouries are the proper province of our restaurants.

But the lack of sweets in restaurants must not lead westerners to the erroneous conclusion that there is no sweet-making tradition in China, and that the Chinese do not know how to make sweets! One has only to eat an egg tart in any authentic Cantonese restaurant to know that the light touch of the Chinese chef is applicable to almost any type of food.

The Peking Glazed Apple

Mandarin: *Pa Ssi Ping K'uo*
Cantonese: *Baat Sì Pihng Gwó*

This dish of sweets consists simply of apples which have been cored, cut into bite-size pieces, battered and briefly deep-fried. The apple pieces are then drained and dipped into a pan of molten sugar, mixed with sesame oil; as they are lifted out of the sugar they pull out a lot of thin sugar threads (from which the Pekingese name *Drawn Thread Apple* is derived). The pieces are plunged into a large bowl of cold water, which gives them a thin, crackling glaze of sugar, coating the surface of the apple (unlike the toffee apple, where the thick sugar coating is often hard and thick enough to break a good many teeth!).

Peking Dust

Mandarin: *Li Tze Feng*

This sweet was invented by the western colony in Peking during the 1920s. It consists simply of a small mound of freshly-ground, mashed chestnut, topped with a blob of whipped cream. Peking is well known for its chestnuts, especially in the winter, when they are roasted at every street corner; Peking, which is just south of Inner Mongolia and the Gobi desert, is equally well known for its dust, especially during every change of season.

Almond Tea (see recipe on page 256)

Mandarin: *Xing Rén Chá*
Cantonese: *Hahn Yàhn Chàh*

This is a creamy drink made with ground rice and ground almonds with water and sugar. Different flavouring essences can be added. The cooking is done slowly in a double-boiler for over two hours, until the mixture reaches a smooth consistency. Water is added to the ground rice and almond, and the mixture is allowed to soak for 1–2 hours; it is then strained through cheesecloth. The liquid thus obtained can be drunk on its own, or as 'punctuation' in a multi-course Chinese dinner.

Almond Jelly and the Water-Melon Pond

Mandarin: *Xìng Rén Dòu Fǔ Xī Gūa Zhong*
Cantonese: *Hahng Yāhn Dauh Fuh Sāi Gwa Jùng*

A jelly is made by simply jellifying the almond tea and cutting it into regular rectangular pieces. It is slightly unusual in that it has a nutty flavour and is best when served with fruits, in a water-melon.

Eight-Treasure Rice (see recipe on page 180)

> Mandarin: *Bà Bǎo Fàn*
> Cantonese: *Baat Bóu Faahn*

This dessert can almost be said to be the Chinese Christmas pudding. It is made by slowly-boiling glutinous rice, with sugar and suet mixed into it, which is then packed into a mould or large basin with eight different types of dried fruits, candied fruits, nuts, barley and sweetened bean paste. The bean paste is placed in it in layers, and the other ingredients are either mixed in or stuck to the sides of the mould, which has been heavily spread with lard; it is then steamed for an hour. When it is turned out it looks like a Christmas pudding, except lighter in colour, and the surface is studded with such ingredients as candied orange-peel, dried lotus-seeds, dried 'dragon eyes', honeyed dates, candied cherries, almonds or walnuts, barley and melon seeds. Most Chinese restaurants should be able to make it if it is ordered beforehand.

Tangerine Soup with Rice Balls

> Mandarin: *Yúan Xiao Jú Zǐ Geng*
> Cantonese: *Yuhn Sìu Gwat Ji Gang*

Yúan Xiao are glutinous rice balls made from glutinous rice flour; sometimes these rice balls are filled with a mixture of sugar, sesame seeds and pork fat. They are dropped into boiling water for 5–6 minutes, drained and added to a pan of tangerine juice, blended with 4 or 5 times its own volume of water and sweetened with sugar; they are allowed to simmer for 5–6 minutes, after which, the sweet soup is ready.

Steamed Honeyed Pears

Mandarin: *Mì Táng Zheng Lí*
Cantonese: *Maht Tohng Jìng Lei*

After cutting off the top fifth of the pear, together with the stem, to reserve as a lid, the pear is cored half way through and filled with honey. The pears are then placed upright in a heatproof dish, sprinkled with a sweet wine, or simply sugared water, and steamed for 25–30 minutes. The lids are replaced before serving.

White 'Wood Ears' in Crystal Sugar Soup

Mandarin: *Riňg Táng Mù Ěr*
Cantonese: *Bìng Toňg Huhk Yih*

The appeal of this dessert lies partly in the texture of the 'wood ears', which can only be described as slippery and crunchy, and the crystalline purity of the soup, which is simply crystal sugar and water. After a multi-course Chinese dinner, during which dozens of savoury foods have been consumed, this soup can be the perfect ending.

Cooking the Chinese Way

What is the fatal charm of Chinese cooking, from which so many, once enamoured, have never recovered? What is its secret, which has caused an American culinary writer to exalt it as the greatest cooking in the world; and some Frenchmen to admit that it is more subtle than French cooking, which is always accepted and respected as the preeminent school in the West? Whether these verdicts or opinions are correct or not, it is certainly worthwhile to conduct a tour of inspection, if not as a connoisseur at least as a gastronomic tourist.

There is one thing of which there is no doubt; that is, during the last couple of decades, Chinese restaurants are establishing themselves and Chinese cooking is prospering in every capital and sizeable city in the world. This must be an attestation to the fact that the number of people in the West who are taking to Chinese food is on a rapid increase. That this rapid expansion should take place without the aid of organized capital or inspired organization, but has gone forward in a purely haphazard, if not chaotic, manner; and that in its expansion Chinese food has never feared any competition from any quarter, generally finding, in fact, most prosperity where the competition is keenest, is a pointer that there must be something intrinsically superior and vital in the foods preferred, in so far, in this case, as the welfare of our two decisive organs are concerned – the palate and the stomach.

If the cat is to be let at once out of the bag, the strength of Chinese cooking simply lies equally in its quality as well as its quantity: to get the right perspective, when thinking of the teeming dishes of China, one must imagine them in terms of China's proverbial teeming millions (here to think of scores or hundreds is to indulge in the extreme of typical Sino-Saxon understatement); when considering the gastronomic poetry of some of China's culinary products one should recall to mind the exquisite delicacy and harmony of Ming bowls, Sung vases and Tang horses. For after all, they are all part and parcel of the life and expression of the same people, and of the same heritage.

To become really 'fatally charmed' by Chinese cooking one has to have some knowledge of certain ranges of its vast repertoire, as well as at least a nodding acquaintance with its first-line top-dishes. One can no more pass a decisive opinion on Chinese cooking by a few visits to some Chinese restaurants in the West, than for an oriental fully to understand and appreciate the wonders and mysteries of western music by listening to a few bands of undistinguished pop.

Although, in this case, it would be wrong to counsel that 'a little learning is a dangerous thing, drink deep or taste not the Pierian spring', remember that so much is cultivated taste, and one requires the palate of a connoisseur to fathom the fullest gastronomic meaning and significance; for every dish has its own gastronomic memories, which are blended with the particular personal memory of the individual diner for the dish; and no dish can attain its full meaning unless both these memories co-exist. It is only through the co-existence of these strains of memories that the quality of the performance of a particular chef can become manifest – his particular interpretation of the masterpiece. In this instance, much as it is in the case of music, the better one is acquainted with a composition, the more desirous one is to hear the performance and interpretation of a famous performer. In order, therefore, to qualify as a connoisseur and a judge, one must have not only the quantitative experience of the whole vast repertoire, but also a keen appreciation and qualitative experience of the historical background of the various interpretations of the compositions as one looks back through the steaming and aromatic corridor of one's own as well as a nation's gastronomic memories.

Still, that is to be a connoisseur and a judge, but much can be gleaned which is highly enjoyable and interesting as a tourist, and so long as one is aware of the topless pinnacles and enormous territories which lie beyond and behind, one is not likely to confuse the Pennines with the Himalaya. Besides, one never knows when one may become enamoured. Some, in fact many, have been known to fall at first taste, and when love is the guiding light and the stomach the driving power, no pinnacle is too high, nor frontier too distant ('though it be ten thousand miles!'). And love in the case of Chinese food is so catching and enchanting – surely to fall is a privilege, whether in youth or age?

To the uninitiated westerner, Chinese cooking appears, like the 'Chinese puzzle', something best left to the Chinese. To the initiated westerner, Chinese cooking has too much of the Himalayan appearance to invite serious tackling. However, the writer believes that this is only their superficial reaction. The challenge of the 'puzzle' (crossword or otherwise) and the challenge of the Himalaya are just the very types of challenge which no true-born Anglo-Saxon can let pass without throwing down his gauntlet. Who knows that one may not some day win the first prize, or cap the top of Everest? This book has been written to give some exercise and skirmishes in the foothills, and also provide some beckoning from greater and more famous heights.

However, the more important reason why the writer would recommend Chinese cooking to the westerner is that it is an extremely useful and practical asset to acquire. Complicated as it might at first appear, yet, like the Chinese language, it is in many ways comparatively simple. One does not have to stick to so many rules and regulations; one is, I think, allowed far more freedom than in comparative western cooking. The point where a very strict and sometimes exalted standard is set is in the *art* of cooking, and not in the pseudo-science, such as in the strict measure of time and exactness of ingredients (Chinese cookery books only give discourse and advice, seldom details and precise measure-

ments); and one has to develop for oneself a high sense of
harmony in blending, the use of contrasts and surprises, and
the right use of ingredients to enhance and bring out the
natural flavour of a given food or to suppress its less agreeable but inherent tastes. It is because of this highly developed artistic sense in Chinese cooking that it is capable of
its incalculable, innumerable variations, and, like the artist,
who is able to produce any number of pictures and designs
with a limited number of colours, so a Chinese chef can
produce a large number of dishes out of a small range of
materials. For this reason, we Chinese are generally less
dependent on and tied down by what is given to us to work
with than the English; it is just because in Chinese cooking
we can make something out of almost anything that it is such
a useful and important art to acquire, especially for the
hard-pressed housewife of today, or a bachelor who is not
indifferent to the gnawing of his stomach.

Because so great a part of Chinese cooking is art and
admits of so many interpretations, for *first-class* cooking
inspiration is imperative. When you have inspiration – which
means that in your mind you have a clear vision of exactly
what you are aiming to do – you can be allowed a great deal
of licence. Whilst, on the other hand, without inspiration,
although you may be measuring your ingredients out
spoonful by spoonful, and keeping your time with a stop-
watch, your production may still be wide of the mark. The
job of the chef in the kitchen is, therefore, precisely the
same as that of the conductor of an orchestra, on a platform, and is often performed with the same flourish.

Since Chinese cooking admits of so much individual
freedom, initiative and inventiveness, it must for all practical
purposes be classified as a liberal art, and as such it can be
taken up and indulged in by anybody, with more or less
success and certain enjoyment. The proof of the pie is in the
eating, and in this case we can only allow our palate and
stomach to be the ultimate judge. For those whose nerves
have been worn to shreds by the hectic strain of modern

living, Chinese cooking can hold the fascination and relaxation of painting, over which it holds one distinct advantage: namely, you can eat the product of your efforts. For those who are artistically inclined, both the cooking and the eating will provide consuming pleasure.

As for raw materials and ingredients, it is a misconception that a great many exotic spices are used. In fact, in at least 80 per cent of Chinese cooking, all the raw materials can be obtained from any ordinary English market or provision shop. The essential thing is that the raw materials should be fresh and good. What few spices and ingredients are necessary or useful for the production of some Chinese dishes can all be obtained from oriental or Chinese provision shops, which now abound in London (see page 259), or if one prefers one can always fall back on such well-known suppliers as Harrods or Fortnum and Mason of Piccadilly, where these days many brands of Chinese foods are prominently displayed. So should any reader feel sufficiently inclined to venture his hand for a trial in the gentle and liberal art of Chinese cooking, he would generally be able to assemble all the raw materials and ingredients he would require in a matter of a few short hours, or certainly in a couple of days. For my part I should sincerely like to wish him very good luck and good cooking! And experience tells that he will be richly rewarded.

Cooking Methods

Before one gets down to preparing a Chinese meal it is necessary to be acquainted with some of the principal Chinese methods of cooking. The majority of the names contain a verb indicating how the dish is cooked. For instance, a dish which is '*Chǎo*' means that it is stir-fried. Hence '*Chǎo Fàn*' is 'Fried Rice', '*Chǎo Cai*', 'Stir-Fried Vegetables'; '*Chǎo Niu Roù Pian*', 'Stir-Fried Sliced Beef'. All 'stir-fried' dishes have one thing in common: they are cooked quickly, and they usually consist of several ingredients, which have been cut small (sliced thin, diced into small cubes, or shredded), and stirred and turned together over a high heat with a small amount of added flavouring and sauces. So, when a dish bears the affix '*Chǎo*', you know more or less what type of dish to expect. The '*Chǎo*' method of cooking has one or two variations, such as '*Gān Chǎo*' which means 'dry-fried', or '*Liu*' which means 'Quick-fried with sauce', or '*Bāo*' which means 'quick stir-fried followed by turning in thick sauce'.

Here is a list of the main methods:

Chǎo	stir-frying
Jiān	shallow-frying
Lin	ladling hot oil over food until it is cooked
Zha	deep-frying
Shāo	Chinese stewing
Mèn	long stewing over low heat
Dùn	slow cooking in a closed receptacle, by steaming, or in a pan of gently boiling water
Zhēng	open-steaming
Jìn	quick boiling followed by cooking in receding heat, after removal of pan from heat
Lǔ	cooking in Master Sauce

Bàn	tossing together of different ingredients
Kǎo	roasting
Hōng	roasting by an open fire
Kòu	fried, steamed slowly and then turned out on a dish
Ye, Xūn	smoked
Fēng	wind-dried
Yān	long-seasoned in salt
T'siāng	long-seasoned in salted soya-bean paste
Zhǔ	cooked in water
Zùi	soaked or marinated in wine or spirits as a concluding process in the preparation
Hùi	several types of food braised together in consommé

I shall now enlarge upon some of these methods of cooking:

'*Chǎo*'

As I have explained, more Chinese dishes are cooked by 'stir-frying' than by any other method. This is because the ingredients are cut small – cubed, sliced thin or shredded – and are therefore suitable for cross-cooking or blending with one another. The cooking is done in a small amount of oil (2–4 tablespoons) over a high heat and is almost instantaneous (in 1–2 or, occasionally, 3–4 minutes). Because of the saving of time, and the speed with which the hot food can be brought to the table, this is the method which is most favoured by restaurants or take-away shops. It is also an economical way to use up small bits and pieces of foods – scrapings of meat from poultry carcasses, or chopped-up ends of vegetables, or small bits of prawns and crabs etc. Dishes cooked by '*Chǎo*' usually contain a small amount of sauce, but never too much.

'*Gān Chǎo*'

Since only a small amount of liquid flavouring (soya sauce, chicken stock, wine) is added when cooking by '*Chǎo*', the dish will become dry if cooked a minute or two too long. This is often done deliberately to produce a slightly firmer and more chewy texture, with an encrustation of sauce on the surface of the food. Dishes so cooked are usually slightly stronger tasting than dishes which are simply 'Chǎo' or cooked by most other methods. They are useful dishes to contrast with the purer or blander ones, especially those which are open-steamed or presented in the form of semi-soups.

'Liū'

In this form of cooking the main ingredients are usually cut into thin slices and then 'poached' quickly in oil, drained and then cooked further for a minute or two in ample sauce. The sauce is often a compound of chicken stock, ginger-water and wine, which has been thickened with cornflour, and is usually translucent. Dishes cooked by this method contrast well with dishes which are dry-fried. Fish and shrimps are often cooked in this manner.

'Bào'

'Bào' is the Chinese word for explosion, although this method of cooking is no more explosive than many others. The cooking is usually done over a high heat; ingredients are either cut into small cubes or thin slices, and are quickly shallow-fried in oil for a minute or two and then drained. A small amount of selected seasonings or flavourings (often soya paste) are then introduced into the pan to mix with the remaining oil into a thick sauce. The main ingredients are then returned to the pan for a short period (1 minute or so) of stir-frying in the sauce. The particular feature of this style of cooking is to combine the fresh flavour of the main ingredients' juices, which are locked into each small piece of food, by rapid cooking in very hot oil, with the strong savouriness of the sauce applied afterwards. The quality of this type of cooking has probably no equivalent in western cuisine.

'*Tang Bào*'

I must mention this form of cooking because it is very closely related to the style of cooking previously described, '*Bào*', except that here, instead of oil, water or stock is used. For an average-sized dish about 250ml ($\frac{1}{2}$ pint) of water or stock is brought to a fierce boil. In this a quantity of well-seasoned or marinated meat, very thinly sliced, is turned and cooked (as if in oil) for a matter of 1–2 minutes, with a few finely-chopped fresh and dried vegetable ingredients. Dishes cooked in this manner combine the qualities of being well-seasoned and extremely fresh at the same time. The *Mongolian Sliced Lamb Hotpot* is a dish of this genre, but here the pieces of sliced lamb are not pre-seasoned; they are eaten dipped into mixed sauces immediately they are taken from the hotpot.

'*Jiān*'

Shallow-frying is often used in China, especially when oil is in short supply and one cannot indulge in deep-frying. The purpose of shallow-frying is much the same as deep-frying, either to crispen food or simply to seal and cook it through very rapidly. It is often used in China in two-stage or multi-stage cooking, where the foods are cooked through quickly by first shallow-frying over a high heat, and then the flavouring sauce is applied when the foods are returned to the pan for another short period of cooking over a medium heat.

'*Zhā*'

Deep-frying is used in Chinese cooking more often to conclude several stages of cooking than to initiate the heating process. For instance, in *Aromatic and Crispy Duck*, the duck is first marinated slowly and then subjected to 2 hours of steaming before it is quickly deep-fried (5–8 minutes) and served. In the case of *Boneless Crispy Duck*, the duck is seasoned first, then steamed, then boned, and then chopped into large pieces. These pieces are then floured and further seasoned, and finally deep-fried. They are then assembled into the shape of a duck and served. In the Chinese Muslim/ Mongolian style of cooking, food materials are often long-boiled (simmered over low heat for 2–5 hours) then cut into large chunks, deep-fried for 3–4 minutes and further cut into bite-sized pieces and served. The pieces of meat are only seasoned or flavoured at the final stage.

Another typical way in which deep-frying or '*Zha*' is used is in the cooking of various types of meat-balls or prawn-balls, or crab-balls. These balls are prepared by mixing meat, fish or seafoods together with coarsely-chopped water-chestnuts (for a crunchy texture) and formed and shaped into suitable sized balls. They are then deep-fried to crisp in 3–5 minutes. When the size of the balls is too large to cook without getting them burnt in hot oil, then the process of deep-frying is often divided into two: an initial deep-fry of 3–4 minutes for the food to cook through (often in batches of 3 or 4 balls at a time); they are then drained and left to cook in their own heat for 5–6 minutes; finally they are all put into the hot oil for 1–1½ minutes of deep-frying before serving. In this way, the food can be well cooked in very hot oil without charring.

'*Shāo*'

Chinese stewing differs perhaps from ordinary western stewing in that fewer vegetables are included. More often than not, only dried ingredients (such as anise, cinnamon bark, cloves, peppercorns, fennel etc.) are used and in quantities of not more than a tablespoonful. These are used in conjunction with soya sauce, a small amount of sugar and wine, and the process of stewing is generally conducted over a low heat for a long period of time (1½–3 hours). When soya sauce is used in the cooking, instead of just salt, the process is called '*Hung Shāo*' (or red-stewing), which is one of the most common and popular forms of cooking in China. But as the process is a slow, time-consuming one, red-cooking is seldom used in restaurants. It should be possible for restaurants to serve red-cooked dishes much more often than they do, because most such meat dishes can be reheated and are often the better for it. They have the further advantage of producing ample gravy, which is a boon to consume with rice, and by prolonged red-cooking all the cheaper cuts of meat can be cooked to a high degree of tenderness.

'*Mèn*'

'*Mèn*' is essentially the same process as '*Shāo*' but is usually more prolonged, and less soya sauce is used (when more soya sauce is used it becomes '*Hung Shāo*' or red-cooking). A '*Mèn*' dish is often produced to present, at least, a contrast in colour to a red-cooked dish.

'*Dùn*'

'*Dùn*' is another form of prolonged cooking where the main ingredients are usually cooked in a closed receptacle with little or no soya sauce but in stock or water, producing a first-class consommé, with a few dried ingredients, wine and seasonings added. It is another one of those dishes which contrast well with red-cooked dishes or stir-fried dishes. It is usually served in a large bowl, or deep-sided dish. But, unfortunately, because of the length of time required to cook a '*Dùn*' dish, and because it is usually done with a whole bird or large piece of meat, it is seldom met with in a restaurant.

'*Zhēng*'

This method of cooking differs from the previous one in that the foods are not cooked in a closed receptacle, but are subjected to the direct action of the steam; consequently the length of cooking is comparatively short: 10–30 minutes. Because of the short cooking time, the foods so cooked are often seasoned or marinated beforehand and usually only very fresh foods are cooked in this manner. Since foods which are open-steamed are very little disturbed during the process of cooking (in contrast to stir-frying) they can be nicely pre-arranged on their serving-dishes before inserting into the steamer.

Dishes which are 'Zhēng' are usually considered very pure dishes, and the method is most often used to cook very fresh fish or shrimps, or crabs, or lobsters. Open-steaming is also sometimes used to keep dishes hot, or just to give them a last blast of heat, so that when they are brought to the table they appear in a cloud of steam, which makes them very appealing, especially in the winter.

'Jìn'

This is a method of cooking which is sometimes also termed *Crystal Boiling* and is often used for 'white cooked chicken'. The idea is to cook food to a turn (without over-cooking it), and it can only be done if the food used is very young and fresh. A freshly-killed free-range chicken is immersed in boiling water for a minute or two and the heat is turned off for it to cook in the receding heat. After a period ($\frac{1}{2}$–1 hour) the chicken is taken out and drained. It is then chopped into bite-size pieces. It is then dipped by each diner into various dips and mixes placed on the table. As this is a delicate form of cooking it is employed only for the best and freshest materials, and for the most appreciative palates.

'Lǔ'

'Lǔ' is quite the opposite of 'Jìn' in that a very strong herbal soya-based sauce is used to cook meats and innards of animals, or giblets of poultry. Undesirable flavours in otherwise appealing food are eliminated when subjected to a period of cooking in the Master Sauce; on the other hand, foods which are comparatively bland, become flavoursome and tasty when cooked thus. Liver, kidney, tripe, heart, trotters are cooked in this manner, as well as other types of foods, which have been previously cooked in another way – say, hard-boiled eggs – to give them colour and extra flavour. Foods which have been cooked in the Master Sauce normally acquire a brownish colour. They are cooked in a whole piece and then sliced, or cut into bite-size pieces before serving. There would usually be a contrast in colour, as well as taste, between the brownish, stronger-tasting outside of the food and the lighter colour and taste of the inside of food cooked in this way.

'Bàn'

This method of cooking or presentation usually involves tossing together a number of food materials and ingredients, some cooked and some uncooked (such as cucumber, and spring onion), with some flavoursome and/or aromatic ingredients thrown over them. The contrasts in texture and character of materials so obtained make the dish both attractive and appealing.

'Kǎo'

Roasting is not practised as universally in China as in the West. Few domestic kitchens are equipped with an oven. Roasting is a method of cooking which is usually carried out on a rather large scale in restaurants in China where the food materials are hung up to roast in a kiln-like oven; one of the purposes of Chinese roasting is to obtain a crispy skin. A typical roast is *Peking Duck*, when a score of birds are usually roasted at the same time. The Canton roasting of long strips of fillet of pork is, however, called *'Chǎ Shāo'*, where the pork is marinated first, then quickly roasted (15–25 minutes) and afterwards, sliced thinly across the grain before serving. The aim here is not unlike cooking in the Master Sauce: to produce meat which is distinguished by the contrast of tasty encrustation of sauce outside and the juiciness of the quickly-cooked meat inside. But unlike '*Lŭ*' only the best fillet meats can be used for this type of cooking.

In Northern cooking the term '*Kǎo*', as in '*Kǎo Rou*', also indicates barbecued roasting, where, instead of a joint, small slices of meat are quickly cooked on top of braziers. This is a method of cooking which has come into China from the frontier regions of Mongolia and Sinkiang and is now one of the favourite forms of cooking in Peking.

'*Hōng*'

As gas or electric grills are little known in China, the usual form of grilling practised is to place the food against the walls inside a big stove or brazier. It is a method used as often for toasting bread and sesame-studded buns as for the cooking of meat, fish or poultry. Food cooked in this manner is usually treated plain, with seasonings and sauces only applied to them at the table.

'*Kōu*'

This method usually involves foods which have been long-steamed in a bowl or basin and are turned out on to a serving dish before serving (as in the case of a pudding). In China small cuts of meat or minced meat are often prepared in this way. In these cases the meats and other ingredients, placed in a bowl or basin, are mixed and built up in layers, flavoured with dried and pickled foods and subjected to a long period of steaming. Because flavouring can be orchestrated by arranging in layers, the method sometimes produces dishes of a high degree of sophistication.

'Ye' or 'Xūn'

In China, as elsewhere, foods are often smoked by using different types of fuels (or smoking materials) such as camphor wood, tea, sugar to give different flavours, and smoking is often employed as one step in a multi-phase cooking process; for example, marinating, smoking, steaming, and deep-frying can follow each other to complete the whole cooking process. Smoking is used more for flavouring than cooking or preserving, and when used in conjunction with other forms of cooking, a short period of smoking is usually sufficient to impart the flavour to the food, whilst a much longer process of cooking (such as steaming) is required to tenderize the food, and deep-frying tends to be used only as a concluding process to crisp the food and give it the final gloss.

In multi-phase fish cookery, it is marinating which takes the longest time (a few hours), smoking the next longest (10–20 minutes) and cooking (deep or shallow frying for 2–5 minutes) the shortest.

'Fēng'

Before the days of deep-freezing and the refrigerator, wind-drying or wind-curing was one of the few methods of preserving the food. Foods which have been dehydrated through sunning or wind-curing often become much more strongly flavoured even after being reconstituted by soaking; in many cases perhaps the majority of people who have come to know the fresh and wind-dried varieties of the same foods prefer the dried (as with Chinese mushrooms: hardly anybody uses fresh mushrooms in China). In the more refined cases, the dried foods are cooked in conjunction with the fresh to impart a special flavour to the dish, which becomes both subtle and more sophisticated. The famous *Nanking Pressed Duck* is an instance of wind-dried food.

Most wind-dried foods are reconstituted through a fairly lengthy period (1–2 hours) of steaming, before being subjected to other forms of cooking, such as stir-frying, shallow-frying, deep-frying or assembling ('*Hui*') before being served. Wind-curing, like smoking, imparts a distinctive flavour to food, which is much appreciated by connoisseurs with sophisticated palates.

'*Yān*'

One of the easiest and most common ways of preserving food is to salt it. Salting is a widely used process, especially for preserving fish. However, apart from preservation, salting also imparts to food a distinctive flavour (as in the case of smoking and wind-curing), which is much appreciated by many who have either sophisticated or jaded palates. Salted foods are usually considered common and earthy – the foods of the peasants and the proletariat. Because of this common earthiness, it has certain or special appeal to the refined and sophisticated.

But for the common people, salted foods – especially fish – are regarded in much the same way as cheese is regarded in the West. When salt fish is slowly fried until it becomes very crispy, it attains an intensity of taste which is equalled by few other foods. Like strong cheese, even a very small amount of it will go a long way as an accompaniment to bulk food. This is exactly how salt foods are used in China, to accompany and help in the consumption of rice. The Japanese, too, have an inclination for salted foods, being an island people for whom salting is one of the most convenient processes for preserving food. Salted hard-boiled eggs are a standard item for breakfast in China. The same egg can be chopped and mixed with minced meat, and steamed into a popular dinner-time dish in south China. Salted pickled greens are often chopped and stir-fried with shredded meat into highly-refined dishes for distinctive flavour.

'T'siāng'

Soya paste is a compound of ground salted black beans, soya sauce, and flour. In fact, it can almost be said to be soya sauce in paste form. Apart from normal cooking it can be used to season or preserve food. When used for the latter purpose, the food is generally heated in a pan with the bean paste added; so, when thus treated, the food can be said to be both cooked and preserved in soya paste. Food so cooked and preserved can be kept for a matter of days, or for a much longer period if, in addition to soya paste, a high percentage of alcohol is added. The food so cooked and preserved has a quality of its own: generally there is a strong contrast between the salty taste of the bean paste outside, and the less salty and much more succulent meaty taste inside. It is this contrast which appeals to a great many people.

'Zhǔ'

Foods are sometimes simply cooked or simmered in water – or by deep-boiling, which means cooking in ample water. Such a form of cooking is usually applied to food materials of good quality, where there is little need for flavouring ingredients and sauces to camouflage taste or flavour. Since a comparatively large quantity of water is employed in the cooking, the foods being cooked are seldom cooked for very long, otherwise much of the taste goes into the water. After the food has had an appropriate period of cooking, it is then drained and cut into bite-size pieces for eating after dipping into dips which are placed on the table. 'Zhǔ' is considered one of the purer forms of cooking.

'Zūi'

Fresh foods which have been seasoned and cooked are often treated to a period of marination in wine or liquor before serving. This period of marination may last for no more than an hour or two, or for a few days to a week. Foods so treated are considered 'drunken', thus *Drunken Chicken, Drunken Spare Ribs, Drunken Shrimps*. Drunken foods are usually served cold and used as hors d'oeuures

'Hüi'

This is a process of cooking in which a wide variety of cooked and uncooked foods are put into the same pot, where they are cooked together before serving. The cooking is usually done in stock or consommé, with each ingredient making its own particular contribution to the orchestration of flavour. Such dishes are usually semi-soup dishes, where the principal ingredients are vegetables and transparent pea-starch noodles, with meats and dried foods (such as dried shrimps or dried scallops) playing only a secondary role. This is another one of those types of dishes which many Chinese regard as indispensable for the consumption of rice.

Materials and Ingredients

There is a popular misconception in the West that we Chinese eat a whole range of strange foods, such as birds' nests, sharks' fins, sea slugs. The fact is that we live on these about as much as western people live on caviare, truffles, cockles and winkles. Certainly we eat them – but only on rare occasions. Some of us have never had them in our lives.

The staple food which we consume day in and day out is much the same as the type of food eaten in the West. This can be divided roughly into four main categories: cereals or grain foods; meats and poultry; fish and seafoods; vegetables.

Cereals or Grain Foods

On balance, we probably consume a greater proportion of rice in our diet than any other people in the world. But this is probably only true of those who live in the Yangtze River valley (central China) and the regions further south. Rice is consumed in China mostly as steamed rice, boiled rice and soft rice. The last is eaten mostly for breakfast and supper. Many of the poorer people often consume rice which is a mixture between boiled rice and soft rice, where a larger than usual proportion of water is used in the cooking; this results in a large volume as well as cheaper food being produced.

Boiled or steamed rice should be fairly dry. They have to absorb the ample gravy which usually comes with the savoury dishes. Many Chinese are so appreciative of good gravy and rice that they often prefer the mixture to meat itself. The excellence of many meat dishes is judged as much by the quality of the gravy as by that of the meat. Many other Chinese dishes, such as most of the semi-soups, the mashed bean-curd with minced meat, or runny-egg dishes, are created especially for eating with rice. On their own they would have very little culinary meaning. The fact is that many Chinese savoury dishes are almost too savoury to consume entirely on their own, or one after another in a whole series; they have to be mixed with plain rice to strike the correct gastronomic balance. Hence in Chinese banquets or party dinners, the earlier series of dishes served are usually served on smallish serving dishes, so that the diners will not be overwhelmed or overloaded by the sheer quantity of savouriness before the banquet has really started. These dishes are only meant to be nibbled at. Westerners sometimes make the mistake of wolfing them.

In the areas north of Yangtze, the Yellow River valley, much more wheat, maize and corn are produced than rice; hence in north China much more bread than rice is consumed. Chinese bread is, however, different from western bread; it is steamed and usually white, rather than baked until brown (there are no crusts). It is usually about the size of a bun, and these are piled up in mounds on the table or in steam-baskets for the diners to pick and take as they require. Like steamed or boiled rice they absorb gravy, and are used to wipe up the savoury juices left at the bottom of the bowl or plate at the end of the meal.

In China we probably serve a far greater variety of noodles than anywhere else. In south and central China noodles are mainly consumed as snacks or 'small meals'; in the north they are often consumed as main meals, for staple food. Noodles are prepared and served in four main ways. *Tossed Noodles* are plain, boiled noodles tossed with a meat sauce, and a number of shredded vegetables are provided on the table for the diners to select and toss with the noodles themselves. *Soup Noodles* are noodles served in bowls immersed in a savoury soup with some shredded meat and vegetables, which have been separately stir-fried and placed on top as 'dressings' or 'toppings'. *Sauce Noodles* are a variant of *Soup Noodles*; here the noodles are served, not in a soup, but in a thickened sauce, which they have sometimes been cooked in. *Sauce Noodles* are normally called '*Lu Mien*' in China, but are sometimes also called '*Lao Mien*'. *Fried Noodles* or *Chow Mien* is the best known Chinese noodle dish in the West; it differs from Italian pasta dishes in that the noodles are not just boiled, but also fried. The frying is done in the gravy/oil which is left in the pan when the supplementary ingredients (meat, prawns, vegetables) have been first of all stir-fried in the pan and then removed. Thus stir-fried, the noodles pick up a degree of savouriness, heat, and lubrication from the pan. It is only after the noodles are laid out on the serving dish that the supplementary ingredients are stir-fried again and laid out on top of the noodles.

Meat and Poultry

The main meat and poultry eaten in China are pork and chicken. The flavours of pork and chicken both have a neutral savouriness which enables them to be combined and cross-cooked with a wider variety of other foods than, say, lamb, beef, duck or pheasant. This does not mean that we do not eat much of the other types of meat or poultry. In north China, and the frontier regions of the north-west (Sinkiang, Inner Mongolia), where there are vast herds of cattle, as much lamb, mutton and beef are consumed as pork. One of the reasons why pork and chicken are produced in greater abundance in central and south China is because pigs and chickens are reared more or less domestically by every household, or on small farms, rather than on farms which specialize in their production on a large scale. Ducks, on the other hand, although also reared domestically are produced in large flocks in the lakes, ponds and waterways of the Yangtze River valley and in the regions further south. When produced in quantity ducks are slaughtered and preserved as 'pressed ducks' which means they are dried and wind-cured; they need long steaming before they are cooked further. Cured ducks have a flavour all of their own which appeals to many people.

Chickens are often cooked whole, then cut into smaller pieces and cross-cooked with other ingredients. Pork is also frequently cooked in large chunks, and, more often than not, these are cut into thin slices, or shredded, and also cross-cooked; when cooked in large pieces the skin is almost always included. We Chinese appreciate the texture and succulence of the skin when it has been cooked for a long time, and its beneficial effect on the gravy. Because of the neutral quality and flavour of pork and chicken, and their ability to combine with most other food materials, the number of dishes which can be produced with them runs into many hundreds.

Beef, lamb and mutton are considered by the Chinese to be stronger tasting meats, and therefore require cooking with the stronger tasting vegetables, such as garlic, ginger and onions or spring onions. Other vegetables which are frequently used with them are leeks, celery and turnips. Beef and lamb (or mutton) cooked with these strong vegetables, plus bean paste, produce dishes which are considered to have a northern flavour. In the south, in Kwangtung or Canton, oyster sauce is often applied to beef, which makes it an ultra-savoury dish; in Fukien, another southern province, a good supply of wine or alcohol is often used in stewing lamb and goat meat, to neutralize their strong flavour. Beef and lamb or mutton are not usually cooked with a lot of fresh vegetables, as in the western stews, but are more often cooked with the addition of the Five Spices (cinnamon bark, anise, fennel, peppercorn, cloves), which give a herbal and spicy flavour to the dishes.

Pheasants are plentiful only in Manchuria, or the north-eastern provinces, and they make only occasional appearances on the Chinese dinner table along with venison (which is cooked and treated as lamb). Turkeys are a more recent arrival but, as the quality and flavour of their meat is similar to that of chicken, it can be cooked in much the same way.

Frogs are eaten as frequently in China as in France. They are called field chickens and are treated and cooked much as chickens, but mostly stir-fried and braised, with slightly stronger tasting ingredients. They are considered delicacies and are seen only on banquet tables.

Fish and Seafoods

The most famous fish dish in north China is the *Yellow River Carp*, which is usually cooked as a dish of crispy sweet and sour fish. But in north China where the rivers are muddy – like the Yellow River – most of the fish taste of mud, and need to be kept in clear-water tanks for several days to eliminate this taste. The best fish in China come from the east and south coasts where they occur in great variety and abundance and the people of these areas consider that the people of north and central China know nothing about fish and seafood.

In China we eat all the fish and seafood which people consume in the West, and possibly more: for instance, one frequently comes across abalone, *bêche de mer* (or sea cucumber), jelly-fish, squid, in addition to the more usual fish, such as bass, bream, carp, clam, cod, crab, eel, flounder, haddock, halibut, herring, lobster, mackerel, mullet, oyster, perch, pike, prawns, rock salmon, sardines, scallops, shad, shark's fin, shrimps, sole, sturgeon, trout, tuna, turbot.

It is customary in China to cook fresh fish by steaming. We first rub it with chopped ginger and salt, then some wine and soya sauce mixed and blended with a small amount of sugar are poured over to marinate the fish, just as the cooking is about to begin. When the fish is cooked, it is dressed and stuffed with ample dried and salted vegetables and pork fat, together with spring onions. Fish so cooked is almost invariably excellent, so long as it is not over-cooked and the material is truly fresh.

We also often deep-fry or shallow-fry fish until it is well browned and crispy; usually braised in soya sauce, mixed with wine, sugar, and spring onions. Fish cooked in this manner – which is called red-cooked, or braised in soya sauce – is unbeatable for consumption with rice. There are of course many other ways of cooking fish, but steaming and red-cooking are the most common and popular.

A well-known Peking fish dish is *Sliced Fish in Wine-Lees Sauce* which entails 'poaching' slices of fish in oil, and draining them before immersing them in the wine-lee sauce, which is translucent and usually concocted from chicken stock, ginger water, wine lees and sugar and thickened with cornflour. This is a method of cooking which is little known in the east and south, where they pride themselves on their knowledge of fish and seafoods.

We also simply fry fish; it is usually cut into cubes or slices and then rubbed with ginger and salt, allowed to season for a while, and coated with flour and fried. Because of the saltiness of the exterior of the fish, and the freshness inside, it can be consumed with great satisfaction and enjoyment with plain rice.

Crustaceans are a very popular form of food in China and vast quantities of them are consumed. Crabs and lobsters are mostly steamed, shrimps and prawns steamed or fried, and clams poached. However, after the initial cooking, whether steamed, poached or fried, some kind of sauce is usually applied. In the well-known dish *Cantonese Crab*, or *Lobster*, the sauce is an egg-sauce, which simply consists of pouring a mixture of chicken stock blended with wine over the frying lobster or crab in the pan, followed by dripping and trailing beaten egg on to the boiling, frothing crustacean and sauce. In all cases, in the cooking of crustaceans, as in the cooking of fish, some chopped ginger, spring onion (occasionally garlic) and salt are applied to the shellfish before or during the cooking. These seem to go well with whatever liquid flavourings are added at a later stage, and blend into some of the most delicious of savoury sauces.

Although Peking is not well known for fish, the Peking and Tientsin areas are very well known for their fat prawns, which are nowadays sometimes called *Pacific Prawns* in the western markets. They are about 7·5 or 10cm (3 or 4 in) long and can be poached, 'crystal boiled', fried in batter, braised in piquant tomato sauce, or in sweet and sour sauce.

There are two principal types of crabs in China, the sea crabs and the fresh-water crabs; both are so popular that special crab-eating parties are often held at specialized restaurants. At such parties the chunks of crab are dipped into mixes such as *Vinegar with Shredded Ginger, Vinegar with Chopped Garlic, Vinegar with Soya Sauce, Soya Sauce with Yellow Wine.*

Abalone is seldom eaten on its own in China. It is more often used as a flavouring (in soups) or eaten as a supplementary ingredient, cut into thin slices to be quickly cooked together with other foods, thus imparting an inimitable flavour to the dish. Scallops and squids are as often used dried, for flavouring, as they are eaten fresh. Scallops can, of course, be cooked in much the same manner as shrimps and prawns. Squids, which have less taste of their own, are often made savoury by cooking in a meat, tomato or black-bean sauce. Sharks' fins and *bêche de mer* only appear on banquet tables. For them to be acceptable and appealing, they need prolonged preparation and cooking; their appeal is a cultivated one and seems to be appreciated only by the sophisticated connoisseur.

Fish and seafoods are often cooked and flavoured with chicken stock laced with wine, rather than with fish stock; the supplementary ingredients used, whether cooked with fish or used as stuffing, usually provide as great a contrast as possible; these can be strong vegetables, dried and salted vegetables, and shredded meats (both lean and fat). The idea is to blend opposites rather than to make the fish more fishy by adding seafoods to them.

Vegetables

The one area of Chinese cooking which is the most easily appreciated by westerners is vegetable cookery. This could be due to the simple fact that they have not themselves given much thought to the cooking of vegetables; or it could be due to the fact that, not having had a Buddhist vegetarian background, there has never been a great tradition of western vegetable cooking. It is only in more recent times that westerners have become more aware of the excellence and freshness of vegetables, and their benefit to human health.

With Buddhism established in China for over one thousand years and with thousands of temples and monasteries, which often fed many hundreds of people at a time on vegetarian foods, all over the length and breadth of the country, a considerable vegetarian tradition has developed in China. The Chinese are deeply aware that vegetables should be exploited both for their richness and for their crunchy freshness, and these qualities can often be combined in the same dish. They are also aware that there is an inherent need for oil and fat which should be added to vegetables to make them smoother, more succulent and appealing; that vegetables can be cross-cooked with meat; and that fresh vegetables can be flavoured, not only with soya and meat sauces, but also with the stronger tasting vegetables, as well as with salted, pickled, and dried vegetables.

The usual Chinese way of preparing vegetables is to cook them first quickly in a small amount of flavoured oil – which has usually already had a small amount of chopped, strong-tasting vegetables, such as garlic, ginger and onion, and salt cooked in it. The vegetables are then turned in the flavoured oil to obtain an initial lubrication, only then are other flavourings added, such as soya sauce, soya cheese, sugar, concentrated chicken stock, meat gravy, some wine. Though the vegetables are shiny when first turned in the oil, once any sauce or stock is added, the vegetables turn dull and opaque again. To improve their appearance in the final presentation, it is a common Chinese practice to add more fat or oil at the last moment to give the vegetables a final gloss before bringing them to the table. The last treatment not only has the effect of improving the appearance, but it also imparts a feeling of smoothness and succulence (anybody who has added butter to vegetables will appreciate this). Spinach, if prepared and cooked in the above manner, can often be the very best dish any restaurant can offer, although the dish may require no more than 4–5 minutes to cook. If the leaves are well selected, the vegetable should be shining green, and one can eat quantities of it on its own, or with rice.

Most of the green vegetables can be cooked in the above manner; vegetables such as lettuce, green or white cabbage, broccoli, sprouts, celery, leeks, Chinese cabbage, etc. Some may require a couple of minutes' longer cooking (such as broccoli, sprouts, cabbage); others slightly less, such as lettuce and bean sprouts, especially if one wishes to retain the crisp, crunchy qualities of the vegetable.

Another favourite way of cooking vegetables is to braise them in a cup or two of chicken stock, further flavoured with additions of small amounts of dried shrimps, scallop muscle, and dried mushrooms, lily-bud stems or chopped salted pickles. Such a dish of vegetables is often produced in the form of semi-soup which is a boon to rice eaters. Cooked in this manner the dish of vegetables is called 'white-cooked' because no soya sauce is used.

Having eaten vegetables cooked in the Chinese way, one soon notices that, although there may be a fair variety of ingredients added to orchestrate and improve the flavour and smoothness of the dish, the principal richness of taste is contributed by the vegetables themselves. This is so partly because of the large quantity of vegetables used, and also because the vegetables are not boiled in water which is drained away, thereby losing much of the vegetable flavour in the process. We seem to consume a much higher percentage of vegetables in China than people do in the West, and this consumption of vegetables is an important part of our enjoyment of food. When a Chinese person is abroad, and has not eaten Chinese food for some time, he not only dreams of the meat dishes he has missed, but also of the freshness and succulence of Chinese vegetables. Can the same be said truthfully of the people of many other countries? When a Chinese dreams of vegetable dishes, he dreams not only of these stir-fried and braised vegetables, as described above, but also vegetables prepared in other forms – wrapped in small *chiaotze* (Chinese ravioli) and poached or steamed, or stuffed inside *paotze* (steamed buns), or, on a larger scale, cooked by steaming inside the excavated cavity of large marrows or pumpkins. He also dreams about the tender hearts of greens, florets of cauliflower, or asparagus tips doused in white *Fu yung* sauce and sprinkled with chopped or minced ham. Then there are the hundreds of dishes where vegetables are cross-cooked with meat, where the quality and richness of one is used to enhance the quality and richness of the other: for instance, where the meatiness and special flavour of dried mushrooms are braised with sliced duck in order to take something from the latter's richness; the sharp piquancy of chopped salted pickles (winter pickles) when stir-fried with shredded pork; or simply the typical aromatic smell of chopped chives or spring onions when sprinkled over a dish of stir-fried Chinese omelette, already made aromatic by the addition of yellow wine and sesame oil; or the sweetness of stir-fried onions and shredded carrots in a dish of dry-fried chewy shredded beef, where the encrustation of soya sauce and paste makes the saltiness of the beef contrast with the sweetness of the vegetables. He dreams of all this, 'and heaven too!' The heaven may consist of a dish of clams, which have been lightly poached in the purest chicken stock laced with a drop or two of yellow wine, and a touch of the best quality soya sauce; or it could be neatly julienned strips of freshest courgettes cooked in the same manner, with a few drops of pink coloured chilli oil sprinkled lightly over them just before serving. What dreams could be more justifiable when standing amidst the coarseness of 'alien corn'?!

Flavourings and Dips

Chinese flavouring differs from western flavouring mainly in the use of soya bean products – soya sauce, soya paste, soya cheese – and salted black beans. Other seasonings, such as salt, pepper, vinegar, sugar, chilli, mustard, are in common use everywhere. We do not use many of the more exotic spices and herbs, which are used much more extensively in other types of cookery, such as Indian. In the West today, where there has been a sudden upsurge of interest in herbs, a wider range is used than in China. We seem to fall back on the Five Spices, which are used mostly in the cooking of meat, especially in the long-cooked meat dishes, to which hardly any vegetables are added, except perhaps for a small amount of ginger; the principal flavouring agent is soya sauce. Chinese long-cooked meat dishes are very often pure meat dishes, where a small amount of sugar and a somewhat larger amount of wine are added; these we believe will help to enhance the richness and flavour of the dish. Indeed, the gravies from such meat dishes are amongst the most mouthwatering things there are in the culinary/gastronomic world.

The Five Spices are hardly ever used in the cooking of fish and seafoods; we rely more on the use of the strong vegetables: root-ginger, garlic, onion or scallion, which are used in conjunction with soya sauce, sugar, chicken stock and wine. Salted black beans are sometimes used as an alternative, or as a complement to soya sauce.

In quick-fry cooking of meat, the flavouring ingredients are much the same as in the cooking of fish and seafoods.

From the above one would note straight away that the common denominator used as a flavouring agent in Chinese cooking is soya sauce, or one of the other by-products of the soya bean. The importance of this flavouring in Chinese food can hardly be overestimated. And perhaps, in order to provide a contrast to the many 'red-cooked' dishes, the Chinese have also produced a whole series of white-cooked dishes, from which soya sauce is strictly excluded. The main flavourings in these dishes are salt, salted pickles, or salted and dried ingredients (such as dried salted shrimps and fish) which do not affect the lightness of the colour of the finished product. The '*Fu yung*' dishes, which are pure white and are produced by beating minced chicken breast with egg-white, are typical of this category.

Viewing Chinese culinary practice as a whole, we have managed to achieve such a wide variety of subtle flavouring in our food, more because of our practice of multi-stage cross-cooking than because of the flavouring agents used. In the creation of any dish, the flavour of its main ingredients or materials is varied by the supplementary ingredients; this is further varied by the flavourings added during the cooking. The ultimate flavour of the dish is, of course, also influenced by the marinade or seasoning used at an earlier stage, and the final taste on the palate is further affected by the dips and mixes into which the foods are dipped by the diners during the meal.

In Chinese cooking, smoking is quite often employed as a method of flavouring, rather than as a method of cooking; hence foods are often only shortly smoked (10–20 minutes). Seasoning and marinating are important, especially in instances such as the majority of steamed dishes where no further flavourings are added during cooking and all the flavours have to be imparted to the dish before cooking starts. Seasoning and marinating are also important in some short-cooked, quick stir-fried dishes, where there is not time for flavours to penetrate the food. In many such cases, the aim of such cooking is actually not to cause the flavour to penetrate the food, but, rather, just to cover it (or each piece of it), and this can often be achieved in an instant. What has to be brought out is the contrast of the strong flavouring outside and the freshness and native flavour of the food inside. In the case of fish and seafoods, seasonings are often used to eliminate or detract from the fishiness of such food. These unwanted smells or flavours are further reduced or eliminated through frying in hot oil, or cooking with strong-tasting vegetables, or both, and the freshness and savouriness of the food materials are emphasized through the use of sugar, wine and good stock.

But in the long-cooked dishes (Chinese stews and casseroles), seasonings and marinades are not as important as in short-cooked or steamed dishes, as a great deal of the flavouring ingredients can be added, if necessary, in stages during the cooking process itself, which may last for several hours. Indeed, sometimes the temperature is kept so low and at such a gentle simmer that the cooking itself can be described as a form of hot marinating. Some of the best flavouring is achieved by subjecting the food to two clear-cut stages of cooking, by cooking the main material, with all attendant flavouring ingredients for some length of time and then allowing it to cool. When cold it can be kept in the refrigerator overnight for the flavours to penetrate. A short while before serving the food is re-heated, with the addition of a small number of ingredients – such as wine – to liven it up; or the food might then be cooked in some other way, such as by deep-frying (as in the case of spare ribs) or cut into smaller pieces and stir-fried and served as fried foods, rather than as stewed foods. This is a reversal of the normal procedure of seasoning or marinating first, followed by hot cooking; here we have hot cooking first, followed by long marinating or seasoning in the cold before final cooking is resumed. Foods treated in the latter manner are usually slightly more highly-flavoured than if they had been cooked in the normal manner – probably because the seasoning and marinating are treated with greater deliberation and seriousness.

In Chinese cooking, deep-frying is a concluding process as much as an initiating process. It often helps to crisp the food and intensify the flavour. The *Crispy and Aromatic Duck* of

north China is a typical case of a dish which is cooked in
this manner. Here the duck is long-seasoned and marinated
in flavourings and herbs. It is then steamed for 2–2½ hours;
finally it is deep-fried until crisp. The meat of the duck is
then scraped off and used to stuff pancakes, and is consumed
in the same way as *Peking Duck*. There are many Chinese
dishes of Muslim/Mongolian origin, where a quantity of
meat, in large chunks, is cooked in a herbal broth for upwards of 3 hours. When ready they are briefly deep-fried and
then sliced into bite-sized pieces for insertion in buns and
toasted cakes (as a kind of sandwich). All meats cooked in
Master Sauce (a soya meaty-herbal sauce) can be treated in
this manner: long slow-simmering in the sauce and a short
period of deep-frying before serving.

There is a good range of Chinese dishes which are plain
cooked in order to bring out the native flavour of the food
itself which is then dipped into dips and mixes on the table
to strike a balance of flavour. Two of the best known of
these dishes are *White Chopped Boiled Chicken*, where a
young pullet has been crystal boiled, which means that it has
been brought to a rolling boil, then the heat is turned off and
the chicken is left to cook in the cooling liquid; when it is
cool the chicken is drained and chopped through the bone
into bite-size pieces. In *White Cut Sliced Pork* a piece of
belly of pork is cooked to a turn (not so long that all the
flavour goes into the soup) and then sliced into thin 5×4cm
($2 \times 1\frac{1}{2}$ in) pieces, and laid out in fish-scale fashion when
served. These plain cooked pork and chicken pieces should
be served with the following dips: the *soya-oil-garlic dip*
(3 cloves garlic, 4 tablespoons soya sauce, 1 tablespoon salad
oil, ¼ teaspoon sugar); *soya-oil-ginger-dip* (1 tablespoon
shredded root-ginger, 4 tablespoons soya sauce, 1 tablespoon
vegetable oil, 1 teaspoon vinegar); *soya-onion-dip* (3 chopped stalks spring onion, 4 tablespoons soya sauce, 1 tablespoon vegetable oil, 2 teaspoons vinegar); *hot soya-oil-dip*
(3 teaspoons chilli sauce, 3 tablespoons soya sauce, 1
tablespoon vegetable oil).

On the other hand, foods which have been deep-fried or shallow-fried require a different category of dip to bring out their best taste. For instance, a good dip to use with crispy *Prawn Balls* or *Meat Balls* or *Chopped Deep-Fried Chicken* or *Deep-Fried Battered Fillet of Pork* is the Salt and Pepper Mix which should consist of a mixture of salt and pepper, which has been heated in a dry pan until it becomes aromatic (or, as they say: when a distinct bouquet arises). Alternatively, such deep-fried crispy foods can be dipped in sauces which are fruity and sweet, such as *plum sauce* (cooked plum and soya), or *soya-sherry-dip* (3 tablespoons sherry, 3 tablespoons soya sauce, ½ teaspoon salt, ¾ teaspoon sugar). To many people these dishes are incomplete without the complementary mixes and dips.

The basic dip for seafoods and fish in China consists of a mixture of shredded root-ginger with vinegar and soya sauce. When seafoods and fish are very fresh they are usually just steamed, poached, or crystal boiled, which means that they are presented fairly plain, and in their white, native state; they therefore need a dark (soya) vinegary and gingery sauce to provide a contrast. Garlic is sometimes used with vinegar instead of ginger; and if tomato sauce is used it is usually made stronger and more piquant by the addition of chilli sauce.

Chinese restaurants abroad are often very slap-dash about providing the essential dips and one of the tests of a restaurant is to see whether its Salt and Pepper Mix has been aromatized by being freshly-heated, or if it has been simply thrown together and served cold. Sometimes restaurants do not even serve them with the appropriate dishes!

Somewhere between supplementary ingredients (secondary food materials with which the main food material is cooked) and flavouring ingredients (the sauces and seasonings) lie dried, smoked, pickled and salted foods, the addition of which during the cooking can often bring fresh interest and new character to a dish. The pickles most often used are the 'snow pickles' and 'winter pickles' (the former taste something like gherkins and they are used to flavour meat); the favourite salted foods employed are salt (duck) eggs, cabbage and fish (often used along the coast to cook with stewed meats); dried or wind-cured foods used for flavouring are pressed duck, Chinese sausage (a kind of salami sausage), dried shrimps, dried mushrooms and dried lily-bud stems (called golden needles); smoked bacon, giblets and beef are often cooked with vegetables or used to flavour soups.

In the practice of cross-cooking it is of great importance to put the right flavours together; scallop, for example, may be cooked with ham, ham with honey, chicken with melon, prawns with egg, pork with chestnuts, beef with peppers, lamb with leeks, lobsters with mushrooms, shrimps with peas, duck with pineapples. Then again the different cooking methods (of which there are over forty) can be used in conjunction, but each one produces a flavour peculiar to itself, and when that type of cooking is incorporated into another a new type of flavour is created.

The above rapid survey of the Chinese 'flavouring situation' is to provide for all those who are interested in Chinese food a bird's-eye view of the numerous factors involved, which interact and have a bearing on the ultimate taste, feel and flavour of food. There are probably more dimensions to Chinese cuisine than any other in the world, which is what makes it so very intriguing.

Cooking of Rice

In China rice is served in three basic forms:

(*a*) Soft rice or Congee, which is used at breakfast time, is in effect a watery-rice gruel, generally eaten with salted or strong-flavoured food, such as salted egg, salted turnips, preserved 'ancient egg', peanuts fried in salt, ham, fried salted fish, Chinese 'cheese' made from soya bean curd, which has an extraordinary captivating flavour when, or if, one gets used to it. It is presumed that at breakfast time one's mouth and palate are still so thick that they require something strong or salty to jolt them into sensibility and awakeness (hence probably the popularity here of bacon and kipper for breakfast).

On the other hand, the thin wateriness of Congee helps to give the mouth a refreshing 'wash-down' effect; in fact, it provides almost a taste of sweetness after the strong-flavoured or salty food. Hence the popularity of Congee in China, not only in the South where it is universally used, but also in the North, where steamed bread or dumpling is the order of the day – used in all three meals – but is served with Congee at breakfast time.

Congee is produced by simply boiling rice in varying quantities of water for about an hour to one and a half hours. Generally four to eight times as much water as rice is used, but the proportion of water to rice really depends upon the final dilution one requires.

(*b*) The second way in which rice is commonly served is the usual plain steamed rice, which is served both during lunch and dinner. Although it is as often prepared by boiling as steaming, if the former method is used (being the simpler of the two, since not everyone possesses an adequate steamer) one has to be extremely careful during the last ten minutes of the cooking not to burn the rice: during this last stage of cooking, the heat should be turned very low, and preferably an asbestos mat should be placed underneath the pan, so that the rice can, in effect, be steamed in its own moisture.

In preparing rice in this manner, one would generally employ about two and a half times as much water as rice. After having washed the rice, place it in a saucepan and pour in the water. Bring it to the boil, keeping the lid securely closed, and leave it to simmer for about six to seven minutes, or until the rice is no longer watery. Now lower the heat to the minimum and insert an asbestos sheet. Leave the pan to simmer for a further ten to twelve minutes. The rice will now be ready to serve. Each grain will be soft but dry.

The established way of cooking this type of rice in China is to steam it in a bamboo basket-steamer, which is placed over a pan of boiling water. Rice prepared in this manner is the staple food of China. In the areas north of the Yangtze River where steamed bread or dumpling (called *Man Tou*) is also the staple food, rice is often served in conjunction with it, at least in all the better-fed families.

Although the Chinese are rice-eaters, it is a misconception to believe, as many westerners do, that the Chinese people eat nothing but rice. Certainly rice is our staple food and forms the main bulk of each meal, but a number of tasty dishes are usually served with it. An average meal will consist of one or two soups – a vegetable soup and a meat soup – a meat dish, an egg or fish dish, and one or two vegetable dishes served in conjunction with rice. In wealthier families where more than half a dozen dishes are served during each meal, rice merely acts as a 'buffer' to all the rich and tasty dishes, which are placed on the table all together in buffet fashion. During banquets or formal parties, no rice is served at all (since there is such an abundance of other types of food), and the dishes – as a rule numbering about one dozen or more – are brought in at ten-minute intervals, and served and consumed course after course.

(*c*) The third way in which rice is prepared and served in China is the semi-solid or 'porridgy' rice, which is made either from steamed rice boiled up with the addition of extra water, or Congee thickened with the use of a greater proportion of rice in the boiling. As this form of rice requires less of the grain to cook than steamed rice and is more sustaining than Congee, it is usually served in the poorer families. For those in greater poverty in the south, rice in this form is often boiled up with shredded dried sweet potato, which gives it further bulk. In the north the bulk is made up of steamed dumplings (a very filling food) and large flour 'big cakes' (like crumpets, but drier and about four times their size) eaten with a lot of garlic.

Apart from these three basic forms in which rice is served in China – here rice more or less takes the place of bread and potatoes in western meals – all the other fancy forms of rice should be classified as snacks or desserts. They bear much the same relation to the three staple forms of rice as sandwiches to bread or potato crisps to plain boiled potato. However, as some of them are quite popular and well known even in the West, and they would probably be more easily found under the classification of rice rather than snacks and desserts, the recipes for several of them are given here:

1. Fried Rice

Although this dish is often and proudly served in European Chinese restaurants, it is never considered a highly presentable dish in China. By that I mean it is not something one would find on the menu of a reputable Chinese restaurant, nor a dish which a proud housewife would wish to place on her table when entertaining any except the most familiar acquaintances. For this dish is in its nature ranked more or less as scrambled eggs on the English menu.

Nevertheless, as a dish it is capable of far greater variations and interpretations than scrambled eggs, and when cooked with the best ingredients can be most appetizing. Being a snack rather than a course or a dish, it is generally eaten on its own rather than served with numerous other dishes at meal-time; but it is generally eaten with a simple soup.

The most common form of fried rice is the egg and ham or the egg and meat, fried with onions, and perhaps with shrimps and mushrooms thrown in for added taste and de luxe effect.

> 2 medium-sized onions
> 2 tablespoons lard
> 1 large plateful of cold steamed rice
> 2 or 3 fresh eggs
> 100g (4 oz) ham or cooked meat
> sauce or salt to taste

Cut the onions into small diced pieces and fry in lard in a large frying-pan over a fierce heat for one minute. Add the rice and break up all the lumpy pieces. Fry until the rice is slightly brown. Pour in the two or three beaten eggs, turn and toss the rice quickly so that the frying and heat are even all over the pan. Add shredded ham, continue to stir and turn for a further two minutes. Add salt or soya sauce (about one and a half tablespoons) to taste. If such things as shrimps and mushrooms are to be added, they should be put in at the same time as the ham.

Properly cooked fried rice is a dry (it must never be messy) aromatic dish, hence it should be served concurrently with at least one soup dish.

2. Soft Rice (Congee) with assorted ingredients

> 1 breakfast cup of rice
>   (glutinous type if available)
> 50g (2 oz) dried shrimps
> 50g (2 oz) dried scallops

2 tablespoons Vesop or soya sauce
1 tablespoon lard
50g (2 oz) cooked chicken meat
50g (2 oz) ham
1 teaspoon salt
pepper

Prepare the rice by boiling in six cups of water for 30 minutes. Meanwhile prepare the ingredients by soaking the shrimps (after removing tails and heads) and scallops in Vesop or soya sauce. Add the mixture with lard, into the boiling rice, together with sliced chicken meat and ham, and simmer over a low heat for another 30 minutes. Season with salt and pepper and serve.

3. Chicken soft-rice

1 spring chicken
2 or 3 slices ginger
1 large onion
1 tablespoon salt
100g (4 oz) rice
6 tablespoons soya sauce
4 spring onions (chopped)
pepper

Dress and clean the chicken and boil it in a pan with six to seven cups of water over a low heat with ginger and onion (sliced) for one hour. Add salt and boil for another 30 minutes. Remove the chicken from the pan and cut it into 4cm (1½ in) pieces.

Meanwhile, wash the rice (use glutinous rice if available) and boil it in the chicken stock for thirty-five minutes, or until it becomes a soft uniform mess. At this point divide the cut chicken into six or so serving bowls, into each of which has been placed 1 tablespoon soya sauce and some chopped spring onion. Pour the soft rice into each of the bowls, and serve after seasoning with a little pepper.

This dish is considered a dainty snack in China and is favoured by society ladies and mistresses, wealthy but corruptible would-be mandarins and merchants. In the West it is highly to be recommended for exhausted business executives with suspicion of duodenal ulcers.

4. The 'eight-treasure' rice

This is the only Chinese rice dish which comes anywhere near to the English conception of a dessert or pudding. This is nothing like the traditional rice pudding of the West, but approaches more nearly in shape and form, the Christmas pudding.

> *400g (1 lb) glutinous rice*
> *6 tablespoons shredded suet*
> *5 tablespoons sugar*
> *2 tablespoons barley*
> *4 tablespoons lotus seeds*
> *4 tablespoons almonds*
> *6 tablespoons honeyed dates*
> *4 tablespoons dragon eyes*
> *6 prunes*
> *4 tablespoons candied cherries*
> *4 tablespoons candied orange peel*
> *4 tablespoons any green candied fruit*
> *2 tablespoons lard*
> *(for anything that is not available*
> *substitute raisins and walnuts)*

Boil glutinous rice in four cups of water until fairly dry. Mix in suet and sugar and continue cooking over a very low heat (insert asbestos mat) for a further five minutes.

Meanwhile blanch the lotus seeds and almond, and cut the fruit into even sizes and slice candied fruits into strips. Now take a large heatproof pudding basin and grease the inside over with lard and then cover with an 8mm ($\frac{1}{3}$ in) layer of glutinous rice. Arrange the fruits and coloured candied fruits in attractive designs on the layer of rice, and press them through to the surface so that they will show when the pudding is later turned out on a plate. Build the ingredients up in the basin in this manner, layer after layer alternately of coloured fruit and rice, until it is full. Place the basin in a steamer and steam for forty minutes. Turn the pudding on to a hot plate when ready to serve.

'Eight-treasure' rice is considered a festive dish in China. It can be recommended to western housewives to try as an alternative to, or as an additional Christmas pudding.

Noodles

We have come next to noodles, because, after rice and steamed bread (or dumplings), they are the next staple food of China. Chinese noodles vary in thickness from the thickest Italian spaghetti to the finest vermicelli. They are all made from dough, which is constituted of wheat or rice flour (mainly wheat flour), or pea starch, mixed with varying quantities of egg and water. But the distinguishing character of Chinese noodles lies not in their constitution, but in the methods of cooking them.

There are four main ways in which Chinese noodles are served:

- (*a*) noodles prepared with sauce (generally a sauce made from bean-paste);
- (*b*) noodles served in gravy;
- (*c*) noodles in soup;
- (*d*) fried noodles.

Under these four major categories, Chinese noodles, having few taboos or limitations as to the ingredients with which they can be mixed, can be cooked, blended and served in several hundred different ways.

Fried noodles and noodles in soup and gravy are generally served as a snack at tea time or at supper time late in the evening. The ingredients most frequently used in conjunction with noodles are shredded meat, chicken meat, ham, shrimps, prawns, lobster, oysters and eggs, together with any form of vegetables, mushrooms or fungi, which might be available.

For a light tea-time snack, as an appetizer to precede an evening of banqueting, on the occasion of a wedding, grand birthday anniversary, funeral, reception or memorial get-together, a light egg-noodle is generally served in a very clear chicken soup garnished with a few strands of shredded ham.

With noodles which are served at ordinary tea time to satisfy a possible appetite far more substantial ingredients are used.

In fried noodles the ingredients, which may consist of meat and prawns together with a number of vegetables, such as mushrooms, 'wood-ears' (a kind of fungi), celery, shredded carrots, are generally cooked independently of the noodles, and are fried together only at the last moment.

A very attractive and tasty way of cooking noodles is to cook them in the gravy of the ingredients which have been prepared separately. This gravy is often thickened with the addition of a little cornflour. In the final stage of the preparation the noodles and ingredients are cooked together for a few minutes which enables the gravy to impregnate the noodles with its generally very tasty flavour.

The favourite 'Birthday Noodle' is distinguished by the addition to the usual noodles in gravy of a hard-boiled egg, which has been dyed or painted red.

By far the tastiest of all noodles are noodles fried or stewed with oysters. In such a preparation oysters are seldom used alone; they are generally used in conjunction with meat and a variety of fungi. Here the interpenetration of flavour is brought to such an effective point that it has an utterly devastating effect on all those who are fond of highly tasty food and inclined to the swallowing of long noodle-like preparations. Its immense value lies in its ability to satisfy and entertain the aged and elderly, who can no longer enjoy the rough and tumble of life and do not possess sufficient teeth to indulge themselves in chewing steaks and chops.

In the North, where noodles are served as one of the staple foods – these are generally larger calibre noodles which resemble the Italian spaghetti – they are, as a rule, eaten with a sauce which has its base in soya bean paste (here minced meat can be added). This preparation, which is served at a regular meal, is a very economical dish, as both large noodles and fermented soya paste are comparatively inexpensive. Yet a dish consisting of these two ingredients, plus a little garlic, minced meat and raw spring onion, can be so appetizing and easy to swallow in quantity that the diner is often unaware of the amount he has eaten until he has to struggle to rise from his seat.

A favourite noodle of the South is the rice-flour noodle. This is generally whiter in appearance than the wheat-flour noodle. In Fukien and Kwangtung, the two southern provinces, rice-flour noodles are often cooked with fresh oysters, dried mussels, together with spring onion, sliced pork, 'wood-ear', mushrooms, dried lily flowers as supplementary ingredients, either in the form of stewed or fried noodles.

Pea-starch noodles, which are completely transparent, are usually reserved for use in soup, or for the preparation and cooking of stewed and fried vegetables. Possibly because of their round slippery shape, and partly because they are able to carry a lot of tasty gravy with them, they have an amazing 'ball-bearing' effect in their ability to help the swallowing of quantities of rice. Invariably when a well-prepared dish of this kind appears on the table, the diners find it difficult to rise after the meal.

Indeed, here I must mention that one of the greatest drawbacks and disadvantages of Chinese food is simply that, if it is well-prepared one is inclined to tuck away so much unawares that one invariably over-eats. This may be attributable to the fact that when one eats in the buffet style and is not limited to the food placed immediately in front, on one's own plate, one invariably develops a knack of gathering all the choicest bits from all the choicest dishes in the most unobtrusive and inconspicuous manner and causing them to disappear, without occasioning the least embarrassment anywhere, except where it matters the longest – in one's stomach.

1. *The northern soya paste noodle*

200g (8 oz) minced pork
1 teaspoon chopped ginger
10 spring onions
2 garlic cloves (crushed)
2 tablespoons oil
4 tablespoons soya bean paste
1 small cucumber
6 radishes
200g (8 oz) pea sprouts
400g (1 lb) noodles (largest calibre)

Mix the minced pork, chopped ginger, half the spring onions (chopped) and crushed garlic together and fry with oil in a large frying-pan for four or five minutes. Add the soya bean paste and, while stirring, add one cup of water slowly. Stir the mixture for a further ten minutes and the sauce is ready.

Now chop the remainder of the onions finely, slice the cucumber into thin strips, peel and slice the radishes lengthwise, and immerse the pea sprouts for three minutes in boiling water and drain. These ingredients are not to be cooked but are to be put into separate dishes on the dining table as an accompaniment to the noodles.

Meanwhile, the noodles should be prepared in the usual way, which is to put them in boiling water and cook for fifteen minutes (use a fork to separate them while boiling). Chinese noodles take a shorter time to cook than Italian spaghetti. Remove from pan, drain. Divide them into equal portions and place them in separate bowls for each individual diner.

Each person at the table helps himself to a tablespoon or two of the soya paste sauce and the other ingredients from the various bowls, which he mixes well with his noodles before eating.

The enjoyment of this type of noodles is very much a cultivated taste; it is particularly indigenous to the Good Earth, especially the Great Northern Plain, of China.

2. Standard fried noodles

100g (4 oz) cabbage
100g (4 oz) bamboo shoots
3 or 4 mushrooms
100g (4 oz) sliced pork
  (in strips)
3½ tablespoons lard
1 teaspoon salt
2 tablespoons soya sauce
2 slices ginger
1 tablespoon sherry
100g (4 oz) shrimps
½ tablespoon cornflour
200g (4 oz) noodles
½ teaspoon sesame oil

Cut the cabbage and bamboo shoots into 4cm (1½ in) long strips. Soak the mushrooms in hot water for ten minutes and cut into slices. Fry the sliced pork, bamboo shoots and cabbage in 2 tablespoons of lard, adding salt, for six to seven minutes, and remove from heat.

Mix 1½ tablespoons soya sauce, ginger, sherry, shelled shrimps and cornflour. Fry the mixture in ½ tablespoon of lard for three minutes. Now mix in the already fried pork, bamboo shoots and cabbage. Fry for a further one and a half minutes.

Now place the remainder of the lard (1 tablespoon) in the frying-pan and pour in the boiled noodles, after draining. Add remainder of soya sauce (½ tablespoon), salt and sesame oil and stir and turn for five minutes. Now add the cooked pork, shrimps, cabbage, etc., stir over a fierce heat for two minutes and serve.

3. Stewed noodles in gravy

200g (8 oz) noodles
100g (4 oz) pork
1 small cauliflower
¼ tablespoon lard or vegetable oil
4 medium-sized mushrooms
salt
2 spring onions
25g (1 oz) 'wood-ear' (fungi)
½ tablespoon soya sauce
1 cup chicken broth
½ tablespoon cornflour
½ tablespoon sesame oil
¼ teaspoon Ve-tsin or gourmet powder or 1 stock-cube

Prepare the noodles in the usual way, by boiling in 1 litre (two pints) of water for twelve minutes. Drain and pass through cold water under a tap.

Slice the pork against grain into 4cm (1½ in) strips. Chop the cauliflower into 1cm (½ in) sq pieces. Fry them together in oil for four minutes with sliced mushroom and a pinch of salt. Now add chopped (about 1cm (½ in) long) spring onion, wood-ear, and soya sauce, and fry for a further two minutes before adding chicken broth into which cornflour has been mixed. Stir and stew for a further ten minutes.

Meanwhile, fry the cooked noodles in the sesame oil for two minutes. Pour the pork, mushroom, cauliflower mixture over the noodles, together with gravy, add the Ve-tsin (or crushed stock-cube), and leave to simmer for three minutes over a low heat before serving.

4. Chicken-ham noodles in chicken broth

(This is the noodle of occasion, served at weddings, funerals, etc.).

    400g (1 lb) thin egg noodles
    100g (4 oz) cooked chicken meat
    100g (4 oz) smoked ham
    1 litre (2 pints) chicken broth
    1 teaspoon salt
    1 teaspoon chopped ginger
    2 spring onions
    ½ teaspoon Ve-tsin or gourmet powder or 1 stock-cube

Prepare the noodles as usual by boiling and rinsing with cold water; divide into eight equal portions and place them in eight separate bowls and keep hot.

Boil the chicken meat and ham in the chicken broth for fifteen minutes. Remove from broth and slice into strips about 5cm (2 in) long. Now add to the broth salt, chopped ginger, spring onion and Ve-tsin or stock-cube. Bring to the boil once more. Pour the broth immediately in equal portions into the eight bowls, garnish with strips of chicken meat and ham and serve.

5. Soup noodles with chicken, ham and oysters

    50g (2 oz) smoked ham
    1 litre (2 pints) chicken broth
    12 medium-sized oysters
    1 teaspoon salt
    ¼ teaspoon chopped ginger
    400g (1 lb) noodles
    2 spring onions
    100g (4 oz) chicken meat
    6 mushrooms
    25g (1 oz) 'wood-ear'

   2 young leeks
   1 tablespoon soya sauce
   1 tablespoon lard
   2 tablespoons sherry

Slice the ham into 4cm (1½ in) strips and boil in chicken
broth for five minutes. Remove oysters from shells and add
them to the broth. Add salt and chopped ginger, simmer for
ten minutes. Add noodles and onions and simmer for a
further two to three minutes.

Fry sliced chicken meat, with sliced mushrooms and
wood-ear (after softening the latter by soaking in hot water)
and sliced leeks, for five minutes, in soya sauce and lard.
Lace with sherry and pour the mixture over the noodles and
serve. If you like shellfish this is one of the tastiest dishes in
creation, wonderful on a cold winter's day.

6. Vegetarian fried noodles

   100g (4 oz) bamboo shoots
   100g (4 oz) spinach
   3 mushrooms
   100g (4 oz) Chinese fermented pickled vegetable
     (Tsa Tsai)
   5 tablespoons vegetable oil
   1 teaspoon salt
   400g (1 lb) noodles
   ½ tablespoon cornflour
   2 tablespoons soya sauce
   ½ teaspoon Ve-tsin or gourmet powder or 1 stock-cube
   2 tablespoons sherry
   pepper

Slice the bamboo shoots into 4cm (1½ in) strips, wash the
spinach, wash the mushrooms and soak in a cup of boiling
water; slice the pickled vegetable into 5cm (2 in) strips.

Fry the bamboo shoots in oil for two minutes; add spinach, mushrooms, pickled vegetable, with salt, and continue to fry for three minutes. Now add the pre-cooked noodles and stir for two minutes, mixing thoroughly. Mix the cornflour with the mushroom water and soya sauce and pour the mixture on to the noodles. Mix well, add Ve-tsin and bring to the boil. Lace with sherry, pepper, and serve immediately.

The fermented pickled vegetable brings out a tastiness which no ordinary vegetable can provide.

Chinese Soups

The ordinary Chinese soup is made from the same base as western soup: bone stock (chicken or pork bone). But the superior type of Chinese soup is made of broth distilled from chicken and pork, with not more than fifteen per cent ham and beef added to enhance taste. To produce a given quantity of soup you require the same quantity in weight of meat (in the proportion of five parts of chicken, seven of lean pork, one each of ham and beef). You start off with one hundred per cent more water, after the first boiling and skimming, you continue to simmer for three or four hours over a very low heat, until the quantity of water becomes reduced to about the same quantity as the weight of meat. This is as you can imagine a very concentrated as well as a very expensive broth, and is practicable to prepare only on a large scale, such as in restaurants. When preparing, so long as no violent boiling is allowed, the broth can always be kept clear; and Chinese soups are as a rule clear soups.

On the other hand, quite a number of Chinese soups can simply be made from tap water, and prepared in next to no time, and yet they can possess an attractive and satisfying taste (several of the soups given below are of this variety) as well as a very presentable appearance.

Because Chinese food is eaten in the buffet style, soup is drunk not at the beginning of the meal, but between mouthfuls of a variety of food. For this reason it has quite a different function from western soups, and probably serves a more useful purpose, both at the moment when it is imbibed and when further afield in the digestive tract, since it is probably helpful to digestion for every couple of mouthfuls of food to be chased down by a mouthful of soup; and especially when rich meat dishes are generally accompanied by fresh vegetable soups, and plain vegetarian food is accompanied and enriched by meat broth.

Since a good-class Chinese meal would consist of certainly more than half-a-dozen dishes (often about ten) the number of varieties of soups served are not limited to one as in the West, but may run up to two or more. Indeed, the people of my home province of Fukien are so fond of soup that one of my Cantonese friends was considerably surprised when he sat down to dinner with a Fukienese family and found that of the ten dishes served seven were soups or semi-soups!

1. Egg-flower soup

> 1 litre (2 pints) bone stock
>   (or tap water)
> 2 fresh eggs
> a little vegetable oil
> 2 spring onions (chopped)
> 1 teaspoon salt
> 2 tablespoons soya sauce
>   (or preferably Vesop)
> $\frac{1}{2}$ teaspoon Ve-tsin or gourmet powder or 1 stock-cube
> 1 teaspoon vinegar
> pinch of pepper

Bring bone stock (or water) to the boil. Remove from fire. Pour beaten egg, mixed with a little oil, slowly into the stock in the thinnest stream. Add chopped spring onions and salt. Bring to the boil again. Add soya sauce or Vesop, Ve-tsin, vinegar and pepper. Stir with ladle, and soup is ready to serve.

This is one of the most commonly served soups in Chinese homes and should not take more than ten minutes to prepare. Although extremely simple, it is quite tasty. The vinegar gives it that extra bite, and also enables it to wash away any excessive richness in other dishes. The addition of sliced mushroom to enhance interest is quite permissible.

2. Sliced pork and watercress soup

> 100g (4 oz) lean pork
> 2 teaspoons cornflour
> 1 litre (2 pints) bone stock or water
> 1 teaspoon salt
> 100g (4 oz) watercress
> 2 spring onions
> 2 tablespoons soya sauce or Vesop
> ½ teaspoon Ve-tsin or gourmet powder or 1 stock-cube
> pinch of pepper

Slice pork into 1cm (½ in) pieces and mix with a cornflour paste (cornflour mixed with tablespoon of water). Bring stock (or water) to boil, add salt and pork and simmer for five to six minutes. Add watercress and chopped onions, as well as soya sauce or Vesop and Ve-tsin. Boil gently for further five minutes. Add pepper and serve.

3. Pork pellet and mushroom soup

Use the same ingredients as above, but substitute mushrooms (six or eight) for watercress. Button mushrooms are preferable in this case, as they don't darken the soup as much as the larger types. If larger ones are used they should be washed and soaked before using.

4. Meat-ball and Chinese transparent pea-starch noodle soup

> 150g (6 oz) minced pork
> cornflour
> 1 tablespoon salt
> pepper
> 1 tablespoon lard

2 spring onions
50g (2 oz) Chinese pea-starch noodles
1 litre (2 pints) bone stock
2 tablespoons soya sauce or Vesop
½ teaspoon Ve-tsin or gourmet powder or 1 stock-cube

Make meat-balls about the size of pigeons' eggs by mixing minced meat with cornflour paste, with the addition of a pinch of salt and pepper. Fry in lard for three to four minutes until quite brown, and remove and drain. Chop spring onions into 6mm (¼ in) lengths. Wash noodles in hot water. After draining, put them in a pan of boiling stock and boil for three minutes. Add the meat-balls and continue to boil for five minutes. Now add the spring onions and the seasoning. Simmer for a further three minutes and the soup is ready to serve.

5. Chicken-noodle-ham and bamboo shoot soup

75g (3 oz) chicken meat
50g (2 oz) bamboo shoots
50g (2 oz) ham
1 litre (2 pints) chicken bone stock
75g (3 oz) egg noodles
1 teaspoon salt
1 tablespoon soya sauce or Vesop
pepper

Slice chicken meat, bamboo shoots and ham into 4cm (1½ in) match-stick strips. Simmer the bamboo shoots and chicken meat in stock for ten minutes. Add noodles and salt and continue to simmer for a further five minutes. Add all the seasonings and sherry. Distribute the sliced ham evenly over the soup. Boil gently for a further minute and serve.

6. Chicken-ham-awabi-bamboo shoot soup

   75g (3 oz) chicken meat
   75g (3 oz) awabi (tinned or dried)
   1 litre (2 pints) chicken bone stock
   2 slices ginger
   75g (3 oz) bamboo shoots
   50g (2 oz) ham
   1 teaspoon salt
   pepper
   1 tablespoon soya sauce or Vesop
   1 tablespoon sherry

Cut chicken and awabi into thin slices. Simmer in chicken bone stock together with sliced ginger, bamboo shoots, which have been cut into match-stick strips, for fifteen minutes. Sprinkle sliced ham over the soup. Add all the seasonings and sherry and boil gently for a further two minutes and serve.

7. Chicken-ham-and-mushroom soup

   6–8 mushrooms (Chinese dried mushrooms if available)
   75g (3 oz) ham
   1 litre (2 pints) chicken bone stock
   75g (3 oz) chicken meat
   1 tablespoon sherry
   1 teaspoon salt
   1 tablespoon soya sauce or Vesop
   ½ teaspoon Ve-tsin or 1 chicken stock cube
   pepper

Cut the mushrooms into quarters after soaking in a cup of boiling water for half an hour. Boil shredded ham gently in chicken bone stock for ten minutes. Add the mushrooms and mushroom water to the pan. Add sliced chicken meat and continue to simmer for ten minutes. Now add the seasonings (sherry, salt, Vesop, Ve-tsin) and pepper to taste.

8. Chicken-and-ham fish soup

200g (8 oz) fish (halibut, bass, sole, skate)
1 tablespoon cornflour
1 litre (2 pints) chicken bone stock
50g (2 oz) ham
1 teaspoon salt
2 slices ginger
2 tablespoons soya sauce or Vesop
1 tablespoon sherry
½ tablespoon vinegar
½ teaspoon Ve-tsin or 1 chicken stock cube
3 spring onions (chopped)

Cut the fish into 1cm (½ in) pieces. Mix with cornflour paste. Boil the fish gently in chicken stock for five minutes. Add sliced ham, and continue to simmer for five minutes. Now add all the remaining ingredients except onions; sprinkle the chopped onions over the soup and serve.

9. 'Won Ton' or Chinese ravioli soup

2 spring onions (chopped)
1 litre (2 pints) pork or chicken bone stock
1 teaspoon salt
1 tablespoon soya sauce or Vesop
½ teaspoon Ve-tsin or gourmet powder
pepper to taste
150g (6 oz) Chinese ravioli

Chinese ravioli or *Won Ton* is made by placing finely minced pork, mixed with chopped onion, a small quantity of garlic soya sauce, and cornflour, in between two very thin sheets

of dough (about 4cm (1½ in) sq). The meat content is sealed
inside by pressing down the edge of the dough with a knife
or fork. Or, alternatively, the meat content can be folded in a
slightly larger sheet (about 6cm (2½ in) sq) of dough and
sealed inside by folding over and pressing the edges together.

Gently boil the chopped spring onions in chicken stock
for five minutes, add all the seasonings. Fry the ravioli in
deep fat until they are distinctly crisp on the outside. Remove the ravioli from pan and drain thoroughly. Pour the
soup into a large Chinese soup bowl (or into as many soup
plates as required). Add the ravioli into the soup immediately before serving. Thus the ravioli will float on top and
the diner will find it still in a cracking state in his mouth
while he is drinking the soup: a pleasant sensation.

An easier and more leisurely way of preparing this soup is
simply to simmer the pieces of ravioli in the stock together
with chopped onion for about ten minutes before adding all
the seasoning and serving. Some people prefer it prepared
this way. The taste of dough cooked in stock has a special,
endearing appeal to the connoisseur of noodle soups.

10. Bird's (sea swallow) nest soup

75g (3 oz) dried bird's nest (dried gelatinous substance)
1 tablespoon sherry
75g (3 oz) white chicken meat
3 egg whites
500ml (1 pint) chicken broth
500ml (1 pint) ham broth
½ tablespoon cornflour
1 teaspoon salt
25g (1 oz) ham (chopped)

Soak bird's nest in boiling water and leave to stand for five
to six hours. Drain and remove any stray feather which may
still remain with tweezers. Add sherry and a cupful of hot
water to the now gelatinous bird's nest. Place the mixture

in a small saucepan and simmer very gently for 30 minutes.

Mince the chicken meat very finely, mix with egg white and beat them up together.

Meanwhile add the chicken and ham broths to the pan containing the bird's nest. Bring to boil and leave to simmer gently for fifteen minutes. Now stir the mixture of minced chicken and egg white into the bird's nest in chicken-and-ham broth, in a fine steady stream. Add cornflour to thicken whilst stirring continually. Add salt and leave to simmer gently for ten minutes before garnishing with chopped ham and serve in a large bowl.

11. Crab and vinegar soup

> 1 large crab
> vegetable oil
> 1 teaspoon salt
> 1 teaspoon chopped ginger
> 2 tomatoes
> 2 eggs
> 2 tablespoons soya sauce or Vesop
> ½ teaspoon Ve-tsin or 1 chicken stock cube
> 2 tablespoons vinegar
> 2 tablespoons sherry
> 2 spring onions (chopped)
> 1 litre (2 pints) chicken bone stock

If the crab is raw steam it for half an hour. Scrape out all the meat, including its eggs, on to a dish. Fry the crab-meat in oil with salt, chopped ginger and sliced tomato for five minutes. Remove from heat and slowly pour in beaten egg in a fine stream. Stir and bring to boil again, and add all the remaining ingredients except spring onions and continue to boil gently for five minutes. Sprinkle with the chopped spring onions and serve.

12. Fishball soup

200g (8 oz) raw fish (halibut, turbot, whiting, sole,
    haddock, etc.)
1 egg white
50g (2 oz) lean pork
1 tablespoon cornflour
1 litre (2 pints) chicken stock
2 spring onions
½ teaspoon Ve-tsin or 1 chicken stock cube
1 teaspoon salt
pepper
2 tablespoons soya sauce or Vesop
2 tablespoons sherry
1 tablespoon vinegar

Chop or mince the raw fish and mix it thoroughly with egg white and minced pork. Add cornflour and one tablespoon of water. Beat the mixture up until it becomes a light homogeneous paste. Make balls of about the size of pigeon eggs with the paste.

Boil the fish paste balls in chicken stock for ten minutes. Add the chopped spring onions, seasonings, sherry and vinegar and serve after simmering for another five minutes.

13. Ham and spring green soup

150g (6 oz) spring greens
100g (4 oz) ham
50g (2 oz) bamboo shoots
1 litre (2 pints) pork bone stock
50g (2 oz) pea-starch noodles
½ teaspoon Ve-tsin or 1 chicken stock-cube
2 tablespoon soya sauce or Vesop
1 teaspoon salt
pepper

Wash the spring greens thoroughly, cut into 2·5cm (1 in) wide slices, and soak in a large bowlful of water for 45 minutes. Slice ham and bamboo shoots into match-stick strips. Bring chicken stock to boil in a saucepan. Add ham, bamboo shoots, and noodles, and simmer for fifteen minutes. Now add the spring greens, Ve-tsin or stock-cube, the seasonings, boil gently for ten more minutes and serve.

14. Beef and turnip soup

> 400g (1 lb) lean beef
> 3 medium turnips
> 3 pieces sliced ginger
> 2 tablespoons soya sauce or Vesop
> ½ teaspoon Ve-tsin or 1 stock-cube
> pepper

Cut the beef into 2·5cm (1 in) cubes. Place them in 1 litre (two pints) of water and bring to boil. Skim all scum and impurities away thoroughly. Place pan on an asbestos mat and simmer over a very low heat for one and a half hours. Cut turnips into 1cm (½ in) cubes. Add them to the beef stock together with sliced ginger. Boil gently for thirty minutes. Add all the seasonings. Stir and serve.

15. Pure beef broth

> 400g (1 lb) beef
> 2–3 slices of ginger
> 3 onions
> 2½ teaspoons salt
> 1 stock-cube
> pepper
> 3 tablespoons sherry

Clean and cut beef into 2·5cm (1 inch) cubes. Place in 500ml (1 pint) of water in a saucepan and bring to boil for three minutes. Pour all this water, with its impurities, away. Place the beef in a double boiler with ginger, onions and salt. Pour 1 litre (two pints) of boiling water on to the beef. Cover tightly and simmer over a very low heat for five hours. Season with stock-cube, pepper and sherry and serve.

16. Vegetarian soup

>   2 carrots
>   1 turnip
>   75g (3 oz) bamboo shoots
>   ¼ cabbage
>   1½ tablespoons vegetable oil
>   2 teaspoons salt
>   2 tomatoes
>   75g (3 oz) pea-starch noodles
>   75g (3 oz) Chinese pickled vegetables (*cha tsai*)
>   75g (3 oz) pea sprouts
>   2 spring onions
>   3 tablespoons soya sauce or Vesop
>   ½ teaspoon Ve-tsin
>   pepper

Shred carrots, turnip, bamboo shoots and cabbage into match-stick strips. Fry them in oil with 1 teaspoon of salt and the sliced tomatoes for five to six minutes. Pour into the fried mixed vegetables 1 litre (two pints) of water. Add noodles. Boil gently for thirty minutes. Slice the pickled vegetables into 4cm (1½ in) slices. Add them, with pea sprouts and chopped spring onions into the vegetable broth. Stir and add the seasonings, continue to boil gently for ten minutes and serve.

Meat Dishes

When we say 'meat' in China we generally mean pork. This is probably due to the fact that, while all the other cattle can be put to some other uses, pigs are primarily reared for food. This does not, however, mean that mutton, beef and goat meat are not popular. Mutton is eaten extensively in the North and goat meat is popular in the South, where, among the hilly regions, probably more goats are raised.

The main reason why the cow is not so often killed for its meat is because it is the main beast of burden in the growing of rice. Besides, south of the Yangtze half of the cattle one sees are water-buffaloes, which have the appearance more of the hippo and rhinoceros than the ordinary cow, and their meat is probably a little too tough for ordinary culinary purposes.

PORK

1. Braised leg of pork

1·25–1·5kg (3–4 lb) leg of pork
1½ cups water
½ cup (8 tablespoons) soya sauce
4 tablespoons sherry
1½ tablespoons sugar

Clean the leg of pork, make a few slashes in the skin, and place in a heavy saucepan with water, soya sauce, sherry and sugar. Heat over a high fire until it starts to boil. Insert an asbestos mat and simmer over a very low fire for three hours. Turn the pork in the gravy two or three times during the process of cooking, so that the whole joint will become evenly brown. Add further seasoning or water, if necessary, or if desired, and simmer for a further half hour. Serve whole in a large bowl or deep, hot plate.

The meat in this case, after the prolonged cooking, will have become so tender that it can, as it generally is in China, be pulled to pieces by a pair of chopsticks. In the West, the carving knife should move through the pork as if through butter. To the connoisseur the fat of the pork is no longer regarded as fat in the normal European way, but as a kind of rich sweet jelly, and can therefore be consumed in very considerable quantities, with great enjoyment and no ill effect. The rich brown gravy, when added to rice, produces such a succulent mixture that it is not far off the mark to describe it as the hungry rice-eater's dream of heaven.

2. Chinese casserole of pork
(Also known as Tung-Po Pork, reputed to have been invented by the famous Tang Dynasty poet, Soo Tung-Po.)

> *1·5kg (4 lb) pork (belly)*
> *1 tablespoon lard*
> *¾ cup soya sauce*
> *2–3 slices of ginger*
> *½ tablespoon sugar*
> *4 tablespoons sherry*

Cut the meat into 2–4cm (1–1½ in) pieces against the grain. Fry the pieces of meat in lard until brown. Place the meat in a heavy pot, pour in soya sauce and cook for a minute or two, stirring continually. Add ginger and one cup of boiling water. Bring to boil. Lower the fire and insert an asbestos sheet under the pan, and leave the pot, tightly covered, to simmer for one and a quarter hours. Add sherry and sugar, stir, and simmer for a further half hour.

This style of pork dish is capable of two further variations:

(1) On opening the pot after one and a half hours of simmering, use a ladle full of the fat and gravy of the pork to fry any of the following vegetables: (*a*) sliced cabbage; (*b*) spinach; (*c*) cauliflower. When cooked, after three to five minutes' frying, place the vegetables at the bottom of a large bowl or deep plate (hot) and pour the cooked pork and gravy over the vegetables. This is one of the most common and popular pork dishes in China.

(2) The pork can also be cooked with whole hard-boiled eggs, turnips, abalone, salted fish (haddock or squid). These ingredients should be added at the beginning and cooked for the full one and three-quarter hours with the pork.

3. White cut pork

   1·25kg (3 lb) pork (leg undercut)
   4 tablespoons soya sauce
   2 teaspoons chopped ginger

Wash the meat and place in a pot. Pour in 750ml (1½ pints) of water. Bring to boil and leave to simmer for 45 minutes. Remove meat from pot and cut against grain into 4mm (⅙ in) thin slices when cold. Arrange the pieces on a large plate. Serve with soya sauce and chopped ginger.

4. Steam minced pork with cauliflower

   400g (1 lb) pork (minced)
   1 egg
   1 teaspoon salt
   ½ teaspoon sugar
   1 tablespoon cornflower
   1 medium-sized onion
   1 tablespoon soya sauce
   1 tablespoon sherry
   1 cauliflower

Mince pork finely and place it in a large bowl with beaten egg, salt, sugar, cornflour, chopped onion, soya sauce and

sherry. Mix thoroughly. Meanwhile, cut the cauliflower into
2·5cm (1 in) pieces and place them at the bottom of a
heatproof basin. Pack the minced pork mixture over the
cauliflower. Place the basin in a steamer and steam for forty
minutes.

5. Steamed pork with salted fish

> 200g (8 oz) salted fish
> 1 tablespoon lard
> 2 slices root ginger
> 600g (1½ lb) pork
> 1½ tablespoons soya sauce
> 1 teaspoon sugar
> 2 tablespoons sherry

Cut salted fish into 2·5cm (1 in) pieces. Fry in lard until well
browned and crispy. Place them in a large heatproof bowl with
ginger and pork which has been cut into 4cm (1½ in) pieces
against the grain. Add soya sauce, sugar and sherry and a
quarter cup of water. Place the bowl in a steamer and steam
over a moderate heat for two hours.

6. Steamed pork with ground rice

> 600g (1½ lb) pork
> 3 tablespoons soya sauce
> 3 tablespoons sherry
> 2 chopped onions
> 2 teaspoons chopped ginger
> ½ cup ground rice (roasted)
> 1 teaspoon sugar

Cut pork into 4cm (1½ in) pieces. Mix them with soya sauce,
sherry, sugar, chopped onions and chopped ginger. Now
add ground rice and mix thoroughly. Place in a heatproof
basin and steam over a low heat for two hours.

7. Fried pork ribbons with young leeks
(Bamboo shoots, celery, pea-sprouts can also be used)

> 3 young leeks
> 400g (1 lb) pork
> 1 egg
> ½ tablespoon cornflour
> 2 tablespoons vegetable oil
> 1½ tablespoons soya sauce
> 2 tablespoons chicken or pork stock
> 1 teaspoon sugar

Wash leeks thoroughly and cut into 1cm (½ in) sections. Cut pork against grain into 4cm (1½ in) long and 4mm (⅙ in) wide ribbons. Mix pork with beaten egg (half an egg will do) and cornflour. Fry the pork with leeks in vegetable oil over a high heat for five minutes, turning quickly and continually. Add soya sauce and stock and fry a further three minutes. Add the sugar and continue to cook for two minutes. Serve immediately on a hot plate.

8. Fried pork ribbons with pickled vegetables
(Tsa Chai, or pickled cabbage, cucumber, etc.)

> 400g (1 lb) pork
> 100g (4 oz) pickled vegetables (chopped)
> 75g (3 oz) bamboo shoots (shredded)
> ½ tablespoon cornflour
> 1 teaspoon sugar
> 1½ tablespoons soya sauce
> 2 tablespoons vegetable oil
> 2 tablespoons stock
> 1 tablespoon sherry

Follow the preparations in the previous recipe. Both the bamboo shoots and pickled vegetables should be fried with the pork from the beginning, before adding soya sauce, stock and other ingredients. It is essential to fry over a high heat.

The resulting dish is one of the most savoury that can be prepared. The impregnation of the pork by the pickle and vice-versa, gives the dish a 'strength' unknown in any other way of cooking.

9. Fried sweet and sour spare ribs

The use of rib-bone meat in the form of miniature chops, when some twenty or thirty chops are served up together in a single dish, seems to be a distinctively Chinese conception.

1·25kg (3 lb) spare ribs (with plenty of meat)
2 tablespoons soya sauce
2 tablespoons sherry
1 egg
1 tablespoon cornflour
4 tablespoons vegetable oil

Cut the bones apart by cutting through the meat in between the bones. Chop the bone (and meat) into 2·5cm (1 in) long pieces. Soak them in a mixture of soya sauce and sherry for 30 minutes. After the seasoning, mix the bones with beaten egg and cornflour. Fry the chops in oil for five minutes over high heat, and drain.

Meanwhile, prepare the Sweet and Sour Sauce as follows: Use 2 onions, 8 skinned tomatoes, 50g (2 oz) pickles, 2 tablespoons vegetable oil, $\frac{1}{2}$ cup of stock, 3 tablespoons soya sauce, 2 tablespoons sugar, 2 tablespoons vinegar, 1 tablespoon cornflour and $\frac{1}{4}$ cup of water.

Fry the mixed vegetables and pickles in the oil for five minutes. Add the stock, soya sauce, sugar and vinegar, and simmer for ten minutes. Thicken by adding the cornflour dissolved in the water. Bring to the boil again and pour it over the fried spare ribs. Continue to fry for one minute and serve.

10. Sweet and sour pork

Repeat the same preparations as given in the previous recipe, only substitute pork cut in 18mm (¾ in) squares for spare ribs.

This is a popular dish in the majority of western Chinese restaurants. Here the pieces of pork are often encased in thick batter, which has the disadvantage of absorbing too much fat when deep-fried. Plain sweet and sour pork is much easier to prepare than sweet and sour spare ribs, if only for the fact that meat is much easier to cut than bones. But fried rib bones is a much better, more classical Chinese dish – if only for the proverbial fact that 'the nearer the bone the sweeter the meat'.

11. Fried diced pork with bamboo shoots, water chestnuts and soya bean paste
(or Sauce 'cracked' diced pork with bamboo shoots, etc.)

> 400g (1 lb) pork (lean)
> 1 egg
> 1 tablespoon cornflour
> 3 tablespoons vegetable oil
> 2 tablespoons soya bean paste
> 2 garlic cloves
> 75g (3 oz) bamboo shoots
> 75g (3 oz) water chestnuts
> 1 teaspoon sugar
> salt
> 1 tablespoon sherry
> pepper

Dice pork into 6mm (¼ in) cubes. Mix with beaten egg and cornflour. Fry in oil over high fire for five minutes. Add soya bean paste and garlic, fry for a further two minutes.

Now add all the ingredients – diced bamboo shoots and diced water chestnuts, and the seasonings (sugar, salt, sherry, pepper) and continue to fry for four to five minutes.

Owing to the great heat of the frying the diced meat jumps and cracks in the pan, and this type of frying is known in China as 'cracked-frying'.

12. Sauce 'cracked' diced pork with pimento and red pepper

400g (1 lb) pork
1 egg
1 tablespoon cornflour
3 tablespoons vegetable oil
2 tablespoons soya bean paste
1 large pimento
2 small red peppers
1 teaspoon salt
1 tablespoon sherry
2 tablespoons chicken broth
1 teaspoon sugar

Prepare according to the previous recipe. Add pimento and red peppers which have been sliced into pieces 2·5cm (1 in) long and 1cm ($\frac{1}{2}$ in) wide, when the diced pork and soya bean paste have been frying for two minutes. Add salt, sherry, broth and sugar and fry for a further four to five minutes. Toss and stir quickly all the time while frying. This is essential in all 'cracked' frying.

13. Fried kidney with spring onions and cauliflower

2 pairs kidneys
1½ tablespoons sherry
½ medium-sized cauliflower
1½ tablespoons soya sauce
cornflour
3 spring onions
3 tablespoons lard
1 teaspoon salt
1 teaspoon sugar
1 teaspoon chopped ginger

Slice kidneys into pieces 4cm (1½ in) long and 1cm (½ in) wide, after removing membrane and gristle. Cut a few criss-cross slashes on top of each piece. Soak them in sherry.

Cut cauliflower into pieces 2·5cm (1 in) square and put into a pan of boiling water to boil for three minutes.

Meanwhile mix the sherry-soaked kidney with 1 table-spoon soya sauce and a little cornflour. Fry them with sliced onions in fat over a very fierce heat for one and a half min-utes, stirring continually. Now add the cauliflower after draining off all water; also add the remainder of the soya sauce (½ tablespoon), cornflour, salt, sugar and ginger. Con-tinue stirring briskly and fry a further two minutes. Serve very hot.

14. Fried liver with spring onions and leeks

400g (1 lb) liver
1 tablespoon cornflour
2 tablespoons sherry
2 tablespoons soya sauce
2 leeks
2 tablespoons lard
1 spring onion
1 teaspoon sugar
1 teaspoon salt

Cut liver into slices 4cm (1½ in) in length. Soak for one minute in boiling water to seal the outside layer. Strain off all water. Mix with cornflour, sherry and soya sauce. Wash leeks and slice into 2·5cm (1 in) sections. First fry liver in very hot fat for one minute. Add leeks and continue to fry and stir for two minutes. Add all the remaining ingredients. Continue to stir briskly for two minutes. Serve very hot.

BEEF DISHES

1. Fried beef ribbons with onion

400g (1 lb) beef (steak)
½ tablespoon cornflour (blend with 2 tablespoons chicken
  stock)
4 medium-sized onions
2 tablespoons fat or vegetable oil
2½ tablespoons soya sauce
1 teaspoon sugar
pepper and salt to taste
1½ tablespoons sherry

Clean beef and slice into 4cm (1½ in) long and 4mm (⅙ in)
wide strips or ribbons. Mix with blended cornflour. Slice
onions into pieces about 6mm (¼ in) wide.

Fry beef in fat or oil for one minute, tossing and turning continually. Add onion and fry for a further one and a half minutes.
Add all the seasonings and sherry. Fry over a high heat for a
further two minutes. Remove from heat and serve immediately.

2. Sliced beef fried with tomatoes

400g (1 lb) beef (steak)
1 egg
½ tablespoon cornflour
4 tomatoes
1 teaspoon salt
ginger
garlic clove
2 tablespoons peanut oil
1 teaspoon sugar
1 tablespoon tomato purée
1 tablespoon soya sauce
1 tablespoon sherry
pepper to taste

Cut beef against grain into thin slices. Mix with beaten egg and cornflour.

Cut tomatoes into thin slices. Add salt and fry for two minutes, remove from heat but keep warm.

Fry the sliced beef over a high heat with minced ginger, crushed garlic in oil, for one minute. Add tomato purée and soya sauce. Stir for a further one minute. Now mix the fried tomatoes in with the beef in the pan. Continue to fry for one and a half minutes. Add pepper and serve.

3. Sliced beef in oyster sauce

400g (1 lb) beef (steak)
1 tablespoon sherry
1 tablespoon soya sauce
1 onion
2 tablespoons vegetable oil (peanut or olive)
1 teaspoon sugar
1 teaspoon salt pepper
1½ tablespoons oyster sauce

Cut beef against grain into 4cm (1½ in) by 5cm (2 in) thin slices, season by soaking in sherry and soya sauce for 30 minutes. Heat oil in pan until very hot. Put the seasoned beef and the onion in and fry over a high heat, stirring briskly, for one minute. Now add sugar and oyster sauce. Stir and cook for a further minute. Serve immediately.

4. Spiced velveteen of beef

800g (2 lb) steak
6 tablespoons lard
½ teaspoon aniseed powder
2 cups chicken stock
½ cup sherry
½ cup soya sauce

Cut beef into eight pieces and fry in a saucepan for two to three minutes with 2 tablespoons lard, until slightly brown. Add chicken stock, aniseed powder, sherry and soya sauce. Boil gently until the pan is almost dry and the meat extremely tender. Remove from heat.

When cold, mince the meat, then place the mince in a pan with 4 tablespoons lard and fry over a very low heat, stirring continually. Fry, never forgetting to stir unceasingly, until the beef is completely dry (about thirty to forty minutes). Remove and pack the velvety beef into a jar or any sterilized container. This extraordinary dish is taken at breakfast with Congee, or used for garnishing any plain white dish, or served as an hors-d'oeuvres (*after* a banquet). In the West it can be used with excellent effect as cocktail canapés.

MUTTON AND LAMB

1. Stewed mutton with turnips

600g (1½ lb) leg of mutton
2 slices ginger
400g (1 lb) turnips
1½ teaspoons salt
3 tablespoons sherry

Cut meat into large chunks about 4cm (1½ in) square. Boil in three cups of water for one minute. Pour all the water and impurities away. Place the meat in a double-boiler, together with ginger and turnips cut into similar-sized pieces. Bring to boil and simmer for two hours. Add salt and sherry and simmer for a further half hour.

2. Fried thin-sliced mutton with leeks (or onion)

400g (1 lb) leg of mutton
3 leeks (or onions)
2 tablespoons lard
2 garlic cloves, crushed
1 tablespoon sherry
1 teaspoon salt
1 tablespoon soya sauce

Cut the mutton into very thin slices, about 5cm (2 in) long and 2·5cm (1 in) wide. Cut leeks (or onions) across grain into 1cm (½ in) sections.

Fry the sliced mutton over a very high heat in lard for one minute. Add sliced leeks, garlic, soya sauce, sherry, salt and stir briskly for two minutes. Serve very hot.

3. Fried ribbons of lamb with pea sprouts and spring onions

400g (1 lb) lamb meat
½ tablespoon cornflour
2 spring onions
lard
2 garlic cloves, crushed
1 teaspoon salt
1 cup pea sprouts
1 tablespoon soya sauce
2 tablespoons sherry
pepper to taste

Cut lamb into thin slices and then cut further into strips or ribbons. Mix thoroughly with cornflour. Cut spring onions into 4cm (1½ in) sections. Fry lamb and onions in lard over a high heat with garlic and salt, for two minutes. Add pea sprouts, soya sauce and sherry. Fry and stir briskly for a further two minutes. Add pepper and serve very hot.

Chicken and Poultry

1. Steamed or boiled chicken

1 medium-sized chicken (boiler or roaster)
2–3 slices of ginger
2 onions (sliced)
½ tablespoon salt
4 tablespoons sherry

Clean the chicken thoroughly and place it whole in a double-boiler (or simply a large basin inside a larger saucepan one-third full of water) with ginger, onions and salt. Bring to boil and leave to simmer for two hours. Add sherry and continue to simmer for one more hour. The chicken should be ready to serve when the meat has become tender enough to be pulled to pieces easily by a chopstick or a blunt fork.

This is one of the most common forms in which chicken is eaten in China. It can be served in this manner whether in home cooking or at an ordinary banquet. It is generally served in a large bowl or a deep dish and the chicken is partly immersed in its own soup.

Apart from the ease with which the bird can be cooked in this manner, it is also considered very digestible and nutritious. Hence it is often used by invalids or expectant mothers.

2. White cut chicken

1 young chicken
½ tablespoon salt
2–3 slices of ginger
2 spring onions
soya sauce
sesame oil

Clean the chicken thoroughly. Boil 1·5 litres (three pints) of water in a saucepan. Add salt. Put the chicken, ginger and onions in the pan and boil for five to six minutes. Remove from fire and leave the contents of the pan to cool while tightly covered. When cold cut the chicken into pieces and serve them on a plate with a sprinkling of soya sauce and sesame oil.

3. Deep-fried spring chicken

1 large spring chicken
6 tablespoons soya sauce
6 tablespoons sherry
1 teaspoon sugar
2 spring onions
flour
400g (1 lb) lard
salt and pepper

Clean the chicken thoroughly and chop it into a dozen or sixteen pieces. Place the cut chicken in a bowl and add soya sauce, sherry, sugar, chopped onions. Let the mixture stand for over an hour, and then dip each piece of chicken in flour so that it is well covered. Fry the chicken in hot lard over a brisk heat for about four to five minutes until golden brown. Drain and serve with a sprinkling of salt and pepper.

4. Braised chicken

1 medium-sized chicken
3 tablespoons vegetable oil (peanut or olive)
½ cup soya sauce
2–3 slices of ginger
2 spring onions
1 teaspoon sugar
4 tablespoons sherry

Clean the chicken thoroughly and fry it in oil for four or five minutes in a saucepan. Now add one cup of boiling water, soya sauce, ginger, onions. Bring to boil again quickly, and leave to simmer for one hour with the lid on. Turn the chicken now and then during the process of cooking so that it gets evenly brown. After one hour add sugar and sherry and continue to simmer for another twenty-five minutes. The chicken is served whole in a large bowl, and cut or taken to pieces with a pair of chopsticks on the table.

5. *Diced chicken meat fried with walnuts*

1 cup walnuts
½ large young chicken
4 mushrooms
½ cup vegetable oil (peanut or olive)
½ tablespoon cornflour
1 teaspoon sugar
1 tablespoon sherry
2 tablespoons soya paste
1 teaspoon salt

Shell and dice the walnuts. Dice the chicken, dice the mushrooms (all to about 6mm (¼ in) square). Fry the walnuts first in some of the oil until they are golden brown. Remove from fire, drain them of oil and place them on thick paper towels which will absorb any remaining oil.

Fry the diced chicken meat in 3 tablespoons of oil over a brisk heat. (This is another case of 'crack' frying.) Stir for one minute or so and add cornflour, sugar, sherry, soya paste and salt, having first of all mixed all the ingredients thoroughly.

Now add the diced mushrooms, which have been soaked in water for ten minutes. Fry and stir for a further three minutes. Remove from heat. Serve the contents of the frying-pan immediately with the deep-fried walnuts, on a hot plate.

6. Diced chicken fried with assorted ingredients

   2 chicken breasts
   3 tablespoons sherry
   3 tablespoons soya sauce
   1 tablespoon cornflour
   2 spring onions
   75g (3 oz) almonds
   4 tablespoons peanut (or olive) oil
   4 mushrooms
   75g (3 oz) water chestnuts
   75g (3 oz) bamboo shoots
   salt
   sugar

Dice the chicken meat (into 6mm (¼ in) cubes) and mix with sherry, 2 tablespoons soya sauce and cornflour, and chopped spring onions.

Soak almonds in hot water, remove inner skin. Fry them in oil for one minute or so until slightly brown and crisp, and remove from fire. Keep crisp and hot.

Use the same oil to fry mushrooms, water chestnuts and bamboo shoots (all diced to the same size as the chicken meat). Fry with salt for two minutes and remove from heat.

Meanwhile, fry the seasoned, diced chicken meat separately over a brisk heat for two minutes. Now add the already fried mushrooms, water chestnuts, bamboo shoots, and the remaining soya sauce (1 tablespoon) and sugar and stir briskly for one minute.

Serve the mixture immediately with the fried almonds on a hot dish.

7. Deep-fried paper-wrapped chicken

 2 cut pieces of chicken, about 200g ($\frac{1}{2}$ lb)
 2 spring onions
 2 tablespoons soya sauce
 1 tablespoon sherry
 1 tablespoon chopped ginger
 $\frac{1}{2}$ teaspoon salt
 $\frac{1}{2}$ teaspoon sugar
 pepper
 16–20 pieces of cellophane paper (10cm by 10cm or
   4 in by 4 in)
 2 cups vegetable oil or fat

Remove bones and skin of chicken and cut into 6cm ($1\frac{1}{2}$ in)
long slices. Mix soya sauce, chopped ginger, salt, sugar and
pepper in a bowl and soak the sliced chicken in the mixture
for half an hour. Now place each piece of chicken on a piece
of cellophane paper and wrap securely in parcel fashion
(with tongue tucked in).

Heat the oil and fry the packages in it, in a deep frying-
pan, over a brisk fire, for two and a half minutes. Serve the
packages of chicken without unwrapping, after draining
them of oil. The packages should be unwrapped by the diner
only on the point of eating. The wrapper helps to hold in the
flavour and heat of the pieces of chicken.

8. Smoked chicken

 1 medium-sized chicken
 5 spring onions
 1 tablespoon salt
 $\frac{1}{2}$ cup soya sauce
 3 tablespoons sherry
 3 tablespoons brown sugar
 3 tablespoons fat

Clean and cut the chicken into ten or twelve pieces. Place the cut chicken in a saucepan with two cups of water, three sliced spring onions, salt, and simmer for thirty minutes. Add soya sauce (reserving 2 tablespoons) and sherry, and continue to simmer for another thirty minutes.

Remove the chicken from the pan. Allow a little while for it to stand and dry. Now place the pieces on a grate or a perforated metal plate, which is in turn placed inside an iron pot, at the bottom of which is deposited 3 tablespoons brown sugar. Cover the pot tightly with a lid and place it over a fierce heat. Allow the chicken to be smoked inside the pot for five minutes.

Meanwhile, heat two tablespoons of fat and add to it two chopped spring onions and two tablespoons soya sauce. Fry the smoked pieces of chicken, together with them, for one and a half minutes and serve.

9. Drunken duck

Method A

> 1 medium-sized duck
> 2 tablespoons salt
> 2–3 pieces ginger
> 2 spring onions
> ½ bottle cooking sherry

Clean the duck thoroughly, removing all entrails.

Rub inside and outside with salt, and put chopped ginger and onion inside the bird. Then place it in a pot or heavy saucepan and simmer in sherry for one hour. Turn the bird every now and then in the process of the cooking. (It is advisable to place an asbestos mat under the pan to prevent burning.) When cold remove bird from pot and cut into sixteen pieces. Serve on plate with spring onions cut into 5cm (2 in) sections.

Method B

1 medium-sized duck
2 tablespoons salt
2–3 pieces ginger
4 spring onions
½ bottle cooking sherry

Clean and wash the duck thoroughly. Place it in a heavy saucepan with salt and two pints of water, ginger and onions. Bring to boil and leave to simmer for forty minutes.

Remove from pot and leave to cool and dry. Now cut the duck into sixteen pieces and place them in a basin or casserole. Pour sherry over them. Leave them to stand for five days to a week. A couple of hours before serving remove the duck from the sherry. Serve with spring onions cut into sections and sweet soya paste jam (if not available use blackcurrant jam).

10. West Lake steamed duck
(*West Lake of Hangchow, the famous Lake District of China*).

1 fat duck
2 stalks of spring onions
100g (4 oz) ham
1 tablespoon salt
6 tablespoons lard
1 small cabbage (or 1 large Chinese cabbage if available)

Clean and wash the duck thoroughly. Stuff the inside with onions, ham and salt. Tie or sew up securely. Fry the duck whole for ten to fifteen minutes in lard until slightly brown. Remove from fat and place the duck in a large basin with cabbage. Place the basin in a large saucepan, one-third filled with water. Simmer continuously for three hours.

11. Roast duck

> 1 fat duck
> salt
> ½ bottle cooking sherry
> 1 tablespoon honey
> 3 tablespoons soya sauce

Clean and wash the duck thoroughly. Place it in a large saucepan with salt and sherry. Cook over a low heat for thirty minutes. Remove bird from pan and smear over with soya sauce. Place it in oven and roast for fifteen minutes at moderate heat. Remove from oven. Now smear the bird with honey (mixed with a little water) and soya sauce. Roast for another fifteen minutes at high temperature. Serve with blackcurrant jam, if sweet soya jam is not available.

Vegetables

The Chinese are great vegetable eaters. Like the French, or even more so, we regard many vegetable dishes as savouries in their own right, which are prepared by eminent chefs with great care and pride. Sliced and shredded vegetables, as the reader has already noted, are often cooked with meat and are impregnated with the meat taste, but even when cooked on their own they can be extremely tasty, as usually very little or no water is used in their cooking. When frying such vegetables as spinach, lettuce and watercress, no water is used at all, as the vegetables contain sufficient water to cook in their own juice. By cooking rapidly – generally in a couple of minutes – without using a lid to close the pan (whether a frying-pan or a saucepan is used) the crispness and green colour of the vegetable can be retained, or even enhanced. The lid is used only in cooking hard vegetables. More often hard vegetables are first fried for two or three minutes, and then water or stock is added together with seasonings, and cooking is carried on for a few more minutes. Thus the vegetable is partly fried and partly braised. Alternatively, a vegetable can be boiled for a minute or two before frying, particularly when the frying is intended to be of extremely short duration, perhaps one minute, although over a very brisk heat.

Those westerners who encounter Chinese food for the first time, are usually most impressed by Chinese vegetable dishes, for these have generally all the positive qualities, such as freshness, crispness, excellent colour, savouriness, and seldom tumble into any of the pitfalls which might confound or repel the uninitiated. Chinese vegetarian cooking is a very fascinating and large world of its own, which should provide an extremely interesting subject of research. It has grown and developed for a couple of thousand years, with Buddhism in China, and around the Buddhist temples and monasteries, which took pride in their culinary products. For its refinements and vastness of repertoire there is probably no parallel in the world.

1. Fried spinach

>   *600g (1½ lb) spinach*
>   *2 tablespoons lard (or butter)*
>   *2 tablespoons vegetable oil*
>   *1 teaspoon salt*
>   *1 tablespoon soya sauce*

Wash the spinach thoroughly and drain it carefully of all water. Cut the leaves to about 7·5cm (3 in) lengths if they are very large, otherwise use them as they are. Heat the fat and oil, preferably in a saucepan, until it spreads and covers the whole of the bottom of the pan. Put the spinach into the pan and fry over a brisk heat with salt for two and a half minutes. When the spinach has turned soft add soya sauce and continue to fry for two minutes.

2. Cream savoury cabbage

>   *400g (1 lb) white cabbage (Chinese if available)*
>   *50g (2 oz) dried prawns (if available)*
>   *2 tablespoons lard*
>   *½ teaspoon Ve-tsin (or 1 chicken stock-cube)*
>   *1 teaspoon salt*
>   *½ cup stock*
>   *cornflour*
>   *½ cup milk*
>   *2 tablespoons Vesop (or soya sauce)*
>   *25g (1 oz) minced ham*
>   *1 tablespoon sherry*
>   *pepper*

Choose a white cabbage. Wash and cut it into 5cm (2 in) squares. Cook in boiling water for three to four minutes and drain.

Meanwhile, fry the dried prawns in lard in a saucepan for one and a half minutes. Add the cabbage and fry for two more minutes. Mix Ve-tsin with stock and pour it on to the cabbage. Cook and stir for ten minutes. Mix cornflour with milk and add to the pan. Stir and simmer for ten more minutes. Sprinkle with minced ham and pepper on top. Serve in a deep vegetable dish with gravy.

3. Braised turnips (or carrots)

400g (1 lb) turnips (or carrots)
2 tablespoons lard
½ cup stock or water
2 tablespoons soya sauce
2 tablespoons meat gravy (pork or beef)
1 spring onion
1 teaspoon sugar
pepper

Peel the turnips and cut them into 1cm (½ in) wedges. Heat the lard in the pan and fry the diced turnips in it for four minutes. Pour in stock or water and leave to simmer for five minutes with lid on. Add soya sauce, meat gravy, chopped onion and sugar. Cook for ten more minutes. Add pepper and serve.

This is a useful vegetable dish to have when there is not enough meat to go round, as it gives a slight illusion of meat.

4. Fried lettuce

1 lettuce
2 tablespoons lard (or butter)
2 garlic cloves, crushed
½ teaspoon salt
1 tablespoon Vesop (or soya sauce)

Wash the lettuce thoroughly. Cut into 5cm (2 in) pieces. Melt the fat and put the crushed garlic into the pan and fry for half a minute. Add lettuce, sprinkle with salt and fry for one minute. Add Vesop, fry and turn the lettuce for half a minute and serve.

5. Fried mushrooms and bamboo shoots with minced ham

12 mushrooms
3 tablespoons lard (or butter)
200g (8 oz) bamboo shoots
½ teaspoon salt
1 tablespoon Vesop or soya sauce
1½ tablespoons sherry
1 tablespoon cornflour
25g (1 oz) minced ham

Wash the mushrooms and soak in half a cup of boiling water for one hour before cooking. Reserve the mushroom water. Fry the mushrooms in half the lard for two minutes and remove from pan. Cut the bamboo shoots into slices and fry in remaining lard with salt for five minutes. Now add the cooked mushrooms and pour in the Vesop and sherry and stir for one minute. Add the mushroom water from the cup and simmer for ten minutes. Meanwhile, mix cornflour with a little water and add to the pan. Sprinkle with minced ham and bring to a quick boil.

When serving arrange the mushrooms over the bamboo shoots on a plate and pour the creamy gravy over them.

6. Brown braised cabbage with mushrooms

2 tablespoons lard
50g (2 oz) dried shrimps
1 small cabbage
2 tablespoons soya sauce
1 teaspoon sugar
1 teaspoon Ve-tsin (or 1 chicken stock-cube)
4 mushrooms

Melt lard in a frying-pan. Fry the dried shrimps in it for two minutes. Cut the cabbage into eight pieces, and boil in two cups of water for ten minutes. Drain, reserving half the water and add to the shrimps and fry for three to four minutes. Add half the cabbage water, bring to boil and leave to simmer for ten minutes. Add soya sauce, sugar, Ve-tsin or stock-cube, sliced mushrooms and simmer for a further ten minutes.

7. Sweet and sour cabbage

   1 carrot
   3 tomatoes
   3 tablespoons lard
   2 tablespoons vinegar
   2 tablespoons sugar
   2 tablespoons soya sauce
   1½ tablespoons cornflour (blended in ½ cup of water)
   1 cabbage
   1½ tablespoons sherry

Prepare the sweet and sour sauce by frying shredded carrot and sliced tomatoes in 1½ teaspoons of lard for five minutes. Add vinegar, sugar and soya sauce, and pour into the pan half a cup of water in which the cornflour has been mixed. Bring to boil and stir until the mixture is thick.

Meanwhile, cut the cabbage into 4cm (1½ in) squares. Fry in the remaining lard for four to five minutes over a brisk heat. Add sherry during the last minute of frying. Pour sweet and sour sauce in and leave to cook for two minutes.

This is a useful dish to serve with roast pork and the like, if eaten with European food.

8. Onion sauce

   4 onions
   1½ tablespoons lard
   ½ tablespoon sugar
   2 tablespoons soya sauce

Slice the onion and fry in lard for four minutes. Add sugar and soya sauce and fry for a further two minutes. Stir and turn briskly while frying.

A very convenient and useful sauce to have for serving with steaks and chops.

9. Chinese vegetable salad

1 stick celery
⅓ cabbage
1 carrot
3 garlic cloves
½ cucumber
1 tablespoon Vesop
1 tablespoon soya sauce
2 tablespoons salad oil
2 teaspoons sesame oil
1 tablespoon vinegar
1 lettuce

Dice the celery, shred the cabbage, grate the carrot, crush the garlic, slice the cucumber. Mix these together first with Vesop and soya sauce and then with salad and sesame oils and vinegar and serve on top of lettuce leaves.

This is, of course, a dish invented by the Chinese for the benefit of foreigners, as in China, at least in the past, if you indulged in uncooked vegetables, which had been freshly manured you'd be dead with cholera, typhoid, dysentery and numerous other famous diseases before you could say Chinese mayonnaise.

Perhaps it should be noted here that the Chinese are so confident of their own culinary art that, like the English men of letters who think nothing of incorporating Latin, French or German expressions into their own language, the Chinese chefs have no qualms whatsoever in incorporating western methods into Chinese cooking. Much as English literature is enriched by European influence, so has Chinese cooking been enriched through the ages by Mogul, Moham-medan, Indian, Japanese and European influence. Because of the vast entity of Chinese cooking, everything that is introduced is immediately assimilated. It has no self-consciousness in the use of methods which were not originally Chinese.

Fish and Shell-fish

It seems strange to say that in China, a continental country with little refrigeration, the fish supplied are, as a rule, fresher than those one finds in this country, but half the time they are supplied alive. All better-class restaurants keep their fish, not dead in refrigerators, but alive in large jars (like those one reads of in the stories of Aladdin) or in tanks. With a coastline of over three thousand miles, several of the world's mighty rivers and thousands of streams, tributaries and lakes, naturally all types of fish abound. Added to all these sources of supply, we Chinese also 'farm' fish from artificial pools. Fish farming is certainly as widely practised in China as dairy farming is in this country. So almost every village has a small lake or pool as an inherent part of its scenery or man-made landscape, and all sorts of waste and feeding-stuffs are thrown into it to feed and multiply the fish.

What of the sea fish? These are eaten either very soon after they are caught, or they are preserved, cooked, or salted. While fresh or cooked fish prepared in the Chinese way, using wine and ginger to disguise any of the less agreeable flavours, is very palatable and easily acceptable to the westerner, they have to be warned in so far as Chinese salted fish is concerned. The normal way in which we Chinese treat this type of fish is to fry it until even the bones are crispy (and melting) which makes it a first-class accompaniment to plain rice. But during the process of thorough frying, to the practised nostril a very beautiful and all-pervading aroma permeates the area within fifty yards of the frying, which to the average uninitiated westerner, unless aided by a vast stretch of imagination, is just undeniable stink. Unless your neighbours are more humorously inclined than can be believed, or you fry with the greatest circumspection, such as in an airtight chamber, they are sooner or later bound to obtain a court injunction against you continuing in your repulsive habits, which amounts to being a public nuisance and may affect the respectability and rateable value of the area in which you reside.

So should you ever be invited to a Chinese home and, whilst you wait for the meal to be served, you smell an unmentionable smell, filling the room, don't be alarmed. It is only salted fish being fried. The Chinese attraction to salted fish is much the same as an Englishman's inclination to ripe cheese. Indeed the two things belong to the same category.

In the recipes given below you will, however, be treading on perfectly safe ground.

1. Steamed fish (whole)

> 1 fish (perch, bass, carp, etc.)
> 1 teaspoon salt
> 1 tablespoon lard
> 2 tablespoons soya sauce
> 1 tablespoon sherry
> ½ teaspoon sugar
> 4 slices ginger
> 6 mushrooms
> 2 slices ham
> 2 spring onions

Clean and scale the fish, and rub both inside and out with salt. Place it in a heatproof long dish or basin. Add soya sauce, sherry, sugar and shredded ginger. Arrange the mushrooms, ham and onions cut in 5cm (2 in) lengths nicely on top. Place the dish in a steamer and steam in a good heat for twenty minutes.

2. Steamed fish in slices

> *400g (1 lb) fish (plaice, sole, halibut, turbot, etc.)*
> *1 teaspoon salt*
> *spring onions*
> *1 tablespoon soya sauce*
> *2 tablespoons lard*
> *½ teaspoon sugar*
> *2 slices ginger*
> *1 tablespoon vinegar*
> *1½ tablespoons sherry*
> *2 slices ham*
> *6 mushrooms*
> *pepper*

Wash and cut the fish into 5cm (2 in) long slices. Rub with salt and place in a heatproof dish or basin with white side up.

Meanwhile, mix the various ingredients together – chopped spring onions, soya sauce, sugar, ginger, vinegar, sherry – pour them over the sliced fish. Place some bits of sliced ham and sliced mushrooms over each piece of fish. Put the dish or basin in a steamer and steam for twenty minutes. Season with some pepper and serve.

3. Deep-fried fish (in pieces)

> *400g (1 lb) fish (cod, halibut, haddock)*
> *1 teaspoon salt*
> *1½ tablespoons flour*
> *1 egg*
> *400g (1 lb) lard*
> *salt and pepper*

Clean fish and cut into 2·5cm (1 in) wide by 5cm (2 in) long pieces. Rub them with salt. Mix flour with beaten egg and add two spoonfuls of water. Coat the fish with this thin flour-egg paste.

Heat and bring the lard to boil. Drop the pieces of fish into it, a few at a time. Remove and drain when slightly brown. Serve on a hot plate with salt and pepper.

Small fish like sprats and herring can be cooked in this manner whole. They should be fried until quite brown, so that the head and tails become crisp.

4. Sliced fish in sweet and sour sauce

400g (1 lb) fish (sole, plaice, turbot, halibut, etc.)
400g (1 lb) lard
2–3 tomatoes
50g (2 oz) pickles
1 tablespoon cornflour
2 tablespoons vinegar
1½ tablespoons sugar
2 tablespoons soya sauce
6 tablespoons stock (bone)

Prepare sweet and sour sauce as in fried sweet and sour spare ribs or sweet and sour cabbage (pages 207 and 227).

Cut fish into 5cm (2 in) long and 4cm (1½ in) wide slices. Rub with salt. Coat the pieces of fish with a mixture of flour and water. Fry until slightly brown. Remove from pan and drain off oil. Place the pieces on a hot plate. Heat the sweet and sour sauce until boiling, and pour it over the sliced fish.

5. Braised eel

400g (1 lb) eel
1·25kg (3 lb) lard
2 spring onions
2 tablespoons sherry
2 tablespoons soya sauce
2 teaspoons sugar
3 garlic cloves
½ teaspoon salt
1 teaspoon cornflour
pepper to taste

Clean and cut the eel into 5cm (2 in) sections. Heat lard and fry the eel in it with chopped onion for five minutes. Add sherry, soya sauce, sugar, garlic, salt and finally a cup of water. Leave to simmer for fifteen to twenty minutes. Stir in cornflour mixed with water. Add pepper, bring to boil and serve.

6. Braised fish

>*800g (2 lb) fish (carp, bream, perch, halibut, haddock, cod)*
>*1 teaspoon salt*
>*4 tablespoons lard*
>*3 tablespoons soya sauce*
>*3–4 slices ginger*
>*2 spring onions*
>*25g (1 oz) ham*
>*2 teaspoons sugar*
>*2 tablespoons sherry*

Scale the fish (if whole) and wash it carefully. Stand for a while to dry, and rub it over with salt. Fry it for about five minutes in lard and baste it continually while frying. Now pour the soya sauce evenly over the fish. Add ginger, chopped spring onion, ham, and braise for a few minutes until the seasonings have penetrated the fish.

Add ½ cup of water. Bring contents to boil again. Add sugar and sherry. Leave to simmer for fifteen minutes.

Cooked in this manner, not only will the frying and stewing have eliminated all the fishy smell, but the gravy of the fish is extremely tasty.

7. Prawns fried in shells

>*400g (1 lb) prawns*
>*4 tablespoons lard*
>*2 spring onions*
>*2 garlic cloves, crushed*

2 tablespoons soya sauce
2 tablespoons sherry
1 teaspoon vinegar
1 teaspoon sugar
½ teaspoon salt

Trim the whiskers and tails of the prawns with a pair of scissors. Wash in water and drain thoroughly

Heat the lard in a frying-pan. Fry the prawns in it for about two minutes over a medium heat. Turn the heat higher; add all the ingredients (chopped onion and garlic) at once, as well as all the seasonings. Fry for a further two and a half minutes and serve immediately. (This is a favourite dish in Peking during the summer, when the prawns attain almost the size of small lobsters.)

8. *Fried shelled prawns with pea sprouts*

400g (1 lb) prawns
½ teaspoon salt
3 tablespoons lard
150g (6 oz) pea sprouts
½ teaspoon sugar
1½ tablespoons soya sauce
2½ tablespoons sherry
pepper

Shell the prawns, wash and drain thoroughly. Season the prawns in salt for one hour before cooking.

Heat the lard in the frying-pan, and fry the prawns in it for two minutes with salt. Add the pea sprouts and fry for one minute. Now add the other seasonings – sugar, salt, soya sauce, sherry – and fry for a further two minutes, tossing and stirring continually as you fry. Serve with a little pepper.

9. Deep-fried lobster

   800g (2 lb) fresh lobster
   1 egg
   2 tablespoons cornflour
   1 teaspoon salt
   6 tablespoons lard
   pepper

Clean and boil the lobsters for three minutes. Remove the meat from the shells. Cut the lobster meat into 1cm ($\frac{1}{2}$ in) pieces. Dip them in batter made from beaten egg, cornflour, 1 tablespoon of water and salt.

Heat the lard to boiling and drop the lobsters into it to fry for three minutes, or until they are golden brown. Add pepper and serve.

10. Braised lobster with egg and pork

   3 lobsters
   lard
   $\frac{1}{2}$ teaspoon salt
   100g (4 oz) lean pork, shredded
   2 eggs
   1 teaspoon chopped ginger
   1 spring onion
   1 tablespoon soya sauce
   1 teaspoon sugar
   2 tablespoons sherry
   $\frac{1}{2}$ tablespoon cornflour

Clean and cut the lobsters lengthwise and then into 4cm (1$\frac{1}{2}$ in) sections with shells on. Fry in lard and salt over a high fire for two minutes. Add shredded pork and fry a further two minutes.

Beat the eggs and mix thoroughly with chopped ginger, onion, soya sauce, sugar, sherry, cornflour and 4 tablespoons of water. Pour the mixture in a very thin stream over the lobster in the pan, stir and toss over high heat for three more minutes.

11. Crab meat in steamed eggs

1 large crab
2 eggs
1 teaspoon salt
1 tablespoon soya sauce
2 spring onions
2 tablespoons sherry
1 tablespoon lard

Wash and steam the crab for fifteen minutes. Remove the meat from the shell.

Beat the eggs, mix them with salt, soya sauce, chopped onion. Add crab meat, sherry and half a cup of water. Mix thoroughly. Add lard. Steam for twenty minutes. The dish is cooked when it attains the semi-solid form of a custard. When serving the basin or dish used is brought in steaming and placed on the dining-table itself. This dish goes well with plain rice and braised pork and is served with soya sauce sprinkled over the top.

12. Fried abalone (or awabi) with oyster sauce

1 tin abalone
1 tablespoon lard
4 tablespoons oyster sauce
1 tablespoon soya sauce
½ tablespoon corn starch
1 slice ham (chopped)

Remove the abalone from the tin, but keep the abalone water in a cup. Cut the abalone into slices 2·5cm (1 in) square and about 6mm (¼ in) thick. Heat lard in a pan and fry the abalone in it for half a minute. Add oyster sauce and soya sauce. Stir for half a minute. Mix corn starch in abalone

water and pour it into the pan. Cook for not more than one
and a half minutes over a high fire. Garnish with chopped
ham and serve.

13. Prawn fu yung (egg-white)

> 400g (1 lb) prawns (shelled)
> 6 eggs
> 3 slices ginger
> 1 tablespoon sherry
> 1 teaspoon soya sauce
> 4 tablespoons lard
> ½ teaspoon salt
> pepper

Shell and wash the prawns. Separate the egg-white from the
yolk. Beat up the egg-white and mix the prawns in with it.
Add the seasoning and mix thoroughly.

Heat the lard in the pan until boiling. Pour the prawn
mixture into the pan, stir and toss over a brisk heat for three
to four minutes. Add pepper and serve on a hot plate.

14. Drunken shrimps

> 400g (1 lb) fresh shrimps
> 2 teaspoons salt
> 2 tablespoons soya sauce
> 3 teaspoons chopped ginger
> ½ cup sherry
> 1 tablespoon vinegar

Choose the freshest shrimps (if possible alive). Trim off tails
and whiskers. Wash carefully. Place the shrimps in a deep
basin. Sprinkle with salt, soya sauce and ginger. Mix well.

An hour later add sherry and vinegar. Stand for a further
hour, drain and serve.

Eggs

In China eggs are more often used as ingredients in conjunction with other foods rather than independently, but there are a number of useful recipes:

1. Egg omelette with assorted ingredients

   6 eggs
   1 teaspoon salt
   100g (4 oz) shredded pork meat (chicken, crab or shrimps
      can also be used)
   2 spring onions
   4 tablespoons oil (or lard)
   100g (4 oz) pea sprouts
   1 tablespoon sherry
   2 tablespoons soya sauce

Beat up the eggs with salt and put them aside.

Cut pork into shreds and spring onions into 1cm ($\frac{1}{2}$ in) sections. Fry them in 1 tablespoon hot fat for two and a half minutes, then add pea sprouts, sherry, soya sauce, and fry for a further one and a half minutes. Remove from pan, but keep hot.

Heat the remaining fat until it has spread completely over the bottom of the pan. Pour in the beaten eggs. Do not stir but lift the bottom of the egg occasionally to see that it does not stick. After about a minute, before the whole of the egg has hardened, add all the cooked shredded meat, spring onion, pea sprouts. After about thirty seconds fold the edges of the omelette over each other with the aid of a fish slice. Serve on a warm plate.

2. Steamed eggs and minced meat

3 eggs
100g (4 oz) minced pork
1 spring onion (chopped)
1 teaspoon salt
1 teaspoon lard
1 cup stock or milk
1 teaspoon soya sauce
25g (1 oz) minced ham

Beat the eggs up with minced pork, chopped onions, and salt. Place then in a deep heatproof bowl or basin with lard and a cup of stock (bone) or milk. Mix well. Place the basin in a steamer or a large boiler, and steam for twenty minutes with lid on. Remove basin from steamer, pour the soya sauce over the now solidified custard-like mixture. Garnish with minced ham and serve on the table in the basin.

3. Scrambled eggs with shrimps (or prawns)

6 eggs
1 teaspoon salt
pepper to taste
3 tablespoons sherry
200g (8 oz) shrimps (or prawns)
2 spring onions (chopped)
2 mushrooms
3 tablespoons lard

Beat the eggs. Add salt, pepper, sherry and mix well.
Shell the shrimps, clean well. Fry them with chopped onion and sliced mushrooms in hot fat for one minute. Pour in the egg mixture. Stir and continue to fry and scramble for two to three minutes. This can be a highly appetizing and aromatic dish.

4. Braised eggs in pork gravy

400g (1 lb) pork
½ cup soya sauce
1 teaspoon salt
2 tablespoons sherry
1 teaspoon sugar
6 eggs

Braise the pork in the usual way by cutting into 2·5cm (1 in) squares, then simmer in a heavy pot or pan for one and a half hours with soya sauce, salt, sherry, sugar and half a cup of water, over a low heat.

Boil the eggs for six to seven minutes and cool afterwards under cold tap-water. Now shell the eggs and place them carefully in the pan with the braised pork. See that each egg is covered by the gravy. Resume simmering for a further thirty minutes.

Eggs braised in this manner can either be served whole, with braised pork or, as they are more often than not, served cold on their own, after they have been cut into quarters or sixes when they are cold, and arranged on a dish with the yolk side turned upwards – a favourite breakfast or late supper dish. They are often sold from market-stalls, as well as sampan-stalls, which ply along the river, selling both to the floating population and travellers who use the river as a highway.

5. Ham and egg dumplings

400g (1 lb) ham
4 eggs
3 slices of bread
1 teaspoon flour
400g (1 lb) fat

Chop or mince the ham. Beat the eggs thoroughly. Mix the eggs and ham well together. Now rub the bread into crumbs and add them together with the flour to the egg and ham mixture to make a thick paste. Make the paste into balls about the size of pigeons' eggs. Heat the oil until boiling, and fry the ham-egg balls in it for four to five minutes, or until golden brown. Serve on a hot plate.

6. Egg-wrapped dumplings

> 1 egg
> 1 teaspoon salt
> 200g (8 oz) pork
> 2 spring onions
> 1 teaspoon chopped ginger
> 2 tablespoons soya sauce
> lard
> 1 teaspoon sugar

Beat up the egg with salt. Mince the pork and mix with chopped onion and ginger and half the soya sauce. Heat 2 tablespoons lard in the pan. When it has all melted and spread over the pan place 1 tablespoon of beaten egg in the centre of the pan. Immediately follow by putting 1 teaspoon of minced pork mixture in the centre of the egg. Fold over and press down the edges. Remove from pan and place it on a plate. Repeat the process until all the materials have been used up. When all the dumplings have been fried, add half a cup of stock to the pan together with sugar and remaining soya sauce. Put back all the fried dumplings into the pan. Cover, and cook for five minutes and serve.

7. Egg threads
(for garnishing)

> 3 eggs
> 3 tablespoons peanut oil

Beat the eggs lightly. Heat the peanut oil in a frying-pan, then spread egg thinly over. Brown both sides of the egg. Cut the thin pancake into narrow strips. Repeat the process until all the eggs are used up. Keep the egg strips for use as garnish over various dishes, such as fried noodles and so on.

Specialities

Among the various Chinese culinary specialities the best-known ones in the West are, of course, Shark's Fin and Bird's Nest Soups. Since we have already dealt with Birds' Nest Soup (under Soups), I think I shall introduce the reader to two other dishes which are more interesting and probably more satisfying. Having spent the last three hours involved in cooking and consuming the first of the following recipes, I can attest to the fact, from first-hand and more recent experience, that it is extremely filling!

1. 'The Boiling Fire Pot'

The literal translation of the Chinese name for this dish is 'Fire Pot', but perhaps a more vivid and descriptive translation of what actually takes place on the table when this dish is being prepared and consumed would be 'the Boiling Fire Pot'.

The main feature of this recipe is that the cooking of the food and eating of this dish proceed in a piecemeal manner, alternately and simultaneously, all on the dining-table. In other words, you eat as you cook, over a period of two to three hours. All the foods provided are prepared, but raw, and arranged in plates all around a round table (in the West a plastic top is necessary if the table is not to become stained). The essential equipment is a large round brass pot with a funnel running up the centre to about 45cm (18 in) in height. At the bottom of this funnel and under the pot is an arrangement either for firing with charcoal, or burning with alcohol; thus sufficient heat can be generated to keep the pot in constant boil. The pot is generally lit and heated in the kitchen and is brought into the dining-room, and placed at the centre of the dining-table with its chimney sprouting fire – a very warming sight during the winter months. Around the 'Boiling Fire Pot' are arranged the following dishes and ingredients for a party of, say, six to eight people.

(1) 2 plates of thinly-sliced chicken meat.

(2) 3 or 4 plates of thinly sliced pork, lamb or beef (1·25kg or 3 lb).

(3) 2 plates of thinly sliced fish (sole, plaice, turbot, halibut, etc.).

(4) 100g (4 oz) of Chinese pea-starch vermicelli, which have been previously soaked in hot water for half an hour to soften.

(5) 6 spring onions, chopped into 2·5cm (1 in) sections.

(6) 200g (8 oz) spinach (carefully cleaned and washed).

(7) 2 plates of thinly sliced liver (400g or 1 lb).

(8) 1 pair of kidneys cleaned and sliced and placed on a plate.

(9) 1 large panful of hot chicken broth, or bone stock, for adding to the pot in the course of the dinner.

(10) 200g (8 oz) shredded cabbage.

The diner can use either a pair of chopsticks or simply a long fork and spoon. He picks up whatever food from one of the numerous plates he chooses – fish, flesh, fowl or vegetable, and dips it in that section of the boiling pot which is immediately in front of him, to cook. Since all the food and ingredients are very thinly sliced or shredded, and a big fire is kept up all the time, the food is cooked in a matter of seconds. The diner thereupon quickly removes the food from the pot and dips it equally quickly in his own bowl, containing the mixed sauces (soya sauce, sesame oil, some chopped ginger or garlic, fermented soya bean paste, mixed to his own liking) before conveying it to his mouth. Rice is not generally served with the 'Boiling Fire Pot'. The usual accompanying food is the Chinese toasted cake, a bun-like

baked cake with sesame seeds studded on top, and less yeast
and more salt used in the dough. Short of this, the ordinary
Chinese steamed dumpling can also be used (in Europe one
can just use bread or toasted buns).

As the meal progresses new platefuls of sliced meat and
ingredients, as well as pans full of boiling stock are brought
in from the kitchen to replenish any food which may have
been finished. It is quite usual for such a meal to last two
and a half to three hours, as so many different types of
things can be cooked and eaten alternately at a sitting. The
finale comes when the majority of the diners feel that they
have had enough, whereupon the soup in the pot, which by
now is extremely tasty, owing to the fact that so much has
been cooked in it, is conveyed to your sauce bowl in large
spoonfuls, until you feel a balance is struck between the
soup and the remaining sauce. You then lift the bowl to your
mouth and drink it in a few big gulps. This last exertion
produces that culminating sweat which is the height of
gastronomic well-being: all this is, of course, a great help
in warming the cockles of one's heart.

Both the 'Boiling Fire Pot' and the 'Brazier Grilled
Lamb' are great favourites as winter pastimes in Peking.
There are several famous restaurants where nothing else is
served.

2. Brazier grilled sliced lamb

3·5kg (9 lb) leg of lamb (for six persons)
6 eggs
6 garlic cloves, crushed (1 for each person)
6 spring onions, chopped
6 tablespoons soya sauce
6 tablespoons fermented soya sauce
6 tablespoons sweet soya bean jam
3 tablespoons chilli sauce
3 teaspoons sesame oil

For this dish a large open charcoal stove or brazier is required, equipped with a well-meshed iron grate over the top. The stove is brought in and placed on the centre of the table after the charcoal has been fanned to blazing.

The lamb is sliced to paper-thin slices, as in the previous recipe, and arranged in plates around the charcoal burner. There should be at least three plates of meat to each person, for meat is more easily consumed when roasted than boiled. In front of each diner, as in the previous recipe, there should be at least two bowls: one containing a beaten egg and the other a mixture of the various sauces (if sweet soya jam and fermented soya paste are unavailable, blackcurrant jam and peanut butter can be used as substitutes) together with chopped onion and garlic.

Each diner uses a pair of long bamboo chopsticks (bamboo because it does not matter so much when damaged by burning). He picks up one or two pieces of sliced lamb meat and places it on the grate over the charcoal brazier. As the heat is so intense, the meat is cooked or roasted in a matter of seconds. Thereupon he removes the meat from the grate with his chopsticks and dips it quickly first into the beaten egg (partly to take on an interesting coating and partly to cool), and then immediately into the mixed sauces before conveying it to the watering mouth. As this process of grilling and eating is both fascinating and repetitive, and generates an appetite, often independent of whether the person is hungry or not, it is difficult to keep track of how much one has eaten. It is, therefore, quite normal for a gentleman to consume say a dozen dishes of lamb at a sitting, so long as he doesn't take too much of the accompanying bread, which in this case, as in the previous recipe, is the Chinese toasted cake (in the West, ordinary toast or toasted French rolls can be served as a substitute).

3. Sharks' fins with crab meat

300g (12 oz) skinless sharks' fins
chicken broth
2 large crabs
3 tablespoons lard
2 eggs
1 teaspoon salt

Prepare the fins by soaking overnight in water, then steaming for two hours in a bowl of chicken broth which has been placed in a large pan of water, to simmer with the lid on, so that the fins, originally as hard as raw hide, become completely soft.

Steam the crabs for thirty minutes. Scrape out all the meat from the shell and claws. Heat the lard in a pan until boiling. Pour in crab meat mixed with the two beaten eggs. Add salt. Fry and stir for one minute.

Now add the softened sharks' fins and fry for a further two minutes, with two or three spoonfuls of chicken broth.

4. Sharks' fin with pork and shrimps

½ cabbage
6 mushrooms
4 slices bamboo shoots
salt
100g (4 oz) shrimps
200g (8 oz) pork
1·5kg (4 lb) lard
6 tablespoons sherry
6 tablespoons soya sauce
1 cup brown pork gravy
chicken broth
300g (12 oz) skinless fins
2 tablespoons cornflour
1 teaspoon sugar

Cut the cabbage into 4cm ($1\frac{1}{2}$ in) square pieces. Fry together with mushrooms for three minutes. Remove from heat.

Fry the bamboo shoots, which have been cut into 4mm ($\frac{1}{6}$ in) thick slices across the grain, for three minutes with a little salt. Remove from pan.

Shell the shrimps and cut the pork into ribbons. Cook shrimps by boiling in a cupful of water with a little salt for two minutes. Drain. Fry them with pork in lard for four minutes over fierce heat. Add sherry, soya sauce and cut cabbage. Stir for five minutes and transfer the contents of the frying-pan to a saucepan. Add one cup of brown pork gravy, and one cup of chicken broth. Simmer for ten minutes.

Now add the softened fins and continue to boil for five minutes. Thicken with half a cupful of a mixture of water, cornflour and sugar. When the saucepan boils again pour the contents into a deep dish. Garnish by placing bamboo shoots and shrimps on top of the fins.

Both of the sharks' fin dishes are regarded as delicacies and are served only at banquets.

5. Fried frogs with chestnuts

 3 fat frogs
 150g (6 oz) chestnuts
 2 tablespoons lard
 $\frac{1}{2}$ teaspoon salt
 6 mushrooms
 1 spring onion
 1 teaspoon chopped ginger
 2 teaspoons soya sauce
 3 teaspoons sherry

Skin the frogs and chop each one into six to eight pieces. Soak the chestnuts in hot water for half an hour. Skin and dry.

Fry the frogs in lard with chestnuts and salt for two minutes over a high heat. Add mushrooms and chopped onion, and all the remaining ingredients, and fry for a further three minutes, stirring continually over a high heat.

6. Velveteen of pork

800g (2lb) lean pork
1 cup chicken broth
3 tablespoons peanut oil
2 tablespoons sherry
4 tablespoons soya sauce
1 tablespoon fermented soya paste
½ tablespoon sugar
½ teaspoon salt

Cut the pork into 1cm (½ in) squares. Boil in chicken broth for one and a half hours over a very low heat, until thoroughly cooked. Remove from pan and drain, if any broth is left at all. Now place the pork in a heavy pot or deep frying-pan, in which the peanut oil has been heated to boiling. Add all the remaining ingredients, and continue the frying over a fierce heat for five minutes, stirring vigorously all the time. Now lower the fire and insert an asbestos mat under the pan, and carry on with the frying, but continue to stir all the time, to prevent any sticking to the bottom of the pan. Continue until the colour of the meat has become rich brown, and the meat itself has become completely dried (this should take about forty minutes). In order to complete the process of dehydration and disintegration of the meat fibre, continue over a minimum fire for fifteen more minutes. When ready the pork should be in a velvety state, dark reddish brown in colour and almost melts on introduction to the mouth.

Velveteen of Pork is more popular than Velveteen of Beef, as it is very much smoother and more 'melting'. It can be fried with almost any vegetable (such as shredded cabbage, pea sprouts, etc.) simply by adding 1 tablespoon pork velveteen one and a half minutes before serving and mixing vigorously. It lends a glorious flavour to the vegetables.

Since it can be preserved simply by keeping it in a jar, it is extremely useful to any housewife, quite apart from the fact that it is a great favourite in China at breakfast and for late supper. In the West, spread on a small piece of buttered toast it makes a delectable appetizer at any party.

Snacks and Desserts

We Chinese are mainly savoury eaters as compared with Europeans, whose inclination to sweets and desserts and comparative obliviousness to the subtle blendings of savoury flavours often baffles us. Although we consume quite a large range of snacks, mostly savouries, in sweets and desserts, our numbers of recipes are comparatively limited as measured against the western counterparts. The following are a few of the most popular snacks and desserts consumed in China.

1. Paotze or stuffed steamed bun

½ cake of yeast
3 cups flour
200g (8 oz) minced pork
1 spring onion
1½ tablespoons soya sauce
1 teaspoon salt
1 teaspoon sugar
½ tablespoon sesame oil (or salad oil)

(a) Savoury Paotze.
Prepare the dough by first of all dissolving half a cake of yeast in one cup of warm water. This water is mixed with the flour to knead into a dough, which is put into a basin and placed in a comparatively warm place to give it time for the dough to rise. After about three to four hours the dough will have risen about three to four times its original size. Now take the dough out and, using a quantity of flour as dusting powder, work each portion (divide dough first into a dozen portions) by rolling into flat round shapes (about 6mm (¼ in) thick and 7·5cm (3 in) diameter).

Meanwhile, mix the minced pork with chopped onion and seasonings and oil and work it into a stuffing. Take a piece of flat round dough in your left hand and place about one to two tablespoons of this stuffing in the centre of the dough. With your right fingers turn up the sides of the dough to wrap around the stuffing until only a small opening is left at the top. This opening is finally closed by pinching the edges together.

Now place all these uncooked buns or dumplings in a hot steamer and steam for fifteen to twenty minutes. These stuffed steamed buns are served at tea-time in China.

(*b*) Sweet Paotze.

The sweet stuffing for, say, twelve pieces of sweet Paotze should consist of $\frac{1}{2}$ cup of almonds, $\frac{1}{2}$ cup of walnuts, $\frac{1}{2}$ cup of sesame seeds, 4 tablespoons sugar, 2 tablespoons honey, 1 tablespoon lard. Grind the nuts and mix thoroughly with the remainder of the ingredients. Use this as the stuffing and proceed exactly as for the previous recipe.

(*c*) Paotze stuffed with crab meat.

Use the meat of two large crabs (instead of pork) which have previously been cooked by steaming. Apart from the other ingredients from which the stuffing is made add $\frac{1}{2}$ teaspoon ground ginger and two extra spring onions.

(*d*) Vegetarian Paotze.

Spinach and leeks are frequently used as stuffings. About 600g (1$\frac{1}{2}$ lb) of vegetables would be required. The vegetables are first minced and mixed with the seasonings. The addition of one piece of chopped pickled vegetable and an extra 1 teaspoon of sesame oil would strengthen the flavour.

It is often interesting or amusing to prepare vegetarian, meat-stuffed, crab-stuffed and sweet-stuffed Paotze at the same time, and steam them all together in the same steamer, but give each type a marking outside to distinguish it from the others.

2. *Chiaotze, or stuffed dumplings*

This is another of our preparations which is capable of a large variety of stuffings, but in this case the stuffings are mainly of meat.

The main difference between this recipe and the previous one is that the wrapping dough is made into a thin skin without the addition of yeast. This dough is prepared by mixing two cups of flour with ½ teaspoon of salt, and sufficient water to make into a very light dough. This is kneaded and rolled into a long strip about 2·5cm (1 in) in diameter. Cut away about 2·5cm (1 in) of it at a time to roll and press into round flat skin-thick cakes, circular in shape and 7·5cm (3 in) in diameter.

In preparing the stuffing for wrapping in the dough, use the same ingredients as in the previous recipe, but cabbage and bamboo shoots are sometimes added into the mixture. Only about ½ tablespoon of stuffing mixtures are used at a time to be wrapped in each piece of circular skin-like dough. The dough is wrapped around the stuffing in a half-moon shape and the edges are pinched or pressed together. Generally several dozen of these dumplings are made at a time. They can be placed in a steamer to steam for ten minutes or they can be boiled for the same length of time. When served, they are generally dipped in vinegar and soya sauce before eating.

3. *Spring rolls*

Spring rolls are so called because they are eaten in the spring, or soon after the Old Chinese New Year, which generally falls in February. The main feature of the spring roll is that it is a stuffed roll (meat and chopped vegetable stuffing wrapped in envelope fashion) fried in deep fat. The same stuffing as in the previous recipe can be used, but half the contents as a rule consist of pea sprouts. The dough skin for wrapping the stuffing is made as follows and requires considerable skill:

Make a mixture of 100g (4 oz) flour with one cup of water. Heat a small frying-pan over a low even heat. Grease the pan evenly with fat. Wipe it over with a grease-soaked cloth. Now pour a tablespoonful of the thin dough mixture in the centre of the pan. Let it run evenly over the flat bottom of the pan. Leave it there until quite dry. Turn it over a plate and peel it off. Repeat until you have a sufficient number of skins for your purpose.

In making the spring rolls place about 2 tablespoons of the stuffing across the centre of the skin, about 6cm (2½ in) long. Fold up both ends of the dough first and then the sides. Finally close the edges with a little water. When you have made a sufficient number of rolls fry them in deep fat for about four minutes, immediately before serving. It is, as a rule, necessary to fry the stuffing for up to two to three minutes before rolling it in the dough to ensure that it will be quite cooked after the final frying, which should render the outside of the roll quite crispy. This is an easily acceptable dish to those people of these islands who are fond of deep-fried food, such as fish and chips, etc.

4. Fried sweet potato

½ cup syrup
400g (1 lb) sweet potato
4 tablespoons peanut oil

Steam the syrup in a bowl in a large panful of water for ten to twelve minutes. Cut the potato, which is often 15cm (6 in) long by 7·5–10cm (3–4 in) in diameter, into thin slices 12mm (½ in) wide by 5–7·5cm (2–3 in) long. Fry them in oil for three to four minutes until they are beautifully golden brown. Remove from heat and arrange them on a hot plate. Pour the hot syrup over them and serve.

5. Almond tea

> 2 cups blanched almonds
> 4 tablespoons rice
> 2 tablespoons sugar
> pinch of salt

Grind the almond and rice in a mortar until they have become a very fine powder. Place this in a basin and add five cups of water. Stir and leave to stand for one and a half hours. Strain through a cheese-cloth. Add a cupful of milk. Simmer in a double boiler for two hours, stirring now and then. Now add sugar, and a pinch of salt. Bring to boil once more before serving.

Almond tea can also be served in the form of a jelly, by dissolving in it 1 tablespoon of gelatine, and placing the mixture in a refrigerator for a couple of hours.

Useful Names and Addresses

LONDON AREA
WEST END
Loon Moon Supermarket Ltd
  9A Gerrard Street
  London W1V 7LJ

Loon Fung Chinese
  Supermarket
  39 Gerard Street
  London W.1

Great Wall Supermarket
  31–37 Wardour Street
  London W.1

Chung Ying Supermarket
  6 Lisle Street
  London W.C.2

See Woo Hong
  19 Lisle Street
  London W.C.2

Walton Cheong Leen Ltd
  4–10 Tower Street
  Cambridge Circus
  London WC2H 9NR

GREATER LONDON
Lees Emporium
  2F Dyne Road
  Off Kilburn High Road
  London N.W.6

Hoo Hing Catering Supplies
  412 Green Street
  Upton Park
  London E.13

Eastyle Ltd
  11–12 Romford Shopping
  Hall
  Market Place
  Romford
  Essex

Good Companions Chinese
  Supermarket
  230 High Street
  Croydon
  Surrey

Patel Grocers
  33 Fife Road
  Kingston upon Thames
  Surrey

Asian Food Centre
  175–177 Staines Road
  Hounslow
  Middlesex

Bargain Grocers
  61 The Broadway Market
  Tooting Broadway
  Tooting S.W.17

OUTSIDE LONDON

Quality Food Products
(Aberdeen) Ltd
Craigshaw Place
West Tullos Industrial Estate
Aberdeen

Wing Yip Supermarket
96 Coventry Street
Birmingham 5

Chung Nam Birmingham Ltd
44–46 Bromsgrove Street
Birmingham

The Delicatessen
162 Old Christchurch Road
Bournemouth
Dorset BH1 1NU

Taj Mahal Stores
216 Old Christchurch Road
Bournemouth
Dorset

Quality Foods
794–796 Leeds Road
Bradford
Yorks

Wah Hing Mini Market
148 Ashley Road
Montpelier
Bristol

Far East Emporium
62–64 Tudor Road
Cardiff

Golden Crown Oriental
Supplies
37 Crouch St
Colchester
Essex

Alma Coventry Ltd
89 Lower Precinct
Coventry

John Mann Supermarket
45 High Street
Dover
Kent

Edinburgh Chinese Company
26 Dublin Street
Edinburgh EH3 6NN

Chung Ying Supermarket
63 Cambridge Street
Glasgow C3

Chong Kee
2–6 Manthorpe Road
Grantham
Lincs

Sui Hing Supermarket
22–23 Story Street
Hull
Humberside

Hong Kong Stores
29 Lady Lane
Leeds 2

Sabat Bros
26–28 Cork Street
Leicester 4E5 5AN

Chung Wah Trading
31–32 Great George Square
Liverpool L1

Woo Sang & Company
19–21 George Street
Manchester 1ML 4HW

Wing Hing Loon Supermarket
46 Faulkner Street
Manchester M1

Wing Yip Supermarket
45 Faulkner Street
Manchester 1M1 4EE

Wing Hing Loon Supermarket
87–89 Percy Street
Newcastle Upon Tyne 1

Gill Bros & Company Ltd
(Trading as – Continental
Food Supply)
166 Kettering Road
Northampton

Wah Yam Company
77 Mansfield Road
Nottingham

Palms Delicatessen
The Market
Oxford

Continental Fruiterers
148 Cornwall Street
Plymouth
Devon P11 1RQ

Wah Lung Supermarket
95 Mayflower Street
Plymouth
Devon

Eastern Stores
214 Kingston Road
Portsmouth

Kung Heng Co.
169 London Road
Sheffield

Yau Food Store
62 Park Road
Freemantle
Southampton

Taj Mahal
69 Derby Street
Southampton

Index

General Index

IMPROVE YOUR COOKING

Pamela Westland
The Everyday Gourmet   75p ☐

Beryl Wood
Let's Preserve It   95p ☐

Bee Nilson
Making Ice-Cream and Cold Sweets   95p ☐
Deep Freeze Cooking   75p ☐
Fondue, Flambé and Side Table Cooking   95p ☐
Bee Nilson's Kitchen Handbook   95p ☐
Bee's Blender Book   75p ☐

Franny Singer
The Slow Crock Cook Book   £1.25 ☐

L D Michaels
The Complete Book of Pressure Cooking   £1.00 ☐

COOKERY HANDBOOKS

Franny Singer
The Slow Crock Cook Book   £1.25 ▣

L D Michaels
The Complete Book of Pressure Cooking   £1.00 ☐

Beryl Wood
Let's Preserve It   95p ☐

Ursula Gruniger
Cooking with Fruit   50p ☐

Bee Nilson
Bee Nilson's Kitchen Handbook   95p ☐
Deep Freeze Cooking   75p ☐

Kenneth Lo
Cooking the Chinese Way   85p ☐

All these books are available at your local bookshop or newsagent, or can be ordered direct from the publisher. Just tick the titles you want and fill in the form below.

Name ....

Address ....

....

Write to Mayflower Cash Sales, PO Box 11, Falmouth, Cornwall TR109EN

Please enclose remittance to the value of the cover price plus:

UK: 25p for the first book plus 10p per copy for each additional book ordered to a maximum charge of £1.05.

BFPO and EIRE: 25p for the first book plus 10p per copy for the next 8 books, thereafter 5p per book.

OVERSEAS: 40p for the first book and 12p for each additional book. *Granada Publishing reserve the right to show new retail prices on covers, which may differ from those previously advertised in the text or elsewhere.*